BEYOND THE RISK PARADIGM IN CHILD PROTECTION

BEYOND THE RISK PARADIGM

Series Editor: Nigel Parton

This important new series argues that a risk paradigm has come to dominate many human services in Western countries over the last twenty years, giving the impression that the social world is calculable and predictable. Each book critically engages with this paradigm, demonstrating the intended and unintended consequences of such an approach for those using and working in services, as well as for wider society, in order to open up new ways for taking policy and practice forward. Designed to challenge readers to think critically and creatively about risk, this fascinating series will develop the understanding and knowledge of students and practitioners alike.

Forthcoming titles:

Beyond the Risk Paradigm in Mental Health Policy and Practice, edited by Sonya Stanford, Nina Rovinelli Heller, Elaine Sharland and Joanne Warner

Nigel Parton is a professor of applied childhood studies at the University of Huddersfield, UK, and has been writing about and researching these issues for over 20 years.

BEYOND THE RISK PARADIGM IN CHILD PROTECTION

EDITED BY MARIE CONNOLLY

First published 2017 by
PALGRAVE

Palgrave in the UK is an imprint of Macmillan Publishers Limited,
registered in England, company number 785998, of 4 Crinan Street,
London, N1 9XW.

Palgrave® and Macmillan® are registered trademarks in the United States,
the United Kingdom, Europe and other countries.

ISBN 978–1–137–44129–4 paperback

This book is printed on paper suitable for recycling and made from fully
managed and sustained forest sources. Logging, pulping and manufacturing
processes are expected to conform to the environmental regulations of the
country of origin.

A catalogue record for this book is available from the British Library.

A catalog record for this book is available from the Library of Congress.

Printed and bound by CPI Group (UK) Ltd, Croydon, CR0 4YY

To my mother
Teresa Connolly (1926–2016)
With love

CONTENTS

LIST OF FIGURES AND TABLES

Figures

Tables

ACKNOWLEDGEMENTS

In 2014 a colloquium was held at the Monash Centre in Prato to discuss the notion of moving beyond the risk paradigm in child protection, criminal justice and mental health. Recognizing the dominating nature of risk discourses within health and human services, experts from across the globe came together to explore ways of shifting dominant risk paradigms and engaging with more responsive policies and practices across these three fields. This book, which is one in a three-volume series, is a result of these deliberations. We are grateful to the Monash University Prato Centre for providing a perfect venue for this international gathering. It is truly an enriching environment that is conducive to the development of important collaborations.

We are also grateful to Professor Nigel Parton, who supported the project as series editor, thanking him for his wise council at all stages of the book's development and production. Thanks also go to Palgrave for their guidance and valuable assistance in bringing the book together, and finally to the University of Melbourne for its continued support.

PREFACE

Marie Connolly

I first came across the phrase 'beyond the risk paradigm' when I read Tony Ward and Shadd Maruna's landmark book *Rehabilitation*, published in 2007. Ground breaking in significance, the book engages in a dialogue that challenges the very nature of how professionals work in criminal justice settings. The authors argue that 'the majority of criminal justice interventions appear more likely to impede the process of going straight by detaching individuals from the families, derailing career paths, and breeding hostility and defiance' (p. 14). What is required is at once incredibly complex, yet at the same time beguilingly simple: to help people build a better life 'in ways that are personally meaningful and satisfying and socially acceptable' (p. 83). Their approach goes beyond a single focus on risk to one that is sensitive to risk but also critically cognizant of the deep human desire to live a good life in ways that are useful, purposeful and rewarding. A singular focus on risk in criminal justice has seen an explosive increase in prison populations across the world. Shifting beyond the risk paradigm, for this reason alone, becomes imperative. Salient are the parallels with child protection.

For decades child protection systems have striven to develop services that are responsive to vulnerable children and families. Reform of child protection is ubiquitous. Waves of change across English-speaking child welfare systems have created unprecedented instability as teams are restructured, systems redesigned and new tools developed to help workers manage an increasingly demanding professional environment. Most practitioners, managers of services and academics working in child protection agree that the bureaucratization of child protection has created a more challenging environment for workers, without an appreciable improvement in service delivery to vulnerable children and families. Rather than redesigning aspects of service delivery systems, then, the argument for cultural change – shifting beyond the risk paradigm – has become a rallying cry in child protection.

This book is directed towards this shift in paradigm. Inspired by the notion of moving beyond the risk paradigm in child protection, the chapter writers are deeply committed to exploring opportunities for change in both child protection organizational culture and service delivery. The book is divided into two parts. Part 1 considers the ways in which notions of risk influence practice and service delivery, providing both critique and opportunities for change. Part 2 explores innovative practices that seek to move beyond dominating risk discourses, effectively mitigating risk but at the same time engaging children, young people and their families in processes that uphold their rights as citizens.

The first two chapters in the book examine notions of risk and the ways in which risk has both influenced and shaped the delivery of child protection services. Nigel Parton begins the discussion by providing an insightful analysis of dominant risk discourses that have promoted the proliferation of forensic practices in child protection. Exploring the concept of risk, Parton examines the 'culture of blame' that permeates child protection systems, one that has become a major challenge for policy and practice. Extending this conversation, Liz Beddoe and Viviene Cree examine the particular influence the media has on public perceptions of child abuse and services that respond to children at risk. Describing the way in which the media frames child protection, they urge practitioners to engage with the media in ways that promote a more tolerant and just society. Recognizing the potential for social workers to shape media perceptions, and thus community expectations, they inspire us to 'stand up and be counted' – by becoming active article and blog writers and taking opportunities to be media spokespeople in areas of critical importance to children and their families.

The following three chapters approach new knowledge in child protection, considering each within a context of risk. Chapter 3, by Irene de Haan and Marie Connolly, looks specifically at predictive risk modelling and how child protection systems are attempting to anticipate future risk through the use of technology. They discuss an initiative by the New Zealand government that investigates whether administrative data could be used to develop a tool that would be capable of assessing the likelihood of a child experiencing a substantiated notification of abuse in the future. Exploring predictive modelling as a potential tool of surveillance versus a tool of early intervention, de Haan and Connolly conclude – perhaps not surprisingly – that its potential to make systems more or less dominated by risk depends on how it is framed and understood. Given Parton's suggestion in Chapter 1 that risk lies at the centre of child protection practice, the framing of predictive risk modelling within a dominant risk discourse might undermine its potential as a signal of adversity.

The influence of neuroscience is the subject of Chapter 4. Messages from attachment research and new discoveries in neuroscience are increasingly used to inform child protection decision making. In this chapter Clare Huntington alerts us to the potential and dangers of the application of neuroscience research, particularly in legal decision making. She succinctly argues that in the context of the risk paradigm, the use of this new knowledge could be used to support or challenge risk discourses. Exploring brain architecture and notions of toxic stress, Huntington concludes that while there is undoubted value in the development of neuroscientific research, it should nevertheless be used with caution. The science is new, and scientific claims are rarely unequivocal.

Chapter 5 discusses the issue of disproportionality and the over representation of indigenous and ethnic minority groups within child protection systems. This is an area that has challenged service delivery for many years. Ilan Katz and Marie Connolly explore the fraught question of disproportionality and the way in which notions of risk frame thinking and action. They argue that there is no reason to assume that ethnic minority families are more likely to maltreat their children or that they are more likely to experience risk factors associated with child abuse. Yet practitioners work within a complex risk-saturated environment, and decisions are invariably influenced by the dominant discourses and, in particular, the risk paradigm. Although the issues are complicated, Katz and Connolly argue that notions of intersectionality offer new opportunities to advance social inclusionary practice, through the interrogation of multilevel factors in ways that are both reflexive and transformative.

The last two chapters in the first part of the book (Chapters 6 and 7) return us to the experiences of the children and families who interface with child protection systems. In Chapter 6 Helen Buckley focuses on service users as receivers of risk-dominated practice. Tracing the tensions and ambiguities of the work, she illustrates how forensic child protection services and the bureaucratization of child welfare have impacted on children and their families. She argues that despite efforts to increase engagement with families, the contemporary risk-saturated child welfare context presents real barriers to engaging families in positive change. Continuing this theme in Chapter 7, Kate Morris and Gale Burford use examples from research to explore the experiences of families who have been involved in systems of child protection. Acknowledging the challenges facing child protection systems, they propose that we nevertheless stop engaging in hollow rhetoric of family engagement while actually framing families as repositories of risk and instead start building family-minded practices that will better serve the interests of children.

Having discussed the influences of the risk paradigm in Part 1 of the book, Part 2 explores innovative ways of moving beyond the risk paradigm in practice. The first two chapters (Chapters 8 and 9) focus on assessment and decision making. In Chapter 8 Aron Shlonsky and Robyn

Mildon look at emerging frameworks that move beyond a single focus on risk. They explore the use of evidence within a systemic decision-making ecology that has the potential to support better outcomes for children, particularly children with complex needs. This is followed by a chapter, by Andrew Turnell, Peter Pecora, Yvonne Roberts, Mike Caslor and Dan Koziolek, on the Signs of Safety approach, supporting participatory practice with children and their families. Widely utilized across child welfare jurisdictions, the approach provides an opportunity to revise concepts of risk and risk assessment in ways that are genuinely partnership oriented. As with many new approaches, building a knowledge base takes time, and Turnell and his colleagues note the complexities of evaluating participatory assessment practices. Their work nevertheless reflects an important contribution to the development of partnership practices within holistic frameworks that manage risk and support engagement.

The following three chapters (Chapters 10, 11 and 12) present innovative approaches from the field across different areas of practice. In Chapter 10 Cathy Humphreys and Nicky Stanley explore notions of risk management within the field of domestic violence. They trace the evolution of interventions in domestic violence, exploring in particular the mother-blaming practices that have negatively impacted on outcomes for women and children. A practice shift in child protection is promoted through a greater focus on men who use violence against women and children. While acknowledging that a stronger focus on perpetrators brings both opportunities and risks, they identify a number of promising examples of interventions that aim to reduce the risk of men's violence. Continuing the theme of family violence into Chapter 11, Joan Pennell then looks at solution-focused practices that engage families and their informal and formal networks. Men who have been violent towards family members are often excluded from this kind of partnership work. Drawing upon research and experience from the field, Pennell promotes a restorative practice approach within a responsive regulation framework to create a space for wise decision-making engagement when working with such men. Pennell also uses examples of restorative practices with traumatized youth – another frequently excluded group within participatory practice models. In Chapter 12 Justine Harris and Robyn Mildon shift our focus to issues of neglect. Reviewing the current knowledge base relating to risk factors in child neglect, they argue that current practices would benefit from more nuanced approaches that consider the particular aetiology of neglect and its responsiveness to change. They argue that taking an ecological perspective when responding to neglect is more likely to impact on recurrence and better support families.

Bringing the book to a close, the last two chapters (Chapters 13 and 14) consider the ways in which child protection systems can mobilize a shift beyond the risk paradigm. In Chapter 13 Robyn Miller examines reform efforts that build capacity within supportive organizational cultures. Positive leadership is critical to the development of supportive cultures, particularly in the context of 'wicked problems'. Miller proposes seven C's of reform leadership: commitment, collaborative leadership, critical reflection, congruence, coherence, champions and community. Miller argues that attention to these areas of leadership will create reform processes that will resonate with practitioners and build strong service systems. Finally, Chapter 14 draws the book to a close with Marie Connolly reflecting upon the challenges in engaging positive and enduring reform efforts in child protection. Moving beyond the risk paradigm clearly presents a complexity of issues at many levels of the system. Connolly nevertheless challenges us to consider whether the reliance on providing professional services might, in fact, be part of the problem. She argues that thinking beyond formal service provision towards a greater emphasis on the mobilization of informal support networks presents us with rich opportunities to better support children and their families.

In bringing together this book, we found both challenges and opportunities in attempting to move beyond the risk paradigm. As Ward and Maruna clearly argue, however, the need to move beyond a single focus on risk is imperative. Ultimately, child protection needs to be all about improving outcomes for children and their families. Democratizing practices not only have the potential to support families and protect children but may also provide the key to more sustainable systems of child protection.

Reference

Ward, T. & Maruna, S. (2007). *Rehabilitation: Beyond the Risk Paradigm*. Oxon, UK: Routledge.

PART 1

NOTIONS OF RISK IN CHILD PROTECTION

1

CONCERNS ABOUT RISK AS A MAJOR DRIVER OF PROFESSIONAL PRACTICE

Nigel Parton[*]

Introduction

An increased awareness about risk seems to constitute one of the key defining dimensions of our contemporary experience and is present in most areas of our social, economic, political and cultural lives (Mythen & Walklate, 2006; Petersen & Wilkinson, 2008; Taylor-Gooby & Zinn, 2006). Nowhere is this more evident than in the area of child protection (see for example Parton, Thorpe & Wattam, 1997; Swift & Callahan, 2009). It is, however, the central proposition of this chapter that concerns about risk in the area of child protection, and child welfare more generally, have taken a particularly narrow, negative and defensive form and that this has had an enormous impact on the priorities and nature of day-to-day policy and practice. Risk assessment, risk management and the monitoring of risk have become key issues for both practitioners and managers, and certain notions of risk have increasingly become embedded in organizational rationales and procedures for both the delivery of services and relationships with users and clients. Ideas about risk have, similarly, become central in making judgements about the quality of performance and what should be the primary focus for professional activities.

A central part of my argument is that particular ideas about risk have taken on a strategic significance for rationing services and holding professionals and others to account in a changing political and economic context where potential need and demand is increasing but where there are insufficient resources. Issues about risk in child protection have come to be intimately related to concerns about professional accountability and

---

[*] Nigel Parton is Professor in Applied Childhood Studies at the University of Huddersfield, UK.

responsibility, such that overly defensive and negative organizational processes have come to dominate. The chapter begins by exploring the concept of risk before analysing how developments have impacted upon child protection more specifically.

The concept of risk

It seems that the concept of risk emerged in the seventeenth century in the context of gambling and insurance and was used to refer to the probability of an event occurring and the size of the associated gains and losses (Douglas, 1992). Up until this time both positive and dangerous events were attributed primarily to divine or supernatural intervention; however, with the emergence of the Enlightenment, rational thought and objective knowledge were seen as crucial for bringing about progress and order (Lupton, 1999). Both the natural and social worlds were increasingly seen as subject to laws and regularities which could be identified and measured so that humans could begin to make calculations in order to intervene to improve the world. It was the time when probability and statistics emerged so that predictions could be made (Hacking, 1975). Risk comes into wide usage only in a society that is future oriented and that sees the future as a territory to be conquered or colonized – a society which *actively* tries to bring the future into the present.

Concerns about risk can be seen to characterize societies which aim to determine their own future rather than assuming the future is predetermined or subject to fate or 'God's will'. At the outset, however, risk was concerned with calculating both losses and gains – in the sense of gambling – and thus pointed to potential positives as well as negatives. It was a neutral concept in the sense that it was associated with the idea of calculating outcomes for the future. Risk understood in this sense is still very important as the primary idea involving a whole variety of different activities, including gambling, investing in the stock exchange and so on.

As Mary Douglas (1986; 1992) has argued, as the idea of risk became more central to politics and public policy, the connection of risk with technical calculations weakened. While it continued to combine a probabilistic measure of the consequences of events, increasingly the concept of risk in terms of public policy became primarily associated with negative outcomes only. As a result, the idea of risk has become much more associated with hazards, dangers, harms and losses. The risk that has become central for policy has now got little to do with neutral probability calculations. 'The original connection is only indicated by arm-waving in the direction of possible science: the word *risk* now means danger: high risk means a lot of danger' (Douglas, 1992, original emphasis). Whereas a high risk originally meant a game in which a throw of the die had a strong possibility of bringing about great joy or great pain, the language of risk has become, in public policy, reserved almost exclusively for talk of undesirable outcomes. Discussions about risk have become primarily concerned with levels of danger and our abilities to predict danger and thereby avert it.

Douglas (1992), however, argues that this shift is not the major significance of the contemporary concerns with risk. 'The big difference is not the predictive uses of risk, but in its forensic functions' (p. 27). The concept of risk emerges as a key idea for contemporary times because of its uses as a forensic resource. Douglas argues that the more culturally individualized a society becomes, the more significant is the forensic potential of the idea of risk. Its forensic uses have become particularly important in the development of different types of blaming systems, and 'the one we are now in is almost ready to treat every death as chargeable to someone's account, every accident as caused by someone's criminal negligence, every sickness a threatened prosecution' (1992, pp. 15–16).

As I will argue further below, however, the situation has been developing in some interesting ways in recent years. While the idea of risk is no longer so dominated by notions of danger and is increasingly influenced by the idea of well-being and bringing about positive improvements, the forensic emphasis on individualized responsibility and accountability seems to have become stronger.

More than ever, risk has become centrally implicated in developments which hold people to account, not just for their actions, but also the *consequences* of their (in)actions; after all, the idiom of risk presupposes not only ideas of choice and calculation but also responsibility. Whether or not the risk attitude prevails depends on the degree to which areas of social life are assumed to be fixed, inevitable and influenced by fate, or subject to human agency and control, and hence responsibility. The more we have assumed that areas of life have moved from the former category (fixed, inevitable and subject to fate) to the latter (subject to human agency and control), the more we have taken them from the sphere of the natural and God-given and made them the objects of human intervention and responsibility. It seems that the more it is assumed that human intervention can have the effect of preventing harm and improving well-being, in an increasingly individualized and forensically driven political and organizational context, the more welfare agencies, managers and practitioners are required to account for their actions when situations or cases in which they might have some involvement are seen to have gone wrong.

A 'culture of blame' can be seen to dominate where a whole plethora of policies and procedures have been introduced to make practice, apparently, transparent so that any negative outcomes can be defended, often in the full glare of the media (Franklin & Parton, 2001; Parton, 1996; Lonne & Parton, 2014; Parton, 2016). The concern thereby shifts from trying to make the *right* decision to making a *defensible* decision. In the process, the concern is not so much 'risk' as 'safety', and a 'precautionary logic' comes to dominate.

Safety and precaution become a fundamental value, such that the passions which might previously have been devoted to the struggle to change the world for the better are now invested in trying to ensure that we are safe (Beck, 1992; Furedi, 2002). Increasingly, it seems that concerns about safety have come to characterize our contemporary social and political culture.

More recently, a number of writers have suggested that in the twenty-first century these concerns with safety are framed within a *logic of precaution* which insists on a politics and practice based on 'strict safety' (Ericson, 2007), where the dominating concern is the pre-emption of harm. Importantly, under the logic of precaution uncertainty is no longer seen as an excuse and, in fact, provides the driver for ever increased surveillance. Assessed against the 'worst-case' scenario, rather than calculative risk probabilities, everyone is required to be responsible for playing their part and thereby preventing future harm (Parton, 2006; 2008; Hebenton & Seddon, 2009).

What I am suggesting, then, is that while risk is a wide-ranging and slippery concept, we can identify a number of key elements which have come to characterize it:

> ➤ It is future orientated.

> ➤ It seems to emphasize calculability, human agency and responsibility.

> ➤ It gives the impression of being predictable and scientific and aims to bring the future into the present, so that the future can be controlled and modified.

> ➤ In public policy and practice, it tends to emphasize the negative consequences and outcomes of behaviour and decision making.

> ➤ It fulfils an important series of forensic functions, with their implication for blame allocation and holding people and organizations to account in the context of an increasing 'logic of precaution'.

These elements can also be seen to have characterized developments in child protection policy and practice, particularly over the last 20 years.

In the process, there has been something of a failure to develop much more positive, creative and empowering approaches to risk.

Changing and competing conceptions of risk in child welfare and protection

The development of modern child welfare and protection policy and practice from the late 1940s in many western countries was based on optimistic notions of improvement and rehabilitation and played a small but key element in the growth of state welfare policies. State welfare, at the time, was premised on the wish to encourage *social* responsibility, the mutuality of *social* risk and the encouragement of *social* solidarity and security. The principal of state intervention was made explicit via the institutional framework for maintaining minimum standards. This involved pooling society's resources and spreading the risks across the population and through the life-course. *Social* insurance summed up the approach and provided the framework for welfare developments in other areas. People were to be governed through *society*, symbolized and coordinated by the state and based on the idea of *social* citizenship. Professional experts were invested with considerable trust and discretion.

The collapse of 'welfarism' and the growth of neoliberal critiques from the mid 1970s ushered in a quite new situation, where notions of risk were not simply recast but given a much greater significance. No longer was the emphasis on governing through 'society' but through the calculating choices of individuals (Rose, 1993; 1996). For neoliberalism the political subject is less a *social* citizen with powers and obligations deriving from membership of a collective body and much more an individual whose citizenship is active. It is an individualized conception of citizenship where the emphasis is on personal fulfilment and individual responsibility. At the same time, the impact of global market forces has hastened dislocation in many areas of economic and social life, reinforcing a whole variety of insecurities, uncertainties and fears. The growing concerns about risks to children can be seen both to reflect these increased uncertainties and insecurities and to provide a rationale for coping, understanding and responding to the new situation (Parton, 2006). While there was a growing range of concerns about the risks facing children in this increasingly 'hostile' world, there was also a greater emphasis on professional responsibility and accountability for the safety and well-being of the children they come into contact with. Concerns about risk can be seen to articulate and represent these challenges.

Following the high-profile and very public criticisms of social workers and other health and welfare professionals in cases of child abuse in the 1970s and 1980s (Parton, 1985; Butler & Drakeford, 2011), the long-established state child welfare services in England came under increasing pressure and came to be dominated by narrowly focused, forensically orientated concern with child protection. Similar developments were evident in the other nations in the United Kingdom, as well as North America, Australia and New Zealand (Waldfogel, 1998; Lonne et al., 2009; Gainsborough, 2010; Connolly & Morris, 2012).

By the early 1990s, the child protection and child welfare systems could be characterized in terms of the need to identify 'high risk', in a context where agencies and professionals 'working together' was set out in increasingly complex and detailed procedural guidelines and where the work was informed by a narrow and defensive emphasis on legalism and the need for professionals to identify forensic evidence (Parton, 1991).

Child protection work had become concerned with trying to identify the 'high risk' or 'dangerous' families and differentiate these from the rest, so that children could be protected; family privacy was not undermined for the vast majority of parents; and scarce resources could be directed to where, in theory, they were most needed (Parton et al., 1997). At the same time, in the context of the increasingly hostile social and political climate in which the work was being carried out, a variety of new procedures, technologies and devices were introduced, which had the effect of subjecting practitioners and the people with whom they worked to a variety of 'systems' for providing safe, reliable, standardized services and, in theory, predictable outcomes. Perhaps inevitably, the plethora of policies and directives become unmanageable for busy practitioners and the proceduralization of practice has the effect of increasing risk rather than ameliorating it. As Carole Smith has argued (2001), the situation is full of paradox: while most agree that certainty in the area of child protection practice is not possible, the political and organizational climate demands it.

At a number of points since the early 1990s, there have been clear attempts in policy to move away from this very narrow and forensic approach to risk and to move beyond overly defensive organizational and professional practices. For example, during the 1990s a major debate opened up in England about how policies and practices in relation to child protection could be integrated with and supported by policies and practices concerned with family support and child welfare more generally (DH, 1995; Parton, 1997). Rather than simply be concerned with a narrow, forensically driven focus on child protection, it was argued there needed to be a 'rebalancing' or 'refocusing' of the work, such that the essential principles of a broader child welfare approach could dominate. Policy and practice should be driven by an emphasis on partnership, participation, prevention and family support. The priority should be on *helping* parents and children in the community in a supportive way and should keep notions of policing and coercive intervention to a minimum.

This change in thinking was evident in Britain in the official guidance published at the end of the decade, *Working Together to Safeguard Children: A Guide to Inter-agency Working to Safeguard and Promote the Welfare of Children* (DH et al., 1999). The guidance underlined the fact that local authority social services had wider responsibilities than simply responding to concerns about 'significant harm' and identifying child abuse and was explicitly located in the much wider agenda for Children's Services being promulgated by the then New Labour government, which had come to power in 1997, associated with social exclusion (Frost & Parton, 2009). The *Assessment Framework* (DH et al., 2000) published at the same time as the 1999 *Working Together*, attempted to shift the focus from the assessment of risk of child abuse and 'significant harm' (DH, 2001) to one which was concerned with the broader idea of risk of impairment to a child's overall development in the context of their family and community environment.

We can thus identify an important change in the nature of the risk that policy and practice was expected to respond to. The object of concern was no longer simply children at risk of abuse and 'significant harm'. Effective measures to safeguard children were seen as those which also promoted their welfare, and they should not be seen in isolation from the wider range of support and services provided to meet the needs of all children and families. This broadening of the idea of risk was taken to a new level a few years later when the British government launched its *Every Child Matters: Change for Children* (ECM) programme (DfES, 2004a), where the overriding vision was to bring about 'a shift to prevention whilst strengthening protection' (DfES, 2004b, p. 3).

The consultative Green Paper *Every Child Matters* (Chief Secretary to the Treasury, 2003) had originally been launched as the government's response to a very high-profile child-abuse public inquiry into the death of Victoria Climbié (Laming, 2003). The changes were, however, much broader than simply being concerned with overcoming the problems of responding to cases of child abuse. The priority was to intervene at a much earlier stage in children's lives in order to prevent a range of problems both in childhood and in later life. The ambition was to improve the outcomes for all children and to narrow the gap in outcomes between those who did well and those who did not. The outcomes were defined in terms of being healthy, staying safe, enjoying and achieving, making a positive contribution, and achieving economic well-being. Together these five outcomes were seen as key to improving 'well-being in childhood and later life'. It was a very ambitious programme of change and was to include *all children*, as it was believed that any child, at some point in their life, could be seen as vulnerable to some form of risk and therefore might require help. The idea was to identify problems before they became chronic.

This shift towards prevention has also emerged across international jurisdictions, with Australia's national framework for protecting children (Commonwealth of Australia 2009) promoting a change in emphasis from responding to abuse and neglect towards the safety and well-being of children. The aim of this 'public health approach' has been to focus on the needs of vulnerable families and through this reduce the occurrence of child abuse and neglect (p. 8). The recognition that not all families reported to child protection necessarily need a child protection response is also one of the reasons why a number of jurisdictions have incorporated elements of differential or alternative response models based on what a child might need (Lonne et al., 2007; Connolly & Morris, 2012).

The growing emphasis on prevention in England coincided with the introduction of a range of new technologies designed to aid early intervention and the sharing of information between different professionals which indicated that there was likely to be much greater surveillance of children, young people, parents and the professionals who operated the system (Parton, 2006; Anderson et al., 2009). In the process the boundaries between the public and the private and between the state and the family might collapse, becoming increasingly difficult to ensure that confidentiality would be maintained and the rights of children improved (Roche, 2008).

While there was, therefore, a clear attempt to move beyond the narrow forensic concerns of the traditional child protection system, it was also clear that new and even more detailed systems of performance management were being put in place, which brought highly prescriptive requirements for recording which relied on new electronic ICT systems. In broadening the focus of what was meant by risk, there was a real danger of an elision of concerns about children and young people who might be *at risk* from a whole variety of threats, including abuse, with concerns about children and young people who might *pose a threat* to others, either now or in the future, particularly by falling into crime or antisocial behaviour. The agendas around the care and control of children and young people as well as those who might be either victims or villains were in danger of becoming very blurred (Sharland, 2006; James & James, 2008).

The aim was to widen and deepen attempts at early intervention while also trying to strengthen the systems of child protection. A key element of this was to integrate communication between different services and professionals and also to increase professional accountability and responsibility. In the process it was highly likely that there would be a growth in, what Michael Power has called, 'the risk management of everything' (Power, 2004), which would tie down practitioners more than ever. Rather than overcoming the defensiveness, risk avoidance and blame culture that are so associated with the child protection system of the 1990s, the danger was that these characteristics would permeate the newly integrated and transformed children's services, making them more risk adverse than they were before. Rather than overcoming the problems associated with the child protection system, there was a real possibility that the situation would be made worse, and there was increasing evidence that this was the case (see for example Wastell et al., 2010; White et al., 2010).

Such concerns were the major focus of the *Munro Review* of child protection in England, which attempted to

> Create the conditions that enable professionals to make the best judgments about the help to give to children, young people and families. This involves moving from a system that has become over-bureaucratised and focused on compliance to one that values and develops professional expertise and is focused on the safety and welfare of children and young people. (Munro, 2011, p. 6)

While many of its recommendations have been implemented, there is very little evidence that it has had any major impact on reducing the defensive and blame culture (Munro, 2012; Parton, 2012). Despite similar efforts internationally, it is clear that the dominance of risk-adverse systems is very difficult to overcome. In many respects the overall political climate has the effect of ensuring that the narrow, forensic and defensive approaches to child protection are more dominant and pervasive than ever (Featherstone, Morris & White, 2014; Parton, 2014). These are major challenges for policy and practice.

Conclusion

In this chapter, I have argued that concerns about risk lie at the centre of contemporary child protection policy and practice such that much of the work is framed in these terms. It is a diverse and slippery concept which varies in both understanding and use, depending on its context. I have argued, however, that it is nearly always operationalized in narrow and defensive ways.

In more recent years there is clear evidence of both a broadening of the concept of risk and its application and serious attempts to recognize the importance of much more positive and proactive approaches. I have explored some of the challenges and tensions involved in such developments in the context of the *Every Child Matters: Change for Children* programme in England and the more recent *Munro Review* of child protection.

I have suggested that these new and more positive approaches to risk may, however, have the effect of both extending systems of surveillance and also posing particular challenges to professional confidentiality and the human rights of service users. Such challenges are heightened in a context where there is a growing emphasis on a 'logic of precaution' which prioritizes an approach to practice based on 'strict safety'. Increasingly, it seems that the language of risk is being stripped of its association with the calculation of probabilities and is being used almost exclusively in terms of not just preventing future harm but also avoiding the 'worst-case' scenario and in a context where there has been a considerable increase in the number of children in the population for whom professionals are seen as having responsibilities and for whom they are seen to be accountable.

References

Anderson, R., Brown, I., Dowty, T., Inglesant, P., Heath, W. & Sasse, A. (2009). *Database State*. York: Joseph Rowntree Reform Trust.

Beck, U. (1992). *Rick Society: Towards a New Modernity*. London: Sage.

Butler, I. & Drakeford, M. (2011). *Social Work on Trial: The Colwell Inquiry and the State of Welfare*. Bristol, Policy Press.

Chief Secretary to the Treasury (2003). *Every Child Matters* (Cm5860). London: Stationery Office.

Commonwealth of Australia (2009). *Protecting Children is Everyone's Business: National Framework for Protecting Australia's Children 2009–2020*. Canberra: Australian Government.

Connolly, M. & Morris, K. (2012). *Understanding Child and Family Welfare: Statutory Responses to Children at Risk*. Basingstoke: Palgrave Macmillan.

Department for Education and Skills (2004a). *Every Child Matters: Change for Children* London: DfES.

Department for Education and Skills (2004b). *Every Child Matters: Next Steps*. London: DfES.

Department for Education and Skills (2004c). *Every Child Matters: Change for Children in Social Care*. London: DfES.

Department of Health (1995). *Child Protection: Messages from Research*. London: HMSO.

Department of Health (2001). *Studies Informing the Framework for the Assessment of Children in Need and their Families*. London: Stationery Office.

Department of Health, Department of Education and Employment, Home Office (2000). *Framework for the Assessment of Children in Need and their Families*. London: Stationery Office.

Department of Health, Home Office, and Department of Education and Employment (1999). *Working Together to Safeguard Children: A Guide to Inter-agency Working to Safeguard and Promote the Welfare of Children*. London: Stationery Office.

Department of Health, Home Office, and Department of Education and Employment (1999). *Working Together to Safeguard Children: A Guide to Inter-agency Working to Safeguard and Promote the Welfare of Children*. London: Stationery Office.

Douglas, M. (1986). *Risk Acceptability According to the Social Sciences*. London: Routledge and Kegan Paul.

Douglas, M. (1992). *Risk and Blame: Essays in Cultural Theory*. London: Routledge.

Ericson, R.V. (2007). *Crime in an Insecure World*. Cambridge: Polity Press.

Featherstone, B., Morris, K. & White, S. (2014). A Marriage made in Hell: Early Intervention meets Child Protection, *British Journal of Social Work*, 44(7), 1735–1749.

Franklin, B. & Parton, N. (2001). Press-ganged! Media Reporting of Social Work and Child Abuse, in M. May, R. Payne & E. Brunsden (eds), *Understanding Social Problems: Issues in Social Policy*. Oxford: Blackwell.

Frost, N. & Parton, N. (2009). *Understanding Children's Social Care: Politics, Policy and Practice*. London: Sage.

Furedi, F. (2003). *Culture of Fear*. 2nd edition. London: Continuum.

Gainsborough, J. F. (2010). *Scandalous Politics: Child Welfare Politics in the States*. Washington, DC: Georgetown University Press.

Hacking, I. (1975). *The Emergence of Probability: A Philosophical Study of Early Ideas about Statistical Inferences*. Cambridge: Cambridge University Press.

Hebenton, B. & Seddon, T. (2009). From Dangerousness to Precaution: Managing Sexual and Violent Offenders in an Insecure and Uncertain Age, *British Journal of Criminology*, 49(3), 343–362.

James, A. & James, A. (2008). Changing Childhood in the UK: Reconstructing Discourses of 'Risk' and 'Protection', in A. James & A. James (eds), *European Childhoods: Cultures, Politics and Childhoods in Europe*. Basingstoke: Palgrave Macmillan.

Lonne, B. & Parton, N. (2014). Portrayals of Child Abuse Scandals in the Media in Australia and England: Impacts on Practice, Policy and Systems, *Child Abuse and Neglect*, 38(5), 822–836.

Lonne, B., Parton, N., Thomson, J. & Harries, M. (2009). *Reforming Child Protection*. London: Routledge.

Lord Laming (2003). *The Victoria Climbié Inquiry: Report of an Inquiry by Lord Laming* (Cm5730). London: Stationery Office.

Lupton, D. (1999). *Risk*. London: Routledge.

Munro, E. (2011). *The Munro Review of Child Protection: Final report. A Child-Centred System*. Cm. 8062. London: DfE.

Munro, E. (2012). *The Munro Review of Child Protection: Progress Report: Moving Towards a Child-Centred System*. London: DfE.

Mythen, G. & Walklate, S. (eds) (2006). *Beyond the Risk Society: Critical Reflections on Risk and Human Security*. Maidenhead: Open University Press.

Parton, N. (1985). *The Politics of Child Abuse*. Basingstoke: Macmillan.

Parton, N. (1991). *Governing the Family: Child Care, Child Protection and the State.* Basingstoke: Macmillan.

Parton, N. (1996). Social Work, Risk and the Blaming System, in N. Parton (ed.), *Social Theory, Social Change and Social Work.* London: Routledge.

Parton, N. (ed.) (1997). *Child Protection and Family Support: Tensions, Contradictions and Possibilities.* London: Routledge.

Parton, N. (2006). *Safeguarding Childhood: Early Intervention and Surveillance in a Late Modern Society.* Basingstoke: Palgrave Macmillan.

Parton, N. (2008). Changes in the Form of Knowledge in Social Work: From the 'Social' to the 'Informational?', *British Journal of Social Work,* 38(2), 253–269.

Parton, N. (2012). The Munro Review of Child Protection: An Appraisal, *Children and Society,* 26(2), 150–162.

Parton, N. (2014). *The Politics of Child Protection: Contemporary Developments and Future Directions.* Basingstoke: Palgrave Macmillan.

Parton, N. (2016). The Contemporary Politics of Child Protection: Parton Two (the BASPCAN Founders Lecture 2015), *Child Abuse Review,* 24(1), 9–16.

Parton, N., Thorpe, D. & Wattam, C. (1997). *Child Protection: Risk and the Moral Order.* Basingstoke: Macmillan.

Petersen, A. & Wilkinson, I. (eds) (2008). *Health, Risk and Vulnerability.* London: Routledge.

Power, M. (2004). *The Risk Management of Everything: Rethinking the Politics of Uncertainty.* London: Demos.

Roche, J. (2008). Children's Rights, Confidentiality and the Policing of Children, *International Journal of Children's Rights,* 16(4), 431–456.

Rose, N. (1993). Government, Authority and Expertise in Advanced Liberalism, *Economy and Society,* 22(3), 283–299.

Rose, N. (1996). The Death of the Social? Re-figuring the Territory of Government, *Economy and Society,* 25(3), 327–356.

Sharland, E. (2006). Young People, Risk Taking and Risk Making: Some Thoughts for Social Work, *British Journal of Social Work,* 36(2), 247–265.

Smith, C. (2001). Trust and Confidence: Possibilities for Social Work in High Modernity, *British Journal of Social Work,* 31(2), 287–305.

Swift, K. & Callahan, M. (2009). *At Risk: Social Justice in Child Welfare and Other Human Services.* Toronto, ON: University of Toronto Press.

Taylor-Gooby, P. & Zinn, J. (eds) (2006). *Risk in Social Science.* Oxford: Oxford University Press.

Waldfogel, J. (1998). *The Future of Child Protection: How to Break the Cycle of Abuse and Neglect.* Cambridge, MA: Harvard University Press.

Wastell, D., White, S., Broadhurst, K., Peckover, S. & Pithouse, A. (2010). Children's Services in the Iron Cage of Performance Management: Street-Level Bureaucracy and the Spectre of Svejkism, *International Journal of Social Welfare,* 19(3), 310–320.

White, S., Wastell, D., Broadhurst, K. & Hall, C. (2010). When Policy O'erleeps Itself: The 'Tragic Tale' of the Integrated Children's System, *Critical Social Policy,* 39(3), 405–429.

2

THE RISK PARADIGM AND THE MEDIA IN CHILD PROTECTION

Liz Beddoe and Viviene Cree[*]

In Chapter 1, Nigel Parton explored some of the concerns about risk that have influenced child protection practice in particular ways. This chapter extends this conversation by examining the influence of the media and both the way it has shaped public perceptions about child abuse and neglect and the way it has influenced professional practice with children and families. Drawing on international literature in media analysis, social identities and representation, as well as the social work and social policy scholarship, we will examine how the media frames child abuse as a significant feature of child welfare and the risk paradigm. Cases will be utilized to demonstrate the potential and real impact on policy and practice. Links will be made to moral panics, addressing cases in various international contexts. Finally, the chapter will briefly describe opportunities to develop a more positive engagement with the press via working with journalists and presenting contrasting ideas in the media through blogs and writing for newspapers.

Introduction

In some respects it is difficult to know where to begin in writing this chapter, because the media (in all its forms) has had such a significant part to play in the creation and maintenance of both everyday and professional ideas of risk and child protection, historically and in the present day. It is, quite simply, impossible to untangle what we know about child abuse from the media as compared with what we know from theory, research or even practice. Whether this has been through the telling and retelling of

---

[*] Liz Beddoe is an associate professor in the School of Counselling, Human Services and Social Work at the University of Auckland, New Zealand. Viviene Cree is a professor at the School of Social and Political Science at the University of Edinburgh, UK.

high-profile scandals over the last 150 years or so or through the incessant 'drip, drip' of television documentaries and dramas and the daily media coverage of court cases, we are constantly reminded that children are innocent victims, who are at risk and in need of protection; that adults (especially men) are dangerous creatures from whom others need protection; and that social workers are a fairly useless bunch, 'damned if they do and damned if they don't'. This is not, however, a phenomenon that is always external to us and that we have no connection with. On the contrary, social work and social workers have sought to engage with the media in order to 'frame' these accounts in ways that foreground our own concerns and agendas, and this, too, has had an impact on the ways that risk, child abuse and child protection are understood.

We will begin with an historical account of risk, the media and child protection before exploring key theoretical underpinnings, which are then examined through two case-study examples. But first, we need to say a word about terminology. The Oxford English Dictionary defines the media as 'The main means of mass communication (television, radio, and newspapers) regarded collectively'. In practice, the media today is much broader than this. The advent of 24-hour news coverage and the arrival of social media over the last ten years or so have meant that 'the media' (through the multiplicity of electronic devices that we are permanently attached to) is taking up increasing amounts of time in all our lives (Cushion and Lewis, 2010). Furthermore, the creators of the messages that the media conveys are no longer simply the powerful press barons of bygone eras. On the contrary, we all have an opportunity to lay claim to the discourses through which we live and work. This offers new challenges, which we will return to later in the chapter.

'The maiden tribute of modern Babylon: the report of our secret commission', July 1885

Between 4 and 8 July 1885, London's *Pall Mall Gazette* published a series of revelations into 'juvenile prostitution' in London. In doing so, it highlighted the presence of an organized traffic in young English girls (what is referred to as a 'white slave trade') to supply brothels on the Continent. The articles were titillating if not downright pornographic, full of graphic stories about the abduction and rape of 'maids' (virgins) by upper-class (often 'foreign') Lotharios in underground rooms where 'the cries of children could not be heard'. At the peak of the revelations, the story of 15-year-old 'Lily' was told in lurid detail. In order to prove that it was possible to purchase a child for sex, she was bought from her mother and taken to France by the newspaper's editor, William Stead, supported by feminist campaigners Josephine Butler and Mrs Bramwell Booth. This story made headline news across the world and led to the passing of UK legislation that raised the age of sexual consent to 16 years and outlawed homosexual acts between men in private and public. It also heralded a wider acceptance by the general public and politicians alike that external agencies (police and vigilance workers) should have the right to intervene in what had, until then, been regarded as private behaviour (Bristow, 1977; Gorham, 1978; Pearson, 1972).

There is not space in this short chapter to rehearse all the arguments for and against the behaviour of the protagonists in the 'Maiden Tribute' series; nor is there time to unpack all the more unsavoury elements within it (for more information, see Cree et al., 2016). What is important, however, is to acknowledge that the media has long understood that child abuse sells newspapers and that by playing the part of the angels – taking the moral high ground, drawing attention to risks, wickedness and wrong-doing – they can build a loyal readership. There have been a great many occasions in which we can see this being played out. The early beginnings of the New York Society for the Prevention of Cruelty to Children in 1874 followed a scandalous story in the national press of the abuse of Mary Ellen Wilson and the court case that followed; the 1948 Children Acts across the United Kingdom were, without doubt, given extra impetus by the death of 12-year-old Dennis O'Neill in England in 1945 and the press coverage that accompanied this case. Since then, many child abuse scandals have preoccupied the media – more recently, the story of 'Baby P', as will be examined in more detail. But first, it is important to take a step back and think a bit more about what it means to 'frame' a story.

Media and the framing of child protection

> The frame is a persuasive invitation, a stimulus, to read a news story in a particular way, so that a specific definition of an event, the causal and treatment responsibility for a societal topic, and a moral judgment of a person come more easily across the receiver's mind. (Van Gorp, 2007, p. 73)

It is clear that child protection has long been a significant topic of media attention. It provokes anger and revulsion as reports of violence against children tap into potent social anxieties about social and familial dysfunction that 'the public' expect to be managed (Parton, 1981; Taylor, Beckett & McKeigue, 2008). As such, child abuse is a target for 'media framing' (as described by Van Gorp above) within strong moral discourses. An understanding of media framing links the psychological concept of framing – the selection of words and concepts in order to suggest relatedness, choices or potential interpretations and deci-sion – to the way the news media influence public opinions on broad social issues such as poverty. Framing is the significant manner in which media emphases 'manipulate salience by directing people's attention to certain ideas while ignoring others' (Kendall, 2011, p. 5). Iyengar (1990) analysed 191 broadcast stories about poverty (1981–1986) and identified two distinct types of story: one in which poverty is 'presented primar-ily as a societal or collective outcome' and a second type where poverty is explored via a presentation of the personal experiences of individuals (p. 21). Reporting can thus be described as episodic – that is, relating to a particular incident in a specific time frame, or thematic, where the author/presenter attempts to link the incident to broader issues and problems. Episodic reporting is most frequent and tends to frame inci-dents in terms of individual or localized responsibility, leading to the 'blame and shame' tactic that is so commonly used to sell newspapers or attract clicks. Thematic frames are less common and tend to locate an incident in some kind of explanatory framework of wider social concerns. Framing of social phenomena in news reporting may thus 'promote a particular problem definition, causal interpretation, moral evaluation' (Entman, 1993, p. 52). In this way, stories of family violence and child neglect can be framed as individual incidents with a basis in morality or alternatively more generally linked to poverty and issues of structure. Both episodic and thematic framing are not recent phenom-ena, and Kendall (2011) reports a newspaper story from 1872 where a child death at the hands of a parent was linked to the poverty and alco-hol abuse affecting her family in the abject social conditions of the time (pp. 85–86). Such stories are more nuanced and can attribute respon-sibility for poverty and misery to individual actions, or they can make structural links to phenomena which affect many people and communi-ties, such as economic recession, unemployment and affordable housing shortages or gendered violence against women and children.

Of course, people engaged in reading and viewing media stories are not passive recipients and will apply their own filters. A social construc-tionist approach acknowledges the importance of the receiver as well as the transmitter (Van Gorp, 2007; Gamson, 1992). Gamson's (1992) con-structionist approach to framing stresses the importance of the audience's engagement in interpreting discourses. Van Gorp further argues that the positioning the frame is not separate from the text, both of them existing within 'culture', here defined as including sets of commonly held beliefs, codes, myths, stereotypes, values and norms that are shared in the collec-tive social consciousness among an audience. Gamson (1992) suggested that the success of media framing is influenced by the strategies employed by audiences: those people who use cultural strategies – received wisdom, 'common sense' and so forth – may be more impacted by framing, while those with 'personal or vicarious experiential knowledge' are more likely to discount or ignore frames (Sotirovic, 2000, p. 274).

Sotirovic argues that media framing is particularly important in influencing opinion on social problems because many audience members will lack direct personal experience when forming their understanding about the needs and experiences of others (2000, p. 276). This is significant in the framing of social problems such as child abuse and neglect where lived experience of abuse may generate nuanced 'explanations' while lack of direct experience may result in strong moral judgements. Social problems are also deeply ideological, and so their response to any issue will reflect deeply held views, preferences and prior judgements. Child abuse and family violence are highly emotive issues, and the language used in reporting stories may trigger ideological and emotional responses, deeply saturated in cultural features. Bullock, Fraser Wyche and Williams (2001), writing about media framing of poverty, note that often as 'well as rhetorical devices such as metaphors, catch phrases and imagery, news-handlers use reasoning devices that draw on causal attributions. ... These powerful (but typically unnoticed) mechanisms affect viewers' judgments of responsibility and causality' (2001, p. 233). Just a short headline (with words such as 'beast' or 'monster') can set the tone for the framing of the story to follow. This leads to moral panics, the second underpinning theoretical framework.

Moral panics, risk and child protection

The concept of moral panic is central to thinking about the media, risk and child protection, because moral panics have, to a very large degree, been the triggers that have set in motion the child protection industry that we find today across the world. The idea of moral panics emerged in the 1970s with the work of sociologists Jock Young and Stan Cohen, who were interested in deviancy amplification, seeking to answer the question, why do some things get blown out of proportion and become widespread social concerns and others do not? Cohen's account of the process of a moral panic is well known but worth repeating:

> Societies appear to be subject, every now and then, to periods of moral panic. A condition, episode, person or group of persons emerges to become defined as a threat to societal values and interests; its nature is presented in a stylized and stereotypical fashion by the mass media; the moral barricades are manned by editors, bishops, politicians and other right-thinking people; socially accredited experts pronounce their diagnoses and solutions; ways of coping are evolved

or (more often) resorted to; the condition then disappears, submerges or deteriorates and becomes more visible. ... Sometimes the panic passes over and is forgotten, except in folklore or collective memory; at other times it has more serious and long-lasting repercussions and might produce such changes as those in legal and social policy or even in the way society conceives of itself. (Cohen, 1972, p. 28)

Cohen's specific interest was in the scuffles between teenage 'Mods' and 'Rockers' on the beaches of England in the 1960s and the social reaction that these engendered. More recently, moral panic theory has been used to interrogate the physical abuse of children (Parton, 1985), child sexual abuse (Jenkins, 1992), child trafficking (Cree et al., 2012) and child protection (Clapton et al., 2013a and b). In each of these instances, a 'folk devil' is uncovered: some individual or group that is portrayed as especially risky and dangerous, a threat not just to vulnerable people but to society as a whole, because of their propensity to undermine societal values and all that we hold to be 'good' and 'true'. Moral panics are, at heart, narratives of 'goodies' and 'baddies', where the 'goodies' are often children and the 'baddies' adults (and especially men). On the rare occasions when children are the 'baddies', such as in the murder in England of James Bulger in 1993 by two 10-year-old boys, the children become presented not just as 'bad' but as evil personified. It is the sex offender that has become the embodiment of all that is to be loathed and feared in the twenty-first century, usually described as the 'paedophile', and the media has played a major part in this construction. This is not, of course, to suggest that social work and social workers should not be concerned about important and worrying issues such as child abuse or child trafficking. Rather, it is to argue that by getting caught up in stereotyping and blame, we may lose sight of the complexities and realities of people's lives. We may also find ourselves focusing too much on some issues (such as the high tariff child protection cases), to the detriment of others (for example, 'routine' cases of neglect) (see Clapton et al., 2013a and b). This takes us to two more detailed examples of the media's involvement in child protection.

Case studies

In this section, two specific examples of media framing will be presented, to make some links between the media representations of social problems and moral panics. While child abuse reporting in itself frequently contains strong elements of moral panics (Parton, 1981; 1985), it is worthwhile examining several cases in detail to examine specifically the role of the media in framing the panic. We will draw on some case studies from New Zealand and the United Kingdom to illustrate how in one case a race discourse dominates and in another a discourse of class does.

Child abuse: a Maori problem?

A racial framing is potent when mixed with emotionally charged events such as a death of a child. Beddoe has written elsewhere about how news media reports in New Zealand tell a racialized story about child abuse in which reporting of child deaths focuses disproportionately on Maori (indigenous) families (Beddoe, 2013; 2014; 2015). Provan (2012) describes the phenomenon of the 'roll of dishonour', where the listed names (and often photographs) of killed Maori children are featured repeatedly in media stories of subsequent and unrelated child deaths. Provan notes that while some versions of the 'roll' do include some European children, there is 'a circular argument whereby a "roll call" with only Maori children's names is used and it is then pointed out that all the names on the list are Maori' (p. 203). Severe child abuse is thus named as a Maori problem. The New Zealand case of the homicide of twin babies Chris and Cru Kahui in 2006 provides a useful example of how framing can be applied in the reporting of family violence. The trial and acquittal of the father of the children means that the contested notions of truth and blame in such events have remained in the public sphere of interest for years. Provan (2012, p. 200) argues that the Kahui family's initial lack of cooperation with the police (which was the subject of widespread and often vitriolic comment) was viewed as an 'outrageous offence which is inseparably intertwined with their being Māori'. The 2012 coroner's inquest provided further opportunities for excoriating comment on family members, in 'opinion' pieces and on talkback radio and other interactive media. Macsyna King, the mother of the twin boys, told her story via a book written by a journalist (Wishart, 2011). Publicity for the book generated a storm of public protest, and the *New Zealand Herald* reported that 40,000 people had signed up to a Facebook page to support a boycott on book sales (*NZ Herald*, 30 June 2011). Barnes et al. (2012, p. 206) argue that even in a general analysis of crime reporting, 'Maori families in which offences have occurred are stigmatised in ways that weaken efforts to remedy contexts that have often arisen from histories of tragedy and trauma'. In a peculiar article published only two weeks after the Kahui babies died, the *New Zealand Herald* published a story under the heading 'Taxpayers shell out for Kahuis', in which residents of two Kahui family homes were listed along with their occupations and the reporter's estimate of the value of benefits and subsidies for which the family was eligible (*NZ Herald*, 27 June 2006).

The impact of media coverage of child abuse on policy and practice is well known, as will be explored below, but a lesser canvassed consideration is the impact of such class- and race-saturated reporting in shaping the views of professionals about the genesis of such problems. In telling 'stories' with strong emotional and moral resonances, dominant discourses of race and class can be brought to the foreground (Warner, 2013b), affecting professional perceptions if unchallenged. In terms of race, the dominant discourse of white culture (in both colonized lands and multicultural societies) can 'other' minority cultures: 'minority and indigenous peoples are constructed as "not us", framed as failing to "fit in" and allegedly threatening the security or way of life of the majority' (Nairn, DeSouza, Barnes, Rankine, Borell & McCreanor, 2014). Nairn et al. (2014) note that in the case of minority health disparities, prevalent explanations can emphasize departures from dominant norms and rely on presumed personal characteristics such as race and ethnicity. Such framing diverts our attention from the wide-ranging societal problem of family violence and specifically child abuse, which occurs across class and race memberships.

'Baby P': a tale of media backlash

In England in 2007, 17-month-old Peter Connelly, known as 'Baby P', was killed in London, resulting in the conviction of his mother, her boyfriend and her boyfriend's brother for causing or allowing his death. Throughout the case and afterwards, intense media coverage and political reaction followed until the local authority children's services director and the social workers involved in Peter Connelly's care were eventually dismissed. In detailed analyses of media coverage of the Peter Connelly case and the political response to it, Warner (2013a) and Jones (2014) describe how politicians, in conjunction with the press, mobilized public hostility towards social work. Warner suggests that this case 'served a powerful function in allowing the articulation by politicians of a particular moral stance' employing highly emotive language to make claims invoking 'moral feeling that simultaneously constructed politicians and social workers in starkly polarised terms' (2013a, p. 1651). In a later paper, Warner (2013b) explores the links between media stories and the elements of moral panic, especially those aspects of social panics that link to moral regulation (Critcher, 2009) and the othering of those sections of society whose lives to do not conform to a largely middle-class way of life. Stereotypes of race, gender and class can also lead to over- and under-reporting of criminal activity; two 2014 examples include the Rotherham inquiry in England

(Jay, 2014) and the case of the Roma child, 'Maria', in Greece (Cree, Smith & Clapton, 2015).

One aspect of the Peter Connelly case that stands out in terms of media role is the development of a public discourse, fed by media and politicians alike, that child protection was really about 'common sense' and that social workers had become mired in bureaucratic procedures (Warner, 2013a; 2013b). Common sense, Warner notes, 'in response to the life Baby P had lived was characterised by a visceral disgust and an impulse to save him that everyone in the country except his social workers was represented as sharing' (2013b, p. 229). In a painstaking analysis of the case, Jones (2014) uncovers not only the general social work blaming of the press, but the very specific scapegoating of the individual social workers – and especially the former director of Children's Services at Haringey Council, Sharon Shoesmith. The media attention on Shoesmith was relentless and frenzied; seven years later, she is still a subject of interest in the UK press.

The Baby P story is instructive for many reasons. It reminds us that it is always easier to blame a public official than it is to face up to the dreadful things that can and do happen within families. The low status of social work (in comparison with, for example, doctors and paediatricians) means that social workers are an easy target when something goes wrong, as Butler and Drakeford (1985) have explored in their earlier investigation of scandals. But perhaps more damaging than all of this is the impact that Baby P and similar stories has on social work practice. There is no doubt that social work has become more risk averse, more likely to 'cover its back', to focus on systems rather than people, as highlighted in the Munro review (2011). Featherstone, White and Morris (2014) bravely call for a 'reimagining' of child protection – one that seeks to work with families, not against them, one that foregrounds care rather than control in social work practice. While this book has received a great deal of favourable attention within social work, it has had little wider media coverage. Will it be remembered when the next child death happens, or will it be criticized as naïve and overly optimistic? At a knowledge exchange project held in Scotland in 2013, children and families' social workers called for a 'critical optimism' in child protection social work (Cree et al., 2014). Whether the subtlety of this message will be understood by the media remains to be seen.

The race and class dimensions illustrated in the Kahui and Peter Connelly case studies outlined above and many other recent examples demonstrate that these situations are not isolated cases but instead reflect dominant discourses and a propensity to moral panic. These discourses and their interplay at micro and macro systemic levels impact on policy and practice, as we will now discuss.

Impact on the worlds of policy and practice

News media work under enormous time pressures as the insatiable appetite for news and 24-hour media outlets raise the stakes in the competition for sales, ratings and 'clicks'. Child abuse injuries, deaths and severe neglect demand explication in the public domain: very private aspects of family life are drawn into individual view, and elected officials and professional employees at managerial and direct service may be excoriated all in the search for responsibility and blame. All parties – families, politicians, investigators and professionals – may want truth and justice, and the impacts of the scrutiny can be severe and long-lasting.

Thomlison and Blome (2012) note three types of media commentaries on the deaths of children in the United States which impact on practitioners and organizations: first, agency service or system distress; second, personal impacts in employment and even criminal charges against child welfare staff; and third, notable shifts in the public support for the child welfare system. The counter-story of over-work, under-qualification and poor supervision is inevitably also heard, but whether or not media and agency statements are valid or exaggerated, 'they communicate to the reader that the child welfare agency offers poor service is a terrible place to work, is mismanaged, and harms children by commission or omission' (Thomlison & Blome, 2012, p. 246). There is a significant literature on the cyclical nature of reporting of abuse and the impact this may have on child welfare practice (Chenot, 2011; Jagannathan & Camasso, 2011; Wilson & Puckett, 2011; Mansell, 2006). While there is a broadly positive aspect to widespread reporting of child abuse because of raised public awareness and consequent engagement of the political process in legislation and resources, the negative consequences of media coverage (as noted above and particularly in the tabloid media) remains sensationalist and advocates simplistic solutions to what social workers know to be complex, enduring and resistant problems (Mendes, 2000). A focus on the criminal justice aspects of high-profile cases distracts attention from the contexts of, causes of and solutions to child sexual abuse, and as a consequence, prevention is rarely addressed (Mejia, Cheyne & Dorfman, 2012), but rather the focus remains on investigation and punishment. An obsessive focus on a small number of individual high-profile cases may prioritize the identification of scapegoats (Mendes, 2000; 2001; Warner, 2013a; 2013b; Jones, 2014) at the expense of building relationships with families in need, as highlighted in the Munro (2011) review of child protection in England.

But there is one final aspect of this discussion of the media, risk and child protection that must be considered, and that takes us back to the historical account at the beginning of the chapter. The newspaper editor in 1885 was able to gain access a child's story because two prominent campaigners helped him to do so. Similarly, all the child abuse enquiries since then demonstrate that social work and social workers have a part to play in drawing risk to the public's attention and then saying what should be done about it. Clapton and Cree (2016) are highly critical of the part that 'claims makers' such as child protection agencies have played in accelerating public fears and anxieties; they argue that social work needs to be more circumspect about evidence and about the possible damaging consequences of its public engagement activities. Today, we can all get involved in the media, through magazine and journal article writing, social media, podcasting and indeed book publication. We have a responsibility to use this wisely – to use our influence to open up discussions and to seek to ameliorate, not heighten, the risk paradigm.

Over the last few years calls have been made to break the negative cycle of child abuse reporting discussed above. In recent literature child welfare workers have been encouraged to utilize media for advocacy, promoting a much less passive relationship between workers and the news media (LaLiberte, Larson & Johnston, 2011; Briar-Lawson, Martinson, Briar-Bonpane & Zox, 2011). Briar-Lawson et al. (2011, p. 187) argue that there is good precedent for this approach, citing how 'pioneering social workers' in our history teamed up with media to promote public awareness about the social problems in our midst:

> In doing so, they recognized the power of the public as client....These professional predecessors understood the powerful interplay between the public's right to know about social ills and the abject community conditions that affected millions of high need families. They harnessed the media's capacity to expose these abject conditions to shape public perceptions and attitudes, propelling action for progressive change and for new policies and practices.

Given the sad fact that poverty, violence, abuse and exploitation are still with us, the example set by our predecessors should encourage us to act. And we are very lucky now to have many more forms of media in we which we can participate.

Conclusions

This chapter has attempted to open up a subject for scrutiny and to invite readers to think about the part the external media has played in creating discourses around children and child protection. It has also, more challengingly perhaps, drawn attention to social work's own role in manipulating the media for its own ends. Michel Foucault (1977) argued that we should not regard power as something that is simply 'top down', always something that is done to us. Rather, we all have power, and with power there is resistance. Perhaps this is a good note to end the chapter, urging that social workers must lay claim to a social work practice that does not demonize and stigmatize, but instead seeks to understand and build a better, more socially just society for all. If we are to do so, then we need to stand up and be counted – to engage with the media, to write articles and blogs, to allow ourselves to be interviewed, to risk disagreeing with each other and, most of all, to be honest about what social work can and cannot do. This has to be a more positive way forward than sitting back and blaming the media for social work's failings.

References

Barnes, A. M., Borell, B., Taiapa, K., Rankine, J., Nairn, R. & McCreanor, T. (2012). Anti-Maori themes in New Zealand journalism: Toward alternative practice. *Pacific Journalism Review*, 18(1), 195.

Beddoe, L. (2013). Violence and the media, in A. Taylor & M. Connolly (eds), *Understanding violence: Context and practice in the human services* (pp. 65–78). Christchurch, NZ: Canterbury University Press.

Beddoe, L. (2014). Feral families, troubled families: The rise of the underclass in New Zealand 2011–2013. *New Zealand Sociology*, 29(3), 51–68.

Beddoe, L. (2015). Making a moral panic – 'Feral families', family violence and welfare reforms in New Zealand: Doing the work of the state?, in V. E. Cree (ed.), *Moral panics in theory and practice: Gender and family* (pp. 31–42). Bristol: Policy Press.

Briar-Lawson, K., Martinson, K., Briar-Bonpane, J. & Zox, K. (2011). Child welfare, the media, and capacity building. *Journal of Public Child Welfare*, 5(2–3), 185–199. doi:10.1080/15548732.2011.566754

Bristow, E. J. (1977). *Vice and vigilance*, Dublin: Gill and MacMillan.

Bullock, H. E., Fraser Wyche, K. & Williams, W. R. (2001). Media images of the poor. *Journal of Social Issues*, 57(2), 229–246. doi:10.1111/0022–4537.00210

Butler, I. & Drakeford, M. (2005). *Scandal, social policy and social welfare* (2nd edn). Bristol: BASW Policy Press.

Chenot, D. (2011). The vicious cycle: Recurrent interactions among the media, politicians, the public, and child welfare services organizations. *Journal of Public Child Welfare*, 5(2–3), 167–184. doi:10.1080/15548732.2011.566752

Clapton, G., & Cree, V. E. (2016). Communicating concern or making claims? The 2012 press releases of UK child welfare and protection agencies. *Journal of Social Work*. 1–20, DOI: 10.1177/1468017316637228

Clapton, G., Cree, V. E. & Smith, M. (2013a). Moral panics and social work: Towards a sceptical view of UK child protection. *Critical Social Policy*, 33(2), 197–217. doi:10.1177/0261018312457860

Clapton, G., Cree, V. E. & Smith, M. (2013b). Moral panics, claims-making and child protection in the UK. *British Journal of Social Work*. doi:10.1093/bjsw/bct061

Cohen, S. (1972). *Folk devils and moral panics: The creation of the Mods and Rockers*. London: MacGibbon and Kee.

Cree, V. E., Clapton, G. & Smith, M. (2014). The presentation of child trafficking in the UK: An old and new moral panic? *British Journal of Social Work*, 44(2), 418–433. doi:10.1093/bjsw/bcs120

Cree, V. E., Clapton, G. & Smith, M. (2015). Standing up to complexity: researching moral panics in social work. *European Journal of Social Work*, 1–14. doi:10.10 80/13691457.2015.1084271

Cree, V. E., Macrae, R., Smith, M., Knowles, N., O'Halloran, S., Sharp, D. & Wallace, E. (2016). Critical reflection workshops and knowledge exchange: Findings from a Scottish project. *Child & Family Social Work*, 21, 548–556. doi:10.1111/cfs.12177

Critcher, C. (2009). Widening the focus: Moral panics as moral regulation. *British Journal of Criminology*, 49(1), 17–34.

Cushion, S. & Lewis, J. (eds) (2010). *The Rise of 24-Hour News Television: Global perspectives*. New York: Peter Lang.

Entman, R. M. (1993). Framing: Toward clarification of a fractured paradigm. *Journal of Communication*, 43(4), 51–58. doi:10.1111/j.1460-2466.1993.tb01304.x

Featherstone, B., White, S. and Morris, K. (2014) *Re-imagining child protection. Towards humane social work with families*. Bristol: Policy Press.

Foucault, M. (1977). *Discipline and punish*. London: Allen Lane.

Gamson, W. A. (1992). *Talking politics*. Cambridge, UK: Cambridge University Press.

Gorham, D. (1978). The maiden tribute of modern Babylon re-examined: Child prostitution and the idea of childhood in late-Victorian England, *Victorian Studies*, 21(Spring), 353–379.

Iyengar, S. (1990). Framing responsibility for political issues: The case of poverty. *Political Behavior*, 12(1), 19–40. doi:10.1007/bf00992330

Jagannathan, R. & Camasso, M. J. (2011). The crucial role played by social outrage in efforts to reform child protective services. *Children and Youth Services Review*, 33(6), 894–900. doi:http://dx.doi.org/10.1016/j.childyouth.2010.12.010

Jay, A. (2014). *Independent inquiry into child sexual exploitation in Rotherham, 1997–2013*, Metropolitan Borough Council. Available at www.rotherham.gov.uk/downloads/file/1407/independent_inquiry_cse_in_rotherham

Jenkins, J. (1992). *Intimate enemies. Moral panics in contemporary Great Britain*, New York: Aldine de Gruyter.

Jones, R. (2014). *The story of Baby P. Setting the record straight*. Bristol: Policy Press.

Kendall, D. E. (2011). *Framing class* (2nd edn). Plymouth, UK: Rowman and Littlefield.

LaLiberte, T. L., Larson, A. M. & Johnston, N. J. (2011). Child welfare and media: Teaching students to be advocates. *Journal of Public Child Welfare*, 5(2–3), 200–212. doi:10.1080/15548732.2011.566757

Mansell, J. (2006). The underlying instability in statutory child protection: Understanding the system dynamics driving risk assurance levels. *Social Policy Journal of New Zealand*, 28, 97–132.

Mejia, P., Cheyne, A. & Dorfman, L. (2012). News coverage of child sexual abuse and prevention, 2007–2009. *Journal of Child Sexual Abuse,* 21(4), 470–487. doi:1 0.1080/10538712.2012.692465

Mendes, P. (2000). Social conservatism vs social justice: The portrayal of child abuse in the press in Victoria, Australia. *Child Abuse Review,* 9(1), 49–61.

Mendes, P. (2001). Blaming the messenger: The media, social workers and child abuse. *Australian Social Work,* 54(2), 27–36.

Munro, E. (2011) *Munro review of child protection: final report – a child-centred system,* London: Department for Education.

Nairn, R., DeSouza, R., Barnes, A. M., Rankine, J., Borell, B. & McCreanor, T. (2014). Nursing in media-saturated societies: Implications for cultural safety in nursing practice in Aotearoa, New Zealand. *Journal of Research in Nursing,* 19(6), 477–487. doi:10.1177/1744987114546724

New Zealand Herald (27 June 2006). 'Taxpayers shell out for Kahuis'.

New Zealand Herald (30 June 2011). 'Macsyna King book author answers your questions'.

NewzText Plus (2012). Media database.

Parton, N. (1981). Child abuse, social anxiety and welfare. *British Journal of Social Work,* 11(1), 391–414.

Parton, N. (1985). *The politics of child abuse.* London: Macmillan.

Pearson, M. (1972). *The age of consent: Victorian prostitution and its enemies.* Newton Abbott: David and Charles Publishers.

Provan, S. (2012). The uncanny place of the bad mother and the innocent child at the heart of New Zealand's 'cultural identity' (University of Canterbury Christchurch, NZ. Retrieved from http://hdl.handle.net/10092/7393

Sotirovic, M. (2000). Effects of media use on audience framing and support for welfare. *Mass Communication and Society,* 3(2–3), 269–296. doi:10.1207/s15327825mcs0323_06

Taylor, H., Beckett, C. & Mc Keigue, B. (2008). Judgements of Solomon: Anxieties and defences of social workers involved in care proceedings. *Child & Family Social Work,* 13(1), 23–31.

Thomlison, B. & Blome, W. W. (2012). Hold the presses: A commentary on the effects of media coverage of fatalities on the child welfare system. *Journal of Public Child Welfare,* 6(3), 243–254. doi:10.1080/15548732.2012.683327

Van Gorp, B. (2007). The constructionist approach to framing: Bringing culture back in. *Journal of Communication, 57*(1), 60–78. doi:10.1111/j.0021–9916.2007.00329.x

Warner, J. (2013a). 'Heads must roll'? Emotional politics, the press and the death of Baby P. *British Journal of Social Work,* 44(6), 1637–1653. doi:10.1093/bjsw/bct039

Warner, J. (2013b). Social work, class politics and risk in the moral panic over Baby P. *Health, Risk & Society,* 15(3), 217–233. doi:10.1080/13698575.2013.776018

Wilson, D. & Puckett, A. (2011). Effects of moral outrage on child welfare reform. *Archives of Pediatrics & Adolescent Medicine,* 165(11), 977–978. doi:10.1001/archpediatrics.2011.177

Wishart, I (2011). *Breaking the silence: The Kahui case.* Auckland, NZ: Howling at the Moon Publishing.

3

ANTICIPATING RISK: PREDICTIVE RISK MODELLING AS A SIGNAL OF ADVERSITY

*Irene de Haan and Marie Connolly**

Introduction

In Chapter 1, Nigel Parton discussed the ways in which notions of risk and danger in child protection have reinforced the idea that we may be able to predict risk and then avert danger for children. This idea of being able to predict future harm has been challenged in the literature, particularly given the complex environment within which services are delivered and indeed the multifaceted difficulties that families face. The issues are certainly complex. This chapter nevertheless explores whether developments in predictive risk modelling might provide opportunities to better support vulnerable families – signalling a need when families experience adversity, rather than functioning as a mechanism that labels and stigmatizes them.

In the past, families experiencing chronic adversity were referred to as 'dysfunctional' or 'problem families'. Sometimes people still use these terms, although less often these days. The terminology suggests a sense of intractability and inevitability about some families' difficulties and a pessimistic attitude towards working with them that lingers more recently in the language used: for example, 'marginalized', 'excluded', 'at-risk', 'hard-to-reach' or 'vulnerable'. Whatever the words used, the situation of the families remains more or less the same – over time their difficulties tend to get worse rather than better. One problem leads to another, multiplying and compounding in 'risk chains' (Rutter, 1999) or 'cascade effects' (Masten & Powell, 2003), to the point of crisis. Adversity becomes

---

* Dr Irene de Haan is a senior lecturer at the School of Counselling, Human Services and Social Work at the University of Auckland, New Zealand. Professor Marie Connolly is a professor and chair of social work at the University of Melbourne, Australia.

entrenched. Children suffer. Child maltreatment is correlated with an array of problems, including mental health issues, substance abuse, chronic financial strain and transience. Exposure to intimate partner violence is increasingly recognized as maltreatment (Hughes & Chau, 2013). Mederos (2004, p. 3) underscores the well-documented overlap between domestic violence and child abuse: 'where one form of family violence exists, there is a likelihood the other does as well'.

As Morris and Burford note in Chapter 7, it is not easy for families to extricate themselves from adversity, and support to do so is seldom easily available when they need it. A common scenario involves struggling with problems for a prolonged period of time with little meaningful support, until a crisis occurs, triggering intervention by police, child protection authorities or health or mental health services. By this time, children may already be suffering cumulative harm, the result of patterns of physical and emotional abuse and neglect, often enmeshed, that undermine security, safety and well-being in ways that are not immediately obvious. Trauma associated with cumulative harm is pervasive and persistent, with effects sometimes becoming apparent only years later (Broadley, 2014), contributing to the intergenerational transmission of trauma. Suffering and marginalization continues. Eventual professional intervention in situations like these commonly results in out-of-home placement, entailing further disruption and trauma (Connolly, de Haan & Crawford, 2014). While the phenomenon of compounding adversity and intergenerational trauma is widely recognized, what is less well understood is what to do about it.

It has been argued that agencies tasked with protecting children's well-being have a 'moral obligation' (O'Donnell, Scott & Stanley, 2008, p. 326) to prevent maltreatment occurring in the first place, thus preventing cumulative harm. Describing child maltreatment as a 'wicked problem' that is unresponsive to linear problem solving, Devaney and Spratt (2009, p. 639) call for the provision of services that will ameliorate the worst effects of adverse childhood experiences, ideally 'even before the point whereby child protection services would traditionally become involved, for example, in cases of intimate partner violence or parental substance misuse'. Identifying these children is complicated by the uncertainty that characterizes professional interaction with families. Recently, a New Zealand study raised the possibility of sharpening focus on these children by using predictive risk modelling (PRM) tools that use algorithms to stratify children's risk of experiencing maltreatment in the future (Vaithianathan et al., 2012; Vaithianathan, Maloney, Putnam-Hornstein & Jiang 2013). Although the term 'predictive' implies future risk, the study focused on using PRM to locate families currently experiencing difficult circumstances. Ideally, supporting families well at this early stage could halt or reverse accumulating problems and make the notion of risk redundant. In the ethical review undertaken as part of this study, Dare (2015) points out that use of PRM in child welfare and protection should be compared with problems embedded in the current system – for example, children continuing to suffer harm; unnecessary intervention causing disruption and distress; stigma; barriers between professionals and families; and workforce demoralization.

Currently, families who experience adversity do not much benefit from supportive services. The boundary between families and professionals sometimes seems impermeable from both sides (Gaye & Campbell, 2011; Featherstone, Morris & White, 2014). Professionals see families as 'hard-to-reach' (Boag-Munro & Evangelou, 2012), and families see acceptance of services as opening their lives to scrutiny by people who will never understand their circumstances. Families in this position are unlikely to seek support. Even in situations of escalating family violence, coping strategies vary so much that both help seeking and help provision are far from straightforward (Nurius, Macy, Nwabuzor & Holt, 2011). A perception that professional service provision is troublemaking interference, threatening rather than supportive, is especially likely when previous encounters with professional 'helpers' were experienced as of little use, or indeed distressing, for example if intervention resulted in children being removed.

Drawing attention to cumulative harm, intergenerational trauma and cascading risk might seem an odd way to begin a chapter in a book entitled 'Beyond the Risk Paradigm'. Nonetheless, we will not get beyond that paradigm unless we take a good look around at where we actually are now. So in the chapter, we will describe strategies for forestalling harm when families are experiencing long-term adversity. We will outline the development of a prototype PRM tool in New Zealand, noting also the reactions when information about this work was published. Finally, we will summarize some of the arguments for and against the use of PRM.

From managing risk to preventing harm

Professionals with a child protection mandate must repeatedly make complex decisions about children's safety (Mansell, 2006; Munro, 2011). In doing so, they must balance two worrying possibilities: overlooking signs that children are unsafe versus overreacting when children in fact are safe (Shlonsky & Friend, 2007; Connolly & Doolan 2007), and they must do so in the knowledge that intervention can be disruptive and traumatic for children, while also knowing that children left in harmful situations may suffer emotional trauma, may be injured or may even die as a result of abuse or neglect. As Beddoe and Cree note in Chapter 2, in reporting high-profile child maltreatment cases the media have at times evoked public outrage, subjecting professionals to public vilification (Jagannathan & Camasso, 2011; Kemshall, 2002). Not surprisingly, this makes professionals even more anxious about leaving children in potentially dangerous situations (Chenot, 2011), so detecting 'risk' has become the main concern of child protection professionals and 'a preoccupation with risk and its management has engulfed public sector services' (MacDonald & MacDonald, 2010, p. 1174). In the context of this risk-focused paradigm, agencies tightened control, making child protection practice a closely scrutinized activity directed and monitored by bureaucratic procedures (Munro, 2005). In an effort to detect risk more efficiently and accurately, a range of consensus and actuarial risk assessment models were introduced. Greater attention to risk assessment, however, has neither significantly fortified confidence in child protection decision making (Schwartz, Kaufman & Schwartz, 2004), nor reduced rates of child maltreatment.

A key message of Munro's review of child protection in England is that 'preventative services will do more to reduce abuse and neglect than reactive services' (Munro, 2011, p. 69). A rationale for promoting prevention is that providing health, education and parenting programmes to promote children's development when they are very young reduces need for remedial services later (Dubowitz et al., 2011; Reynolds, Mathieson & Topitzes, 2009; Manning, Homel & Smith, 2010; Parton, 2014). Family support models developed in the 1980s and 1990s conceptualized early intervention as supporting families to resolve difficulties at an early stage, reinforcing self-efficacy and benefiting adults as well as children (Mason, 2012). Lately, however, the focus of prevention efforts has been the individual child, in the belief that parenting programmes and early childhood education may mitigate consequences of growing up in families considered to be lacking in capacity to promote children's optimal development. A service response focused on early intervention with children has been critiqued as part of a neoliberal agenda of 'investing' in children as a future benefit to society while neglecting to address the current needs of their families (Featherstone et al., 2014; Gray, 2014).

If early intervention services of any description are considered worthwhile, there is still the problem of identifying and engaging families who prefer to avoid professional service providers. 'Proportionate universalism' or 'cascading service delivery' (OECD, 2009) has been proposed as a non-threatening, non-stigmatizing way of making supportive services available to families. In this model, services designed to promote the well-being of all children, such as free maternity and infant health services, are used to introduce intensive or specialized services for children and families who need them. Making a case for a preventive approach based on universal services, O'Donnell et al. (2008, p. 329) say that for this to work, service providers must be able 'to identify vulnerable families early enough to change risky behaviours and avoid pathways to abuse'. Yet there is evidence that many children are not identified as 'at risk' even when actually suffering harm, especially when that harm is because of neglect or emotional abuse (Gilbert et al., 2009). It is not easy to distinguish families who are in particular need of extra support.

While there is a strong association between child maltreatment and poverty, a particularly prevalent aspect of adversity, most poor families do not ill-treat their children (NSPCC, 2008). Yet the hardships of poverty may overwhelm a family's equilibrium and capacity to keep coping when problems are compounding (Pelton, 2011; Waller, 2001). In a recent New Zealand study dealing with poverty and maltreatment, Wynd (2013) notes that maltreatment occurs against a background of individual stresses and capabilities, changing household circumstances, extended family issues and community characteristics. This complexity makes it hard to design programmes that will successfully enhance children's well-being, so as Wynd (2013, p. 13) says, 'accurately identifying at-risk children and designing programmes that are effective at protecting children in the long-term remains the Holy Grail of child abuse research'. In a meta-analysis of how low-income families experience support, Atree (2005, p. 335) found that parents' accounts 'underscore the often fragile nature of the social resources available to them' and agencies 'failed to offer support relevant to families needs'. PRM could contribute to preventive strategies by identifying families who need extra support so that relevant programmes could be designed and delivered.

Tackling the problem of identifying families in particularly troubling circumstances in order to offer support, Dubowitz et al. (2011) undertook a prospective longitudinal study of children from low-income families with no prior involvement with child protective services. Having looked at community and societal features as well as characteristics and experiences of individual families and children, they identified several factors that could be detected by professionals who routinely see children, and they concluded that screening families could enhance the delivery of targeted preventive services that complement universal policies and programmes. We suggest that PRM could be part of a similar strategy.

We will now turn to the development of PRM for child protection purposes in New Zealand, focusing on issues inherent in its use. Rather than going into the technical aspects of the development of PRM, we refer you to Vaithianathan et al. (2012; 2013) for a comprehensive account. The following discussion looks at broader imperatives influencing the development of the PRM initiative and reflects on challenges and opportunities associated with using technology of this type to identify children who might be deemed 'at risk'.

Development of PRM for child protection in New Zealand

New Zealand experiences persistently high rates of child maltreatment and intimate partner violence (Connolly & Doolan, 2007; Family Violence Death Review Committee, 2014; MSD, 2011; UNICEF, 2003). In recognition of this and the high levels of reporting of child abuse and neglect to the statutory services, the Vulnerable Children Study was commissioned by the New Zealand government in 2012. The aim of the study was to ensure that families received the services they needed and thus ease pressure on child protection resources, an issue of concern in New Zealand as in other countries (Mansell, 2006). The study was undertaken by a cross-university team of researchers based at the University of Auckland's Centre for Applied Research in Economics (Vaithianathan et al., 2012; 2013). Under strict confidentiality agreements, the researchers had access to a data set that linked administrative records from the income maintenance and child protection agencies, both of which are responsible to the New Zealand Ministry of Social Development (MSD), and both hold information collected on a nationwide basis. A literature review undertaken for the study sought previous applications of PRM in child maltreatment but found only one foray into computational intelligence techniques in this field (Schwartz, Jones, Schwartz & Obradovic, 2008). The Vulnerable Children Study included an ethical review by an expert in health ethics (Dare, 2015) and a Maori ethical review (Blanket al., 2015), both of which explored potential benefits and negative consequences of using PRM. The Maori ethical review was an essential component of the study, reflecting the government's commitment to the Treaty of Waitangi, New Zealand's founding document, and to Maori rights to self-determination that are reinforced within it.

The question addressed by the Vulnerable Children Study was whether administrative data could be used to produce a PRM tool capable of correctly assessing the likelihood that a child will have a substantiated maltreatment finding. The sample comprised the 57,986 children born between January 2003 and June 2006 and whose family received a main income support benefit (intended to cover basic living costs) for any length of time (termed a 'benefit spell') between the child's birth and fifth birthday. The data supplied by MSD to the researchers is routinely collected and relatively easily retrievable, and it contains information about parents' own history of maltreatment as well as more recent information associated with adversity, such as imprisonment, mental health issues or addictions. The researchers started with 224 potentially predictive variables that could be harvested from the data and sequentially dropped variables that were not statistically significant (P<.20) or perfectly correlated, leaving 132 variables selected for inclusion in the algorithm. As noted above, these variables related to both past and present circumstances. Since the data set extended into 2011, the researchers were able to retrospectively 'follow' children to establish whether they had a substantiated finding of maltreatment during their first five years. The methods utilized a stepwise probit regression technique, which was estimated on a randomly chosen 70 per cent of the sample and then validated on the remaining 30 per cent of the sample. Probit regression is a technique used when the predicted variables (in this case, substantiated maltreatment by age five) takes on one of two values: 'maltreated' or 'not-maltreated'. The algorithm was applied at the start of any new 'benefit spell'; that is, whenever the benefit system recorded alterations in a family's circumstances, such as a new address, new partner or new baby. A steep increase in risk rating in succeeding spells signals the possibility of increasing adversity.

The study indicated that notwithstanding the limited range of data sets available to the PRM tool, it was capable of very early identification of children about whom there was a later substantiated finding of maltreatment. Of the 57,986 children included in the sample, there was for 11,878 of them a finding of maltreatment by age five. The study showed that the families of 9,816 of these children received a main benefit before the child turned two and therefore would have been risk scored by the algorithm. This indicates that 'an algorithm that risk scores children while on a benefit in the first 2 years of their life has the ability to capture 83% of all children with maltreatment findings by age 5' (Vaithianathan et al., 2012, p. 12). Some children (13 per cent) were under two years old when the finding of maltreatment was made, suggesting that families should be offered support when children are very young. By comparison, for children whose families did not receive a benefit by the child's second birthday, only 1.4 per cent had a substantiated finding of maltreatment by age five. The algorithm was used to sort the children into deciles according to how likely they were to be maltreated during a particular spell. This showed that while only 5 per cent of an annual birth cohort will be identified in the top 20 per cent of risk, this group of children account for 37 per cent of all children who had substantiated maltreatment by age five. Depending on perspective, this group can be seen either as particularly 'at risk', thus raising professional alarm, or as likely to be coping with significant adversity, thus particularly in need of relevant support.

The Vulnerable Children Study suggests that PRM can help to prospectively identify some children who will later be maltreated, but not all. It indicates that PRM could identify families experiencing a set of circumstances *likely* to produce chronic adversity and *possibly* leading to cumulative harm and maltreatment. It is important to note that there was no substantiated finding of maltreatment for 52 per cent of the children in the top decile (i.e. highest risk) and for 71 per cent of those in the second top decile. The PRM tool variables are not causal. In devising the algorithm, the aim was not to ask 'What contributes to maltreatment?' but rather 'What variables can help us best discriminate between spells that are high risk and spells that are low risk?' (Vaithianathan et al., 2012, p. 11). By interpreting a family's 'high-risk decile' categorization as an indication of adversity, and a steep increase in risk as a crisis builds, constructive gains could be made in enhancing well-being and safety by offering families services carefully designed to be non-threatening and relevant to their needs.

Reactions to the PRM initiative

The publication of information from the Vulnerable Children Study drew media attention (NZ Herald, 2012) and created considerable reaction in New Zealand. One particularly vociferous reaction was that the PRM tool further stigmatized people receiving income support benefits. Another was that in stratifying families showing no signs of ill-treating children, PRM is a form of intrusive surveillance, infringing human rights. Others, however, saw the PRM tool as providing a genuine opportunity to facilitate early intervention, shifting child and family service provision away from its current reactive mode, where support is made available only after children have suffered harm. The ethical review linked to the study (Dare, 2012) strongly articulated this counterargument. Taking a human rights stance, and noting that UNESCO recently deplored 'staggering' rates of child maltreatment in New Zealand, Dare (2012) concluded that the harm done by maltreatment creates an ethical imperative to find ways to protect children and that potential concerns about PRM are outweighed by potential benefits. Adding weight to this view, the study confirmed the disturbing scale of maltreatment in New Zealand. Noting the problems involved in implementation, Dare (2012) concluded that the application of PRM should be preceded by a careful review of practical and ethical issues involved in implementation, including issues of privacy and stigma.

Surveillance and stigma

When a database contains disproportionate numbers of people from particular socioeconomic or ethnic groups, then the intensity of surveillance will fall most heavily on these people, who may then be perceived as particularly liable to exhibit the behaviour which the database records. The label thus created may then be applied to everyone in those groups, creating or exacerbating stigma. Since the Vulnerable Children PRM tool was constructed from data held by MSD, families with minimal interaction with MSD were 'invisible' to the tool, whereas families with a long history of interaction were highly visible. When the Vulnerable Children Study report was released, concerns were expressed that PRM would further stigmatize people receiving income support benefits. Commentators worried that the tool's linking of data from the state income support agency and the state child protection agency suggests that people receiving benefits have a propensity to child maltreatment. This concern is warranted. There are significant problems with superficially conflating child maltreatment and beneficiary data. To access benefits, families must interact with agencies, so data about them accrues, making these families subject to greater surveillance. It is important to note, however, that the Vulnerable Children PRM tool was an exercise in *possibility*, a trial prototype rather than an operational model. Discriminatory issues relating to using beneficiary and child protection databases could be ameliorated by incorporating more extensive sources of data, such as health, tax and birth records.

The practicalities and vagaries of administrative data collection are part of what makes a high PRM risk score a signal, not a forecast. PRM is certainly not infallible. The PRM tool will inevitably sort some children into 'wrong' risk deciles because the variables from which it is built are not causal. PRM will produce 'false positives' – that is, some children in high PRM deciles will never be maltreated; and it will produce 'false negatives' – that is, children deemed 'low risk' will suffer maltreatment. As a family's circumstances change, for better or worse, this may or may not be reflected in administrative data. Even when change in PRM scores indicates significant change in circumstances, this does not explain what this means for particular families (Spratt, 2008). Finding out what a change in PRM score means requires exploratory follow-up, notably comprehensive assessment or perhaps referral to a support provider or self-help group. The use of PRM presents issues of practice that need careful consideration. Families offered extra support as a result of high scores may feel either that this is an unwanted intrusion or that at last someone is offering help they badly need. Acceptance of support is likely to depend, first, on whether services offered are perceived as useful and, second, on how much stigma is associated with the support offered.

In the field of child and family welfare, professionals are now urged, and increasingly required, to collaborate more closely and share information more readily than they were in the past. This is in response to repeated findings that inadequate information sharing was a factor in family violence deaths. Adding information about PRM scores would add another layer of complexity to the maintenance of stringent confidentiality. If a PRM score is shared around a number of professionals, and a high score is interpreted as meaning that children are unsafe in that family, then a 'risky' label might stick (Pollack, 2010) to the family, compromising their privacy and reputation and maybe affecting professionals' perceptions of them in the future. Yet, the family may not know that information about them was shared, nor who received that information (Garrett, 2005). Hence, an important criticism that could be levelled against PRM is that it breaches confidentiality and subjects families to an unacceptable level of surveillance, creating ethical and human rights issues salient 'when service users are unaware that professionals are conducting risk assessments on them and communicating the findings of those assessments to others' (Langan, 2010, p. 96). Concern about confidentiality may be appeased by assurances that only the minimal amount of information is shared for professional purposes. Nevertheless, in the context of increased expectations about information sharing across agencies, several professionals may hear about a high PRM score, so even when a high score is a definite 'false positive', a family might still carry vestiges of the 'risky' label. Further, agencies with knowledge of a child's high PRM score may feel compelled to intervene, fearing consequences of inaction, to themselves as well as the child. Families may be pressured into accepting help. This is where the complex dynamics of pressure, coercion and discrimination become a real risk for families. There is potential for PRM to push families further into marginalization. In a context of misinterpretation of PRM, warning about danger rather than signalling adversity, even the provision of services intended to address families' problems, might unintentionally create negative perceptions about families who receive those services. Nonetheless, there are grounds for overcoming potential adverse consequences of using PRM. Arguments expressed in favour of its use hold that data in the custody of authorities should be used for the good of those to whom it pertains and that all information sharing is warranted because the consequences of family violence may be dire. These arguments presumably derive from the belief associated with a recent UK trial of a system for sharing information for safety reasons (Carter, 2012). We must return nevertheless to the fallibility of PRM and to the critical appreciation of what it can and can't tell us.

There are ways that PRM could contribute positively to the support needs of vulnerable families. PRM could streamline the introduction of targeted services to families who would benefit from them, perhaps through cascading service delivery, as mentioned above. Targeting, however, brings its own set of problems. Supporters of targeted services for 'high-risk' groups warn of the need to 'be sensitive to social inequalities and not to inadvertently widen them' (Reading et al., 2009, p. 337). The prototype PRM tool was criticized for potentially reinforcing an existing notion that families who receive income support benefits are more likely to abuse their children. This is a New Zealand stereotype that is no doubt common in other countries. Yet, if use of PRM is accompanied by the development of relevant preventive services, this stereotype may actually be dispelled through revitalizing the notion that families and their environment are interdependent and that, with relevant support, families can resolve problems. The Vulnerable Children Study showed that for most of the 57,986 children whose families received income support benefits, there was no evidence of maltreatment, while 2,062 children with a substantiated finding of maltreatment came from families who did not receive benefits. As noted above, research has repeatedly shown that maltreatment is associated with an 'accumulation' of personal, relational and environmental factors (MacKenzie, Kotch & Lee, 2011). It is by providing opportunities to address these difficulties that PRM has potential to dissipate the notion of risk, not only for individual families, but also more generally by reinterpreting 'high risk' as an opportunity to promote well-being.

Interestingly, PRM challenges child welfare policy and practice to hone the delivery of preventive services. At the same time, concern expressed in New Zealand is that PRM may be used to target services at the notionally 'vulnerable', with resources concomitantly diverted away from universal services. New Zealand's long tradition of universal services, including 'well child' services grounded in a model established in 1907, however, makes this an unlikely possibility. It is more likely that universal services would be used as a solid base for introducing targeted services for families who need them. At present this occasionally happens anyway, but the use of PRM would strengthen the case for a range of carefully designed preventive services aiming to meet families' actual needs, such as the intensive family support services widely resourced in the 1990s but now much less common, having largely been replaced by 'manualized' parenting programmes delivered according to a schedule or formula. Spratt (2008) argues that economic and social justice considerations demand that services be targeted at those most likely to benefit. For fear of professional scrutiny, however, parenting programmes are more likely to be voluntarily used by parents who are already functioning fairly well rather than parents whose capacity is destabilized by serious issues like addiction or intimate partner violence. For the latter families, motivation to participate can be compromised by fear of professional scrutiny. Mitchell and Campbell (2011, p. 422) call for a conceptual model that recognizes context and integrates practice, programme and policy approaches 'to intervene in the causative processes which create and maintain exclusion, while at the same time helping excluded families to leave the excluded state'. There is a convincing argument that screening should be undertaken only in a context where a remedy can be offered. The use of PRM, which is essentially a screening tool, might illuminate a need for more, or different, targeted services to assist families whose lives are affected by adversity.

PRM as a tool of early prevention

One of the distressing aspects of child protection work is that by the time children receive 'protection', they have already suffered harm. Often, families' problems become complex and entrenched long before their children come to the notice of child protection agencies (Boag-Munroe & Evangelou, 2012; Darlington, Healy & Feeney, 2010). Early intervention has the potential both to promote children's immediate safety and well-being and to interrupt the intergenerational cycles of deprivation and violence in which many families are caught (Reading et al., 2009). Since experiences of being parented influence children's eventual parenting capacity (Conger, Belsky & Capaldi, 2009), promoting the ability to raise children in a nurturing, secure environment may underpin beneficial change that will endure into the future. Few would disagree that it is preferable to support families to find positive solutions before problems tip them into crisis or that it is better to provide families with support to overcome chronic adversity rather than to react when serious events occur. Yet troubled families tend to avoid professional service providers, and service providers are constrained both in their ability to identify such families and to provide support in ways that engage them. Reasons that families reject professional support include mismatch between services provided and actual needs; the attitude or demeanour of professional workers; and fear that children will be 'taken away'. In Boag-Munroe and Evangelou's (2012, p. 209) systematic review of literature on families that have been dubbed 'hard-to-reach', the authors reframe the problem as 'how to reach' these families.

If seen as a way of identifying families with problems early, PRM could function as an aspect of a public health model of child welfare, providing ways to make secondary prevention services more easily accessible. Reading et al. (2009, p. 340) portray a public health approach as elevating children's rights, seeing provision of a wide range of preventive services as 'a highly effective instrument of change in policy, professional activity, and public values'. At the same time, investment in improved delivery of preventive services saves resources that would otherwise be required for tertiary prevention. Although PRM might be attractive to governments interested in the cost-effective targeting of resources, it takes time to see financial benefits from early intervention. Savings are typically not evident within relatively short political terms of office. Meanwhile, continued resourcing is required across the tertiary, secondary and primary levels.

Conclusion

Curiously, depending upon how it is framed and understood, PRM has the potential to make systems more, or less, risk dominated. Extending PRM to all children could set the scene for notions of risk to completely dominate the field. Conversely, PRM could lower the threshold at which families receive services, not in a way that ushers them into a confined space where all are deemed 'risky', but rather in a way that opens doors to an environment where they get what they need.

If PRM is to be used in the field of child and family welfare, what is required is a reframing of risk: from risk to opportunity; from hard to reach to under-resourced; from ignoring troubled families to caring enough to work out how best to support them. Certainly, advances in technology will make it easier to use administrative data sets to assist the identification of families who are experiencing difficulties. Insufficient attention to how support is provided, however, might reinforce forensically oriented child protection practice, stigmatizing and labelling families, creating extra work for professionals and potentially inundating the system to the point that it is unable to provide a well-organized, considered response. This scenario would only reinforce the risk paradigm. A different paradigm might nevertheless eventuate if a 'high-risk' score came to be viewed as a signal that a family may be experiencing adversity, and if this signal triggered, then an offer of support could be made easily available through responsive, capable services. In this way, the risk paradigm might be overlaid by a paradigm of prevention encompassing accessible support for problems identified by families themselves, as opposed to problems deemed important by professionals. A revitalized preventive paradigm might transport us to a point where professionals see opportunities and potential rather than problems and dysfunction and where service provision is welcomed rather than feared.

References

Atree, P. (2005). Parenting support in the context of poverty: A meta-synthesis of the qualitative evidence, *Health & Social Care in the Community*, 13(4), 330–337.

Blank, A., Cram, F., Dare, T., de Haan, I., Smith, B. & Vaithianathan, R. (2015). *Ethical issues for Māori in predictive risk modelling to identify new-born children who are at high risk of future maltreatment.* Wellington, NZ: MSD.

Boag-Munroe, E. & Evangelou, M. (2012). From hard to reach to how to reach: A Systematic review of the literature on hard-to-reach families, *Research Papers in Education*, 27(2), 209–239.

Broadley, K. (2014). Equipping child protection practitioners to intervene to protect children from cumulative harm: Legislation and policy in Victoria, Australia, *The Australian Journal of Social Issues*, 49(3), 265–284.

Carter, C. (2012). Police launch pilot scheme allowing queries about domestic violence history. *The Guardian*, 6 September. Retrieved from www.guardian.co.uk/society/2012/sep/06/police-scheme-queries-domestic-violence-history.

Chenot, D. (2011). The vicious cycle: Recurrent interactions among the media, politicians, the public, and child welfare services organizations, *Journal of Public Child Welfare*, 5(2–3), 167–184. doi:10.1080/15548732.2011.566752

Conger, R., Belsky, J. & Capaldi, D. (2009). The intergenerational transmission of parenting, *Developmental Psychology*, 45(5), 1276–1283.

Connolly, M., de Haan, I. & Crawford, J. (2014). Published online before print December 8, 2014. A cohort of young children in statutory care in Aotearoa New Zealand. 10.1177/0020872814554855.

Connolly, M. & Doolan, M. (2007). *Lives cut short: Child death by maltreatment.* Wellington, NZ: Dunmore Press Ltd.

Dare, T. (Due for publication February 2015). *Predictive risk modelling and child maltreatment: An ethical review.* Wellington, NZ: MSD.

Darlington, Y., Healy, K. & Feeney, J. (2010). Approaches to assessment and intervention across four types of child and family welfare services, *Children and Youth Services Review*, 32(3), 356–364.

Devaney, J. & Spratt, T. (2009). Child abuse as a complex and wicked problem: Reflecting on policy developments in the United Kingdom in working with children and families with multiple problems, *Children and Youth Services Review*, 31(6), 635–641.

Dubowitz, H., Kim, J., Black, M., Weisbart, C., Semiatin, J. & Magder, L. (2011). Identifying children at high risk for a child maltreatment report, *Child Abuse & Neglect*, 35(2), 96–104.

Duncan, J., Bowden, C. & Smith, A. (2005). *Early childhood centres and family resilience.* Wellington, NZ: Centre for Social Research and Evaluation, Ministry of Social Development.

Duvnjak, A. & Fraser, H. (2013). Targeting the 'hard to reach': Re/producing stigma? *Critical and Radical Social Work*, 1(2), 167–182. doi:10.1332/204986013x673245

Fallon, B., Trocmé, N., Fluke, J., MacLaurin, B., Tonmyr, E. & Yuan, Y. (2010). Methodological challenges in measuring child maltreatment, *Child Abuse & Neglect*, 34, 70–79.

Featherstone, B., Morris, K. & White, S. (2014). A marriage made in hell: Early intervention meets child protection, *British Journal of Social Work*, 44(7), 1735–1749.

Garrett, P. (2005). Social work's 'electronic turn': Notes on the deployment of information and communication technologies in social work with children and families, *Critical Social Policy*, 25(4), 529–553.

Gaye, G. & Campbell, L. (2011). The social economy of excluded families, *Child & Family Social Work*, 16(4), 422–433. doi:10.1111/j.1365-2206.2011.00757.x

Gilbert, R., Kemp, A., Thoburn, J., Sidebotham, P., Radford, L., Glaser, D. & MacMillan, H. (2009). Recognising and responding to child maltreatment, *Lancet*, 373, 367–380.

Gray, M. (2014). The swing to early intervention and prevention and its implications for social work, *British Journal of Social Work*, 44(7), 1750–1769.

Hughes, J. & Chau, S. (2013). Making complex decisions: Child protection workers' practices and interventions with families experiencing intimate partner violence, *Children and Youth Services Review*, 35, 611–617.

Jagannathan, R. & Camasso, M. (2011). The crucial role played by social outrage in efforts to reform child protective services, *Children and Youth Services Review*, 33(6), 894–900.

Kemshall, H. (2002). *Risk, social policy and welfare*. Buckingham, UK: Open University Press.

Langan, J. (2010). Challenging assumptions about risk factors and the role of screening for violence risk in the field of mental health, *Health, Risk & Society*, 12(2), 85–100.

Macdonald, G. & Macdonald, K. (2010). Safeguarding: A case for intelligent risk management, *British Journal of Social Work*, 40, 1174–1191.

MacKenzie M., Kotch, J. & Lee, L.-C. (2011). Toward a cumulative ecological risk model for the etiology of child maltreatment, *Children and Youth Services Review*, 33(9), 1638–1647.

Manning, M., Homel, R. & Smith, C. (2010). A meta-analysis of the effects of early developmental prevention programs in at-risk populations on non-health outcomes in adolescence, *Children and Youth Services Review*, 32(4), 506–519.

Mansell, J. (2006). The underlying instability in statutory child protection: Understanding the system dynamics driving risk assurance levels, *Social Policy Journal of New Zealand Te Puna Whakaaro*, 28, 97–132.

Mason, C. (2012). Social work the 'art of relationship': Parents' perspectives on an intensive family support project, *Child & Family Social Work*, 17(3), 368–377.

Masten, A. S. & Powell, J. (2003). A resilience framework for research, policy and practice. In S. S. Luthar (ed.), *Resilience and vulnerability: Adaptation in the context of childhood adversities*. Cambridge, UK: Cambridge University Press.

Mederos, F. (2004). *Accountability and connection with abusive men: A new child protection response to increasing family safety*. Massachusetts Department of Social Services: Family Violence Prevention Unit – Family Violence Prevention Fund.

Ministry of Social Development. (2011). *The statistical report*. Wellington, NZ: MSD.

Mitchell, L. & Campbell, G. (2011). The social economy of excluded families, *Child & Family Social Work*, 16(4), 422–433.

Munro, E. (2005). Improving practice: Child protection as a systems problem, *Children and Youth Services Review*, 27(4), 375–391.

Munro, E. (2011). *The Munro Review of child protection: Final report: A child centred system*. London: Department for Education.

NSPCC (2008). *Poverty and child maltreatment*. London: NSPCC.

Nurius, P., Macy, R., Nwabuzor, I. & Holt, V. (2011). Intimate partner survivors' help-seeking and protection efforts: A person-oriented analysis, *Journal of Interpersonal Violence*, 26(3), 539–566.

NZ Herald (20/10/2012). *Predicting trouble: Child abuse database raises eyebrows*. www.nzherald.co.nz/nz/news/article.cfm?c_id=1&objectid=10841709

O'Brien, M. (2011). Poverty and violence, and children, in M. C. Dale, M. O'Brien and S. St John (eds), *Left further behind: How policies fail the poorest children in New Zealand. A Child Poverty Action Group Monograph*. Auckland, NZ: CPAG.

O'Donnell, M., Scott, D. & Stanley, F. (2008). Child abuse and neglect – is it time for a public health approach? *Australian and New Zealand Journal of Public Health*, 32(4), 325–330.

OECD (2009). *Doing better for children*. www.oecd.org/els/familiesandchildren/doingbetterforchildren.htm

Parrot, L. & Madoc-Jones, I. (2008). Reclaiming information and communication technologies for empowering social work practice, *Journal of Social Work*, 8(2), 181–197.

Parton, N. (2006). *Safeguarding childhood: Early intervention and surveillance in a late modern society*. London: Palgrave Macmillan.

Parton, N. (2014). *The politics of child protection. Contemporary developments and future directions*. Hondmills, Basingstoke: Palgrave Macmillan.

Pelton, L. (2011). Concluding commentary: Varied perspectives on child welfare, *Children and Youth Services Review*, 33(3), 481–485.

Pereda, N., Guilera, G., Forns, M. & Gomez-Benito, J. (2011). The prevalence of child sexual abuse in community and student samples: A meta-analysis, *Clinical Psychology Review*, 29(4), 328–338.

Pollack, S. (2010). Labelling clients 'risky': Social work and the neo-liberal welfare state, *British Journal of Social Work*, 40, 1263–1278.

Quinton, D. (2004). *Supporting parents: Messages from research*. London: Jessica Kingsley Publishers.

Reading, R., Bissell, S., Goldhagen, J., Harwin, J., Masson, J., Moynihan, S., Parton, N., Santos Pais, M., Thoburn, J. & Webb, E. (2009). Promotion of children's rights and prevention of child maltreatment, *Lancet*, 373(January 24), 332–343.

Reynolds, A., Mathieson, L. & Topitzes, J. (2009). Do early childhood interventions prevent child maltreatment? A review of research, *Child Maltreatment*, 24(2) 182–206.

Rutter, M. (1999). Resilience concepts and findings: Implications for family therapy, *Journal of Family Therapy*, 21, 119–144.

Schwartz, D., Kaufman, A. & Schwartz, I. (2004). Computational intelligence techniques for risk assessment and decision support, *Children and Youth Services Review*, 26(11), 1081–1095.

Schwartz, I., Jones, P., Schwartz, D. & Obradovic, Z. (2008). Improving social work through the use of technology and advanced research methods, in D. Lindsey

& A. Shlonsky (eds), *Child welfare research: Advances for practice and policy* (pp. 214–230). New York: Oxford University Press.

Shlonsky, A. & Friend, C. (2007). Double jeopardy: Risk assessment in the context of child maltreatment and domestic violence, *Brief Treatment and Crisis Intervention*, 7, 253–274.

Spratt, T. (2008). Identifying families with multiple problems: Possible responses from child and family social work to current policy developments, *British Journal of Social Work*, 39(3), 435–450.

UNICEF (2003). *A league table of child maltreatment deaths in rich nations, Innocenti report cards*. Florence, Italy: UNICEF Innocenti Research Centre.

Vaithianathan, R., Maloney, T., Jiang, N., Dare, T., de Haan, I., Dale, C. & Putnam-Hornstein, E. (2012). *Vulnerable Children: Can administrative data be used to identify children at risk of adverse outcomes?* Wellington, NZ: Ministry of Social Development. Retrieved from www.msd.govt.nz/about-msd-and-ourwork/publications-resources/research/vulnerable-children/index.html

Vaithianathan, R., Maloney, T., Putnam-Hornstein, E. & Jiang, N. (2013). Children in the public benefit system at risk of maltreatment: Identification via predictive modeling, *American Journal of Preventive Medicine*, 45, 354–359.

Waller, M. A. (2001). Resilience in ecosystemic context: Evolution of the concept, *American Journal of Orthopsychiatry*, 71(3), 290–297.

Wynd, D. (2013). *Child abuse: An analysis of child, youth and family data*. Child Poverty Action Group Inc.

4

NEW KNOWLEDGE IN CHILD PROTECTION: NEUROSCIENCE AND ITS IMPACTS[1]

*Clare Huntington**

Introduction

Scholars, practitioners, courts and policymakers are increasingly drawing on the growing field of neuroscience to inform decisions. Educational experts, for example, are pressing for reforms to the classroom based on neuroscientific research about how students learn (School of Education at Johns Hopkins University, 2015). Doctors and sports medicine experts are using research on the lasting damage to the brain from repeated concussions (Aronson, 2011) and accordingly advocating for changes to the practice of many sports. And courts are using neuroscience to justify changes to settled doctrine, such as a series of decisions by the U.S. Supreme Court finding that the sentencing of juveniles should account for their ongoing brain development (*Montgomery* v. *Louisiana*, 2016; *Miller* v. *Alabama*, 2012; *Graham* v. *Florida*, 2010; *Roper* v. *Simmons*, 2005).

Research into brain development during early childhood and adolescence is equally salient to child protection and perceptions of risk that inform so much policy in this area. It is an area of knowledge that informs decision making. This research holds tremendous potential for the development of child protection policy and is gaining currency in the practice of child protection, particularly in judicial decision making. Yet operationalizing this still emerging science in itself presents considerable dangers. Given its indeterminacy, the research is highly susceptible to political cooptation and can be deployed in support of different, and sometimes incompatible, policies.

---

* Professor Clare Huntington is the associate dean for research and a professor of law in the School of Law at Fordham University, USA.

46

In the context of the risk paradigm in child protection, neuroscientific evidence could be used either to support or challenge the paradigm. Policymakers and other stakeholders could use the research into brain development to argue in favour of a defensive approach to child protection. Advocates could contend that too much is at stake, neurologically speaking, to risk leaving very young children with questionable caregivers. By contrast, policymakers and other stakeholders could use the research into brain development to argue that the child protection system should do far more to support and strengthen families early on to prevent child maltreatment because reactive intervention comes too late.

After explaining the current research into brain development, this chapter describes the recent use of neuroscience to explore this question of malleability, concluding that the danger is considerable.[2]

Neuroscience and child development

A growing body of neuroscientific research is clearly relevant to the child protection system. In a system ostensibly designed to protect the well-being of children, it is important to understand the basic building blocks of child development across childhood and through adolescence. To make the process of brain development more understandable to non-scientists, some neuroscientists use the concept of brain architecture – the idea that during the prenatal period and the first few years of life, children develop a framework that is the foundation for all future learning (National Scientific Council on the Developing Child, 2010a, p. 1). The interaction between caregivers and children is essential to building this architecture, but when this relationship is deeply compromised because of child abuse or neglect, extreme poverty, maternal clinical depression or similar challenges, children's brains are affected in ways that can last a lifetime. Similarly, neuroscientists are beginning to identify a second period of rapid growth and development, during adolescence, that is a particularly important window for intervention.

Brain architecture

Neuroscientists have found that during the prenatal period and early childhood, the brain lays down neural pathways that become the foundation for future brain development, with brain cells – neurons – forming circuits. The neural circuits that are used repeatedly grow stronger, but those that are not used regularly die off through a process called pruning. Neural circuits become the basis for the development of language, emotions, logic, memory, motor skills and behavioural control (Center on the Developing Child, 2007). With repeated use, the circuits become more efficient, connecting different areas of the brain more rapidly and thus affecting a person's ability to think effectively and regulate emotions (Id.). If the foundation is strong, it is easier to build upon in later years, but if the foundation is weak, it is much harder for the brain to develop the higher-level skills that rely on efficient connections between different areas of the brain (Id.; National Scientific Council on the Developing Child, 2007a, pp. 1–4).

Much of the critical development occurs before a child enters formal schooling at age five, although some processes continue into adulthood (National Scientific Council on the Developing Child, 2007a, pp. 1–5).[3] Different capacities develop during so-called 'sensitive periods', with the basic neural circuitry for vision and hearing developing shortly before and soon after birth and the circuits used for language and speech production peaking before age one (Id., pp. 2–3). The higher-level circuits used for cognitive functions develop throughout the first several years of life (Id., pp. 3–4). The so-called executive functions refer to the brain's ability to hold information in the short-term, ignore distractions and switch gears between contexts and priorities (or, to use slightly more formal terminology, 'working memory', 'inhibitory control' and 'cognitive flexibility'). Executive functioning is developed from birth through late adolescence, but with a particularly important period occurring from ages three to five (National Scientific Council on the Developing Child & National Forum on Early Childhood Policy and Programs, 2011, pp. 1–8).

Genetics provide a blueprint for brain development, but it is a child's environment and experiences that determine the strength of the brain architecture.[4] Beginning with environment, the prenatal and postnatal context for development can affect the expression of genes. For example, if a foetus is exposed to certain toxins, such as alcohol, during pregnancy (and especially during certain periods of the pregnancy), this harms the development of neural circuits. Similarly, after birth, the availability of nutrients and the absence of toxins also affect the construction of the neural circuitry.

Turning to a child's experiences, a critical mechanism for making and strengthening neural connections is what some neuroscientists refer to as 'serve-and-return' interaction between an attentive, responsive caregiver and a child. The child initiates interaction through babbling, movements and facial expressions, and the adult responds with sounds and gestures. Through this serve-and-return, neural connections between different areas of the brain are established and reinforced. As neuroscientist Daniel Siegel explains, 'where you are focusing attention stimulates the firing of certain neurons. And when neurons fire, they increase their synaptic connectivity to one another' (Siegel & McIntosh, 2011, p. 513). In other words, 'relational experience drives neural firing, and neural firing drives neural wiring' (Id.). The neural connections forged through interactions with a caregiver become the basis for future communication and social skills (National Scientific Council on the Developing Child, 2004a, p. 1; National Scientific Council on the Developing Child, 2007a, p. 5; National Scientific Council on the Developing Child, 2004b, pp. 1–3).

Sensitive developmental periods are a time of particular vulnerability for neural circuits. Significantly adverse environments and experiences during the sensitive periods can have lasting impacts on the circuitry as the circuits develop in response to the adverse conditions. Compromised circuits are harder, although not impossible, to repair later in life (National Scientific Council on the Developing Child, 2007a, p. 4).

Toxic stress

A relationship with an attentive, responsive adult may be the key to building strong brain architecture, but the absence of such a relationship can be devastating. This can be demonstrated through the concept of toxic stress. Learning how to cope with stress is an important part of child development. For example, the temporary disappearance of a caregiver or a minor injury may trigger a child's stress response system, with an increased heart rate and increased levels of stress hormones (National Scientific Council on the Developing Child, 2007b, pp. 9–10; National Scientific Council on the Developing Child, 2005, p. 1). When a caregiver promptly comforts the child, the response system is quickly deactivated and the child develops a sense of mastery over stressful events (National Scientific Council on the Developing Child, 2005, p. 1). Neuroscientists refer to this as positive stress (Id.).

By contrast, prolonged, severe or frequent stress stemming from abuse, neglect, extreme poverty and maternal clinical depression can create 'toxic stress' (Id.).[5] When there is no caring adult able to relieve this stress – or when the caregiver is the source of the stress, as in the case of abuse and neglect – the child's stress response remains activated. This constant activation overloads the developing brain and impedes the construction of neural pathways. In cases of moderate toxic stress, the brain can change such that it develops a hair trigger for stress, activating the stress response system in reaction to events that others might not perceive as stressful (Id.).[6]

This lasting effect occurs because the neural circuits involved in the transmission of stress signals are particularly flexible during early childhood. Toxic stress leaves an enduring impression on the creation of these circuits, affecting how easily the stress response is turned on and off (Id.,

p. 2). This, in turn, creates a greater vulnerability to physical and mental illnesses, such as diabetes, strokes, cardiovascular disease, depression and anxiety disorders (Id.).

Further, the heightened level of cortisol, the hormone triggered by stress, has consequences for the development of the areas of the brain dedicated to memory and learning, weakening the neural connections to these parts of the brain (Id., pp. 2–3). Responsive caregivers help to prevent the production of cortisol, even in a child temperamentally predisposed to be anxious. By contrast, when a caregiver is depressed, abusive or neglectful, a child's cortisol levels increase during the stressful period and remain high even after that period ends (Id., p. 4).[7]

The effect of toxic stress is particularly strong during sensitive periods when neural circuits are forming and maturing (National Scientific Council on the Developing Child, 2007a, p. 2). During these periods, the genetic plan and brain architecture can be significantly modified. By contrast, once a circuit has matured, environment and experiences affect the genetic plan and architecture to a much lesser degree (Id.). For example, the loss of an important caregiver during the period of critical growth – say at age nine months – can change the child's brain development in a way that affects the child's ability to regulate her emotional state in the future (Schore & McIntosh, 2011, pp. 506–507). For a nine-year-old child, this loss may result in temporary disorganization and regression, but for the infant, the loss may have a lasting effect on brain functioning (Id.).

To appreciate the effect of toxic stress on serve-and-return interactions, consider maternal depression. In this context, maternal depression refers to clinical depression, not the 'baby blues' that many women experience after giving birth. Instead of engaging in serve-and-return interactions, a clinically depressed mother typically is either hostile and aggressive to her children or withdrawn and disengaged (National Scientific Council on the Developing Child & National Forum on Early Childhood Program Evaluation, 2009, p. 3). Both parenting styles negatively affect the serve-and-return interaction that is crucial for brain development, either because the mother's serve is unappealing to the child or because the mother does not return a serve from the child (Id.). When this pattern continues for a prolonged period, the child's brain architecture can be affected (Id.). Indeed, brain scans conducted through an electroencephalogram, or EEG, reveal that children with depressed mothers show brain activity similar to depressed adults. This result was found both with infants and toddlers (children in their second and third years) (Id., pp. 3–4).

Maternal depression is particularly worrisome because it is widespread and highly correlated with poverty. For example, one study of mothers with nine-month-old infants found that 10 per cent of the women with income levels over 200 per cent of the poverty level were severely depressed, but 25 per cent of the women living below the poverty level were severely depressed (Id., pp. 1–2).[8] Further, maternal depression often occurs alongside other adverse conditions – depressed mothers are more likely to be young, have had stressful childhoods and be socially isolated (Id., p. 4). They are also more likely to be victims of domestic violence, have poor health and struggle with substance abuse (Id.). This raises complex questions about the cause and effect of maternal depression, but the correlation – and impact on neural development – is clear.

Adolescence as a second period of brain development

Adolescence and young adulthood are another critical period for brain development, and neuroscientists have begun to map the changes. Much has been made of the fact that brain development continues into the 20s, typically with an emphasis on the incomplete nature of adolescent brains. During this period, the prefrontal cortex, which is involved in judgement and impulse control, is still maturing. In addition to developing this part of the brain, there are other critical processes underway as well. The brains of adolescents and young adults, for example, are undergoing another period of pruning and strengthening (Steinberg & Morris, 2001; Sowell et al., 1999).

The effectiveness of intervention

Even when a child has been exposed to toxic stress during a sensitive period, and even if the child has a genetic predisposition to be harmed by that stress, early interventions can still be effective. Take, for example, mental illness in children. Widely under-recognized and under-diagnosed, mental illnesses in young children often stem from a combination of a genetic predisposition and adverse environment and experiences (National Scientific Council on the Developing Child, 2008, pp. 1–9). A child with an anxiety disorder, for example, may have inherited a gene that is associated with adult anxiety. If the child grows up in a stressful environment, the child is particularly at risk for developing an anxiety disorder. But this child is also a candidate for effective intervention, especially if undertaken at a young age (Id.). If the child is provided with experiences in an environment rich with appropriate emotional supports, stable relationships with nurturing and skilled caregivers, and preventive mental health services, she may well overcome the anxiety disorder, or at least develop far better coping mechanisms (Id., p. 6). Similarly, studies on severe maternal depression have found that intensive interventions focusing on the mother–child interactions have positive outcomes for both parent and child (National Scientific Council on the Developing Child & National Forum on Early Childhood Program Evaluation, 2009, pp. 5–6). Finally, adolescence appears to be another fruitful time for intervention and healing (Jim Casey Youth Opportunities Initiative, 2011).

The use of neuroscientific evidence in legal decision making

Findings from neuroscience are clearly relevant to child protection. The research strongly supports the notion that caregiver–child relationships are essential to child well-being, that there are particularly important periods for brain development and that the early years are critical to a child's future capacity for learning, social skills and self-regulation. The question, then, is how legal decision makers are using the research.

Court decisions

Consider several cases from around the United States.[9] In an unpublished opinion, *In re G.V., C.A., Z.H.* (2009), a North Carolina appellate court reviewed the trial court's decision, which had relied, in part, on neuroscientific evidence about neglect and brain development to terminate parental rights to two children. The mother in the case had left the children, both under the age of three, alone in repeated instances, and one time the children were found playing in the middle of the road. In its findings of fact, the trial court recounted testimony and concluded that 'the effects of neglect on the brain are profound' and that 'there is research available over the past 10 years of what we can now see in children's brain development, and it is astounding, as it looks like organic damage, so when we see the brain scans it is quite striking. These will and can affect the child the rest of his life' (Id.).[10] The trial court (Id.) further found that

> With children under three, professionals in the field are now asking the Courts, Attorneys and Counselors to protect the children's brain function at this important stage of development, as when parents have not shown an ability to take care of themselves, raising a child is the most stressful thing they will do in their lives and parents that are trying to keep clean, work, should be rewarded, but not with a child.

Although the evidence clearly influenced the trial court, the appellate court was more guarded in its use of the research. It concluded that the evidence was not relevant to the question of whether the parents were likely to repeat the past neglect, which was one of the statutory bases for terminating parental rights. In other words, the neuroscientific evidence showed what was at stake in the case, but could not establish a parent's likelihood to reengage in child neglect.

In a second example, the Supreme Court of Indiana drew on evidence about brain development to uphold the termination of a father's parental rights. One of the questions facing the trial court was whether the father's physical abuse of the mother in front of a toddler and infant was sufficient to find that the father had abused the children, under Indiana law. The court concluded that this was sufficient, justifying its decision by quoting research finding that 'even in the earliest phases of infant and toddler development, clear associations have been found between exposure to violence and post-traumatic symptoms and disorders' (*In re E.M.*, 2014, p. 644).[11] The court further stated that '"[t]he developing brain is most vulnerable to the impact of traumatic experiences" *before age one* – and during the first three years, those experiences actually change the organization of the brain's neural pathways' (Id.).[12]

In this case, then, the neuroscientific evidence was relevant to the legal question of which kinds of conduct constituted abuse. In assessing this determination, the court relied on general neuroscientific evidence about the long-term impact of witnessing domestic violence on brain development.

A third example also involved the impact of domestic violence committed in front of young children. In the case, *In re Hazekiah G.* (2013), a trial court in Connecticut issued a written opinion in conjunction with its decision, ordering the removal of an infant from the parents' custody based on the past violence between the parents in front of older children. At the trial (Id., p. 3), a clinical psychologist who had conducted evaluations of the parents testified as follows:

Q: What would be the impact of domestic violence of – within the home on – on an infant?

A: So one of the primary concerns is that it results in trauma because it creates a level of stress response in a child, fear, and that can have, we know now from the research, significant implications on brain development. And infants and young children can develop PTSD symptoms at a very early age, and then that goes on to disrupt their appropriate and normal pathway of development if it's not addressed.

The court relied on this testimony as well as other evidence to conclude that the child should not be left in the care of the mother and thus should be removed from the home. As with the Indiana case, the court drew on general neuroscientific evidence about brain development to support the legal decision.

Finally, in *Gore* v. *Gloucester County Department of Social Services* (2012), a Virginia appellate court reviewed the evidence used by the trial court to order the termination of parental rights. The parents had subjected their six-year-old daughter to extreme torture by keeping her locked in a small cage at all times, including when the parents went to work and by depriving her of medical care, adequate food and access to a toilet. A child abuse specialist examined the girl and reported that she was severely underweight and nearly eight inches shorter than normal for her age and that her head circumference was equivalent to a three-year-old child. The doctor stated that '[w]hen a child is malnourished such that the brain is not growing, severe developmental deficits take place that will never be overcome' (Id., p. 2).[13] The doctor also found that 'the devastating effects of prolonged starvation and emotional abuse on her development remain to be seen. [The child] will need intensive medical and psychological intervention for years' (Id., p. 3). Based on this evidence, the appellate court had little difficulty in upholding the trial court's decision to terminate parental rights.

Judicial training

It is not surprising that courts are drawing on neuroscience in light of the considerable effort to integrate neuroscientific research into judicial decision making. The National Council of Juvenile and Family Court Judges (NCJFCJ), for example, has released a video (2014) about the issue, introduced with the following text:

> This 5-minute video, narrated by NCJFCJ President Judge Peggy Walker, depicts a call to action for the legal community to learn as much as possible about brain science to make sure our law and policy are aligned with the focus on the latest information for building the capabilities of caregivers and strengthening the communities that together form the environment of relationships essential to children's lifelong learning, health, and behavior.

The video describes the current reactive approach to child well-being and argues for an early intervention approach that is based on neuroscience. After explaining the basics of brain development, the video describes the effectiveness of evidence-based interventions that target trauma, such as cognitive behavioural therapy. The video is then followed by a series of links to resources with more information about neuroscience and child development. This video is not limited to the brain science about young

children and instead highlights the importance of interventions for adolescent children as well.

Another example of the integration of neuroscience into family court
is the work of Cindy Lederman, the presiding judge of the Juvenile Court
in Miami-Dade County, who has partnered with scholars from several
disciplines to develop the Miami Child Well-Being Court model (Fraser
& Casanueva, 2013). This model is based on neuroscientific research and
is focused in particular on court-based interventions for parents and very
young children. The court refers the mother and child to a team of clinical
experts in infant mental health for evaluation and treatment, which can
include child–parent psychotherapy and parenting programmes proven
to improve outcomes. The court works with the team in developing an
appropriate treatment plan for the family. Coordination and cooperation
among the court, the caseworkers, the treating therapists and the attor-
neys is at the core of the approach. Judge Lederman and her team are
working to replicate the model around the country.

Reasons for caution

Threshold questions

As the description of legal decision making illustrates, the still emerging
field of neuroscience can help inform the field of child protection, under-
scoring the importance of protecting and promoting children's well-being.
There are, however, concerns about using this research. As an initial matter, it is important to ask whether non-neuroscientists are competent
enough to draw on this complex research, whether the field is sufficiently
mature to form the basis for decisions and how the research should be
used, both in individual cases and at a policy level.

Beginning with the concern about competence, it is true that layper-
son readers may adopt study findings uncritically, and readers should be
particularly cautious about research summaries that necessarily contain
elisions in the underlying science. But this challenge is no more pointed
in the context of neuroscience than in many other interdisciplinary
undertakings. Courts have long used expert psychological testimony and
have developed tests for evaluating and admitting this kind of evidence.
The use of neuroscientific evidence in child protection cases is no different
from the widespread use of other kinds of evidence.

Turning to the concern about whether the field is too young, neuroscientists are quick to identify gaps in our understanding of brain development (Rose, 2005, pp. 187–220). But this does not mean that the evidence
is irrelevant, only that consumers should be cautious. One answer is to

rely on findings that are well established by multiple sources and studies. The role of serve-and-return interactions in developing neural circuitry, for example, is widely accepted.

As reflected in the judicial training and reported cases discussed above, courts appear to be taking this conservative approach. Judicial actors are not relying on novel claims about the effects of child abuse on the brain. Instead, courts are drawing on the abundant research establishing that trauma in early childhood can have a lasting detrimental impact on child development. In particular, courts are relying on the finding that maltreatment can affect stress levels or, in the terminology set forth above, create 'toxic stress'. Although courts must be careful not to assume that this is true in every instance of maltreatment, as a general matter the proposition is well supported by the research.

Finally, there is a real danger when courts and other decision makers use evidence in individual cases. For example, even if they had the resources to do so, participants in the child protection system should not scan the brain of a depressed mother and a child and then base a removal decision on the extent to which the child's brain activity mimics that of the mother. The studies to date tell us only that there are reasons to be concerned about clinical depression and child development, but not that any given child should be removed from the care of a depressed mother. We simply do not know enough about how a particular child might fare in the care of a particular mother, what other protective factors might be in place or what hardships the child might face in a different placement.

The survey of cases as well as the judicial training provide some indication that courts are drawing only on general findings about brain development. It does not appear that courts (or social service agencies) are trying to apply the research in a more particularized fashion. In the first case concerning neglectful parents, for example, it appears that the trial court was relying on the evidence about brain development to support the termination of parental rights. But the court was doing so only in a generalized way, to explain what was at stake. And the appellate court made clear that the trial court could not simply conclude that early childhood is an important period for brain development. The trial court also had to find that the parents before the court were unfit. As the appellate court explained, the evidence about brain development was irrelevant to this inquiry and instead showed merely why neglect would matter at this age. In extreme cases, such as the severely malnourished child in Virginia, the evidence of head circumference was used to make a particular finding about the physical effect of the maltreatment, but neither were there brain scans of the child nor was there the introduction of extensive neuroscientific evidence.

As a tentative matter, then, there does not appear to be cause for concern about the *current* use of neuroscientific research in the courtroom.

Instead, courts are relying on well-established propositions to clarify what is at stake in particular cases. Moreover, the larger-scale efforts to help judges understand how best to work with the families before them are encouraging. The Miami Child Well-Being Court is an excellent example of the potential benefits of drawing on neuroscientific research to develop more effective, court-based interventions.

Despite this cautious optimism, it is important to remain alert to potential dangers, which may come to fruition if courts begin to use neuroscientific evidence in troubling ways.

Malleability

At present, the biggest concern with neuroscientific research is that it can be used to support different, and sometimes incompatible, policies. Some may look at the research, for example, and use it in support of a defensive approach (as embodied in the risk paradigm) to child protection. The argument would be that the child protection system should do more to remove very young children from questionable caregiving situations. Especially in a time of budget cuts and a political unwillingness to incur short-term costs for long-term gains, policymakers and legislatures could argue that this research demonstrates that there is no time to lose. Advocates of this approach might use the research to buttress policies that emphasize removal and termination, with short time limits for parents to address the issues underlying the abuse or neglect. The argument would be that there is a basic mismatch between the time line of child brain development, with the need for attentive care during the all-important sensitive periods, and the time line of a troubled parent, who may need prolonged assistance with issues such as substance abuse and may well experience relapses that are often part of recovery (McLellan et al., 2000, p. 1689).[14]

By contrast, others may use the research to argue against a reactive approach to child well-being and in favour of prevention programmes. The argument might be framed as follows: If early adverse experiences and environments can deeply affect a child's neural development, with lifelong consequences, then surely the child protection system – and the state more generally – should try its hardest to improve the conditions in which children live. Programmes that work with pregnant women and new parents to improve parenting are particularly well suited to improving both the prenatal and postnatal environment and a child's early experiences with a caregiver.

The new research into brain development, then, does not settle these longstanding debates so much as give each side additional evidence for its arguments.

One promising outgrowth of the research is the development of new interventions. The Miami County Child Well-Being Court, for example, does not necessarily reflect either a defensive or a preventive mindset. Instead, it starts with the families that are before the court and asks how the court can best serve these families. Using the research into the importance of parent–child interactions, the court uses that relationship as the basis for supporting and strengthening the family.

Another promising example is the work of the Jim Casey Foundation. Funded by the larger Annie E. Casey Foundation, the Jim Casey Foundation is advocating for a different approach to adolescents in the child welfare system. Drawing on the emerging research about brain development during adolescence and early adulthood, the Jim Casey Foundation is advocating for greater supports for youth ageing out of foster care. The foundation is using the research to show that supportive relationships during this critical period are essential for foster youth. It suggests that we need to be much more attentive to the developmental work going on during this period and to be alert to the potential to heal past trauma (Jim Casey Youth Opportunities Initiative, 2011).

Conclusion

Based on a growing body of research by neuroscientists, there should be little disagreement about the value of attentive, responsive caregivers to the healthy development of children. In light of the neuroplasticity of children's brains and the importance of sensitive periods for brain development, early childhood is a critical period for child development.

Determining the precise policies that should flow from the evidence about brain development is nevertheless a fraught endeavour. The research can be used in support of multiple and sometimes competing policies. There are examples, however, such as the work with adolescents in the child protection system and interventions at the level of the parent–child relationship, that are less controversial and can provide a model moving forward for how to use this important and promising research to develop appropriate responses to the problems in the field of child protection.

Notes

1 This chapter is adapted from an article in the *Journal of Law and Policy* entitled 'Neuroscience and the Child Welfare System', published by Brooklyn Law School (Huntington, 2012).

2 Wise & Connolly's (2014) article presents an excellent discussion of the use of neuroscience in child welfare.

3 The National Scientific Council on the Developing Child (2007a, p. 1) explains that although 'the foundations of brain architecture are established early in life', neural circuits continue to adapt throughout adulthood.

4 The mechanism through which experiences affect the expression of genes is the epigenome. In a useful analogy, neuroscientists liken genes to the hardware of a computer, setting the limits of what the body can do, but useless without an operating system. The epigenome is that operating system, determining which functions the hardware will perform. Experiences and environment shape the epigenome, leaving 'signatures' on the epigenome, which in turn affect which genes will be turned on and off. The example of identical twins helps explain this process. Although identical twins have the same genetic makeup, their different experiences in life will lead to different epigenomes, meaning that some genes will be expressed differently. Thus, although identical twins may be very similar in many aspects of their lives, their health, behaviour and skills can differ because of the different expressions of their genes (National Scientific Council on the Developing Child, 2010a, p. 1).

5 The National Scientific Council on the Developing Child (2005, p. 2) defines toxic stress.

6 'Tolerable stress' falls between positive stress and toxic stress. Tolerable stress has the potential to affect brain architecture but is mitigated by both its brevity and also the presence of responsive caregivers who are able to help children learn to cope with the stressful event. Examples include the loss of a loved one or an alarming accident (National Scientific Council on the Developing Child, 2005, p. 1). The National Scientific Council on the Developing Child (2010b, pp. 5–6) further discusses the effect of toxic stress on the brain.

7 Although adverse experiences such as abuse (including neglect) put children at risk for poor outcomes, some children are genetically predisposed to be particularly affected by adverse experiences. For these children, toxic stress is correlated with later physical and mental health illnesses, such as clinical depression (National Scientific Council on the Developing Child, 2008, p. 1).

8 The National Scientific Council on the Developing Child & National Forum on Early Childhood Program Evaluation (2009, pp. 1–2) cite calculations using the Early Childhood Longitudinal Study, Birth Cohort nine-month restricted use data.

9 These cases were chosen after a search of the child protection cases in the 'allstates' database on Westlaw, using a variety of search terms, such 'brain' in the same sentence as any variant of 'develop'. It is difficult to comprehensively assess the use of neuroscientific evidence in child protection proceedings because most trial courts do not publish opinions describing the evidence introduced by the parties and detailing the bases for the courts' orders. Some appellate courts publish detailed opinions, but these, too, are not particularly common. Thus, the cases described below are not a representative sample of judicial decisions using neuroscience in child protection cases. The cases do, however, shed some light on the place of neuroscientific evidence in judicial decisions.

10 The appellate court in *In re G.V.* (2009) quotes the trial court's findings of fact.

11 The court quotes research conducted by Joy D. Osofsky (1995).

12 The court further quotes research conducted by Abigail Sterne et al. (2010) and Allan N. Schore (2001).

13 The Court of Appeals in *Gore v. Gloucester County Department of Social Services* (2012) quotes the treating doctor's report.

14 McLellan et al. (2000, p. 1689) note that active substance use relapse occurs in 40 to 60 per cent of patients, and such common relapses should not be viewed as evidence of treatment failure due to the chronic illness-like nature of substance abuse.

References

Aronson, E. (2011). Concussion research aims to help athletes, study of the brain. *Princeton University*. [Online] 17 October. Available at www.princeton.edu/main/news/archive/S31/80/06C59/index.xml?section=featured [Accessed 23 September 2015].

Center on the Developing Child (2007). The science of early childhood development. *InBrief*. [Online] Available at http://developingchild.harvard.edu/wp-content/uploads/2015/03/InBrief-The-Science-of-Early-Childhood-Development.pdf [Accessed 23 September 2015].

Fraser, J. G. & Casanueva, C. (2013). *The Miami Child Well-Being Court Model: Essential Elements and Implementation Guidance*. [Online] Miami, FL: Miami Child Well-Being Court Initiative. Available at www.floridaschildrenfirst.org/wp-content/uploads/2013/02/MiamiChild.pdf [Accessed 23 September 2015].

Huntington, C. (2012). Neuroscience and the child welfare system, *Journal of Law and Policy*, 21(1), 37–57.

Jim Casey Youth Opportunities Initiative (2011). The adolescent brain: New research and its implications for young people transitioning from foster care, *Success Beyond 18*, [Online] 1–49. Available at www.jimcaseyyouth.org/sites/default/files/documents/The%20Adolescent%20Brain_prepress_proof%5B1%5D.pdf [Accessed 23 September 2015].

McLellan, A. T. et al. (2000). Drug dependence, a chronic medical illness, *The Journal of the American Medical Association*, 284(13), 1689–1695.

National Council of Juvenile and Family Court Judges (2014). *Child and Family Law Courts Meet Brain Science*. [Online Video]. 21 July. Available at www.ncjfcj.org/child-and-family-courts-meet-brain-science [Accessed 23 September 2015].

National Scientific Council on the Developing Child (2004a). Children's emotional development is built into the architecture of their brains: Working paper 2, *Center on the Developing Child*, [Online] 1–9. Available at http://developingchild.harvard.edu/wp-content/uploads/2015/05/Childrens-Emotional-Development-Is-Built-into-the-Architecture-of-Their-Brains.pdf [Accessed 23 September 2015].

National Scientific Council on the Developing Child (2004b). Young children develop in an environment of relationships: Working paper 1, *Center on the Developing Child*, [Online] 1–8. Available at http://developingchild.

harvard.edu/wp-content/uploads/2015/04/Young-Children-Develop-in-an-Environment-of-Relationships.pdf [Accessed 23 September 2015].

National Scientific Council on the Developing Child (2005). Excessive stress disrupts the architecture of the developing brain: Working paper 3, *Center on the Developing Child*, [Online] 1–9. Available at http://developingchild.harvard.edu/wp-content/uploads/2015/05/Stress_Disrupts_Architecture_Developing_Brain-1.pdf [Accessed 23 September 2015].

National Scientific Council on the Developing Child (2007a). The timing and quality of early experiences combine to shape brain architecture: Working paper 5, *Center on the Developing Child*, [Online] 1–9. Available at http://developingchild.harvard.edu/wp-content/uploads/2015/06/Timing_Quality_Early_Experiences-1.pdf [Accessed 23 September 2015].

National Scientific Council on the Developing Child (2007b). The science of early childhood development: Closing the gap between what we know and what we do, *Center on the Developing Child*, [Online] 1–13. Available at http://developingchild.harvard.edu/wp-content/uploads/2015/05/Science_Early_Childhood_Development.pdf [Accessed 23 September 2015].

National Scientific Council on the Developing Child (2008). Establishing a level foundation for life: Mental health begins in early childhood: Working paper 6, *Center on the Developing Child*, [Online] 1–12. Available at http://developingchild.harvard.edu/wp-content/uploads/2015/05/Establishing-a-Level-Foundation-for-Life-Mental-Health-Begins-in-Early-Childhood.pdf [Accessed 23 September 2015].

National Scientific Council on the Developing Child (2010a). Early experiences can alter gene expression and affect long-term development: Working paper 10, *Center on the Developing Child*, [Online] 1–9. Available at http://developingchild.harvard.edu/wp-content/uploads/2015/05/Early-Experiences-Can-Alter-Gene-Expression-and-Affect-Long-Term-Development.pdf [Accessed 23 September 2015].

National Scientific Council on the Developing Child (2010b). Persistent fear and anxiety can affect young children's learning and development: Working paper 9, *Center on the Developing Child*, [Online] 1–13. Available at http://developingchild.harvard.edu/wp-content/uploads/2015/05/Persistent-Fear-and-Anxiety-Can-Affect-Young-Childrens-Learning-and-Development.pdf [Accessed 23 September 2015].

National Scientific Council on the Developing Child & National Forum on Early Childhood Policy and Programs (2011). Building the brain's 'air traffic control' system: How early experiences shape the development of executive function: Working paper 11, *Center on the Developing Child*, [Online] 1–17. Available at http://developingchild.harvard.edu/wp-content/uploads/2015/05/How-Early-Experiences-Shape-the-Development-of-Executive-Function.pdf [Accessed 23 September 2015].

National Scientific Council on the Developing Child & National Forum on Early Childhood Program Evaluation (2009). Maternal depression can undermine the development of young children: Working paper 8, *Center on the Developing Child*, [Online] 1–13. Available at http://developingchild.

harvard.edu/wp-content/uploads/2015/05/Maternal-Depression-Can-Undermine-Development.pdf [Accessed 23 September 2015].

Osofsky, J. D. (1995). The effects of exposure to violence on young children, *American Psychologist*, 50(9), 782–788.

Rose, S. (2005). *The Future of the Brain: The Promise and Perils of Tomorrow's Neuroscience*. New York: Oxford University Press.

School of Education at Johns Hopkins University (2015). *Neuro-Education Initiative*. [Online] Available at http://education.jhu.edu/research/nei/ [Accessed 23 September 2015].

Schore, A. (2001). The effects of early relational trauma on right brain development, affect regulation, and infant mental health, *Infant Mental Health Journal*, 22(1–2), 201–269.

Schore, A. & McIntosh, J. (2011). Family law and the neuroscience of attachment, part I, *Family Court Review*, 49(3), 501–512.

Siegel, D. & McIntosh, J. (2011). Family law and the neuroscience of attachment, part II, *Family Court Review*, 49(3), 513–520.

Sowell, E. R. et al. (1999). Localizing age-related changes in brain structure between childhood and adolescence using statistical parametric mapping, *Neuroimage*, 9(1), 587–597.

Steinberg, L. & Morris, A. S. (2001). Adolescent development, *Annual Review of Psychology*, 52(February), 83–110.

Sterne, A. et al. (2010). *Domestic Violence and Children: A Handbook for Schools and Early Years Settings*. New York: Routledge.

Wise, S. & Connolly, M. (2014). Using early childhood development research in child protection: Benefits, boundaries and blind spots, *Developing Practice*, 39(July), 16–27.

Cases

Gore v. *Gloucester County Department of Social Services* (2012) 2012 WL 1835537 [Unpublished].

Graham v. *Florida* (2010) 560 U.S. 48.

In re E.M. (2014) 4 N.E.3d 636.

In re G.V. (2009) 674 S.E.2d 479 [Unpublished].

In re Hazekiah G. (2013) 2013 WL 7084483 [Unpublished].

Montgomery v. *Louisiana* (2016) 136 S. Ct. 718.

Miller v. *Alabam* a (2012) 132 S. Ct. 2455.

Roper v. *Simmons* (2005) 543 U.S. 551.

5

DISPROPORTIONALITY AND RISK DECISION MAKING IN CHILD PROTECTION

*Ilan Katz and Marie Connolly**

The fraught question of disproportionality in child welfare has challenged practitioners, policy makers and managers across the world. On the one hand, there is no doubt that children from indigenous and ethnic minority groups are overrepresented in the child protection system (CPS), including reports to the CPS, substantiations of maltreatment and numbers of children in out-of-home care. Although parenting behaviour differs between different social groups, no culture or social group condones the abuse of children. Historical disadvantage, alienation and injustice impact on indigenous and ethnic minority families, and child protection practice responds to these families by over- or under-reacting to perceived risks to these children. Frontline practitioners are left to manage risk and make decisions within an environment where resources are constrained, and anxieties surrounding race have the potential to impact on decision making around risk and protection. This chapter explores the nature of disproportionality, including the theories that have sought to explain why children from different ethnic, cultural and racial backgrounds appear to elicit different responses from the child protection system. The chapter teases out the multiple causes of disproportionality and then explores what this means for child protection decision making and service delivery.

* Ilan Katz is a professor at the Social Policy Research Centre at the University of New South Wales, Australia. Marie Connolly is a professor and chair of social work at the University of Melbourne, Australia.

Defining disproportionality

Disproportionality refers to the fact that children from indigenous and minority ethnic communities are overrepresented in the child protection system compared to their numbers in the general population. While this is a deceptively simple concept, discussions of disproportionality contain a number of implicit assumptions which need to be unpacked in order to better understand the policy and practice implications which arise. The first assumption is that all racial groups should have similar rates of involvement in child protection systems. At its heart, the idea of disproportionality assumes that children should be represented in the child protection system (as well as other human service systems) in proportion to the numbers of their ethnic group in the population as a whole. This is particularly the case for child protection and other systems such as justice and mental health, where involvement in the system is largely involuntary. Underlying the concern about overrepresentation are two other presumptions: contact with the child protection system is damaging for children, and overrepresentation in the system is an indication of discrimination within the system or by society as a whole. This is in contrast to concerns about underrepresentation of minority groups in other areas of society, such as business and politics.

Disproportionality overwhelmingly focuses the overrepresentation of children from cultural or racial groups. Children in child protection systems are, nevertheless, dissimilar from the population as a whole in a number of domains other than race and culture. Other domains of overrepresentation include gender (girls are much more likely to be reported as victims of sexual abuse), age (babies and toddlers), socioeconomic status (low socioeconomic status families), family structure (children of single parents and children from large families) and parental well-being (children of parents with mental health and/or alcohol and drug issues). However, these factors are seldom included in discussions of disproportionality other than as correlates of racial or ethnic characteristics. In fact it is more or less taken as a given that children from disadvantaged families are more likely to be abused, and many of the risk factors associated with child abuse and (especially) neglect are very closely linked to poverty and disadvantage.

The problem

At its most basic, the debate around disproportionality revolves around (1) whether the overrepresentation of certain cultural and ethnic groups in the child protection system is a result of racism within the system, either at the institutional level or by individual practitioners, or (2) whether it is justified because of differences in the risk of maltreatment in different communities.

In virtually every country in the world, minority ethnic and indigenous children are overrepresented in child protection systems, although the level of disproportionality varies between different populations and across different countries. In the United State, around double the proportion of African American children are involved with the CPS compared to the general population (Drake et al., 2011; Putnam-Hornstein, Needell, King & Johnson-Motoyama, 2013) and Native American children are around one and a half times as likely to have a substantiated report as white children (14.5 per cent vs 10.7 per cent) (Wildeman et al., 2014). Australian indigenous children, by comparison, are overrepresented by a factor of 7 to 10 in different parts of the child protection system (Australian Institute of Health and Welfare, 2015; Tilbury, 2009). On the other hand, some minority groups such as Chinese and other Asians are underrepresented in some systems.

For several decades, across many countries, disproportionality has been examined empirically, and a number of different theories have been developed to explain the phenomenon. In many jurisdictions there have been attempts to reduce or eliminate disproportionality by developing interventions aimed at preventing children from indigenous and/or minority communities from entering into the child protection system or progressing through it. These initiatives have ranged from large-scale policy interventions through to individual community programmes, cultural awareness and anti-racism training for practitioners. While there have been some successes in some systems, the overall pattern of disproportional representation nevertheless continues in virtually all jurisdictions. Indeed disproportionality is one of the most persistent features of child protection systems, as well as other human services, such as justice and mental health. The ubiquity of overrepresentation of minority families raises significant issues about the nature of child protection systems themselves.

Most explanations of disproportionality focus on the behaviour and attitudes of child protection workers or the historical developments of the child protection systems in specific jurisdictions. As we have noted, however, overrepresentation occurs in every system and persists over decades, irrespective of changes in structure, funding, legislation, training, workforce and procedures within the CPS. This suggests that disproportionality may represent something basic and deep-seated about the nature of child protection itself (and possibly all state mandated interventions in human services, as there are similar patterns in other areas such as mental health and especially criminal justice), rather than a particular manifestation of historical developments in the systems, structural factors or the behaviours and attitudes of child protection workers. This disproportionality must be viewed at two levels: child protection policy and system design; and day-to-day child protection practice, particularly in relation to risk assessment and decision making.

Disproportionality raises some of the most fundamental challenges for the delivery of child protection services – the balance of individual needs and risks with structural forces which result in disadvantage and exclusion. This has been a constant dilemma for practitioners and an ongoing tension within social work for several decades (Bailey & Brake, 1975). Social work theory acknowledges that most social problems are ultimately caused by structural features of societies which create differential risks for people in different social groups. Thus the actual behaviours of individuals are not the primary causes of social dysfunction but are manifestations of inequality and lack of access to resources for some sectors of the population (Welshman, 2007). The children and families with whom social workers come into contact, however, have very real, immediate needs and are facing risks which social workers inevitably have to address; they cannot wait for the structural changes in society which will alleviate their risks. In addition, addressing the risks to individual clients may even worsen the structural inequalities by keeping in place the very power relationships which cause the inequalities. In the case of disproportionality, practitioners are working with the knowledge that overrepresentation of minorities is potentially damaging to minority communities and perpetuates the oppressive power of the state over indigenous and minority communities. Yet they must make individual judgements relating to specific families in order to safeguard the best interests of the children, irrespective of the broader social implications. Recent research has found that, all other things being equal, black children in the United States are no more likely to be taken into care (Drake et al., 2011), and in the United Kingdom, Bywaters has found that, taking into account socioeconomic factors, children from white families are in fact more likely than minority children to be taken into care (Bywaters, Brady, Sparks & Bos, 2014a; 2014b). Nevertheless, the fact that children from minority communities are overrepresented in the system can indicate to those minority groups that the system is biased against them and that that their families are under increased scrutiny by the statutory authorities. For individual practitioners, this presents not only the dilemma of working with risk across cultures but additionally the challenge of working with the intense hostility and/or fear which can be generated within different communities by the intervention of child protection systems in their families.

Explaining disproportionality

There are a number of theories which have been developed to explain the overrepresentation of minority and indigenous groups in child protection systems. Although the theories overlap and are not mutually exclusive, they fit into two broad categories:

(a) that there are no differences across demographic groups, which means that disproportionality is essentially related to institutional racism in the child protection system itself and not the behaviour of families;

(b) that disproportionality is a result of higher prevalence of maltreatment in particular communities and not a consequence of the actions of child protection workers or the structure of the child protection system.

In each of these broad categories, there are a range of other theories to explain disproportionality.

No differences

These theories assert that levels of maltreatment are similar across all demographic groups, and therefore disproportionality is explained by the operation of the child protection system as a whole and/or of the actions and beliefs of child protection workers.

Cultural insensitivity theory proposes that parents from indigenous or minority communities have different standards or approaches to parenting from those of parents from European backgrounds. Child protection workers are unable to recognize that these children are being parented appropriately according to their own cultures. Parents are assessed as posing a risk to their children using Eurocentric criteria for good parenting and for risk to children. Furthermore, most minority and indigenous communities come from collectivist cultures in which the family and community are given priority over the individual and in which group norms are emphasized over individual autonomy. The child protection system is, however, based on individualist cultural assumptions in which individual rights and protection are more important than preservation of group or family harmony. Thus there is a fundamental tension between the child protection system and these communities in terms of how they see the role of the child and the family in society.

Institutional racism is also included in this category. This refers to the idea that institutions (including the child protection system) can be racist or culturally insensitive if their policies, procedures or practices disproportionately negatively affect particular racial or cultural groups. For example, risk assessment tools can be constructed in such a way that minority parents are disproportionately assessed as being risky, or court processes can be conducted without interpreters so that families with poor English are disadvantaged. Institutional racism can exist even if individual practitioners or managers within the institution do not hold racist views.

According to *exposure theory*, the actual rates of abuse are similar, but children from indigenous and minority ethnic families are more likely to be reported because they depend more on public services; are therefore more likely to come into contact with mandatory reporters or other potential referrers; and are subjected to much more scrutiny. The reasons for their high levels of exposure include that they tend to be from lower socioeconomic communities and also that they have fewer resources to support each other than other families have.

One of the reasons presented for the overexposure of families from indigenous and minority communities to child protection is that they have less access to preventive services or that the services which are available are inadequate or not culturally responsive to their needs. Because of the lack of early intervention, family problems are likely to escalate to the point where child protection systems become involved. Again there are a number of explanations for a lack of engagement with preventive services, including the cultural insensitivity of those services and the reluctance of some communities to voluntarily seek support from services, thus creating a situation where service provision tends to be associated with coercive intervention (Tilbury, 2009).

The implications of the 'no differences' theories, and their focus on the system rather than the family, are that the most appropriate ways of dealing with disproportionality are to develop culturally responsive practices and assessment methods for child protection practitioners. It is expected that culturally responsive services and culturally aware practitioners and caseworkers will ensure that families from indigenous and minority communities will be treated equitably and that ultimately the numbers of children in the system will reflect their proportion in society as a whole.

Different rates

These theories claim that disproportionality is a result of higher prevalence of maltreatment in particular communities and that child protection systems respond to people from all races and cultures equally – although they encounter more child abuse and neglect risk with some groups than others.

According to the *cultural deficit* theory, parents from indigenous or minority groups have parenting styles which have been appropriate in the past or in different contexts but are not appropriate for modern society and therefore constitute a risk to their children. Typical examples of this are allowing young children to take responsibility for even younger siblings, encouraging young children to do household chores such as cooking and cleaning, allowing young children to go out alone or stay in the house alone. This is a very similar theory to the cultural insensitivity theory except that in the cultural deficit theory it is the parenting practices which are portrayed as being deficient rather than any cultural insensitivity on the part of child protection systems to parenting practices differing from the Eurocentric norm.

Parental education and support are the most appropriate modes of intervention to ameliorate these problems. In this view, parents are essentially well meaning but need to better understand the risks posed by modern family life and need to adapt their lifestyle to ensure that their children are safe. This contrasts with the cultural insensitivity model, which emphasizes that it is practitioners who need to be educated about the parenting practices of other cultures and to accommodate different cultural parenting practices.

The distinctions are nevertheless rather subtle. Consider this quote from a recently released report by the Children's Commissioner for England on intra-familial child sexual abuse:

> Some groups of children and young people are underrepresented in the criminal justice system as victims of child sexual abuse in the family environment. Victims from some Black and Minority Ethnic groups may face additional barriers to accessing statutory services. In some Black and Minority Ethnic communities, victims of sexual abuse and their families are blamed, particularly if they are supportive of the victim and the 'honour' of the perpetrator is brought into disrepute by the allegation. Family members may also feel that they can manage allegations of child sexual abuse themselves, though these solutions generally involved silencing the victim. They were disinclined to involve statutory services, primarily as a result of distrust. (Children's Commissioner (England), 2015, p. 9)

Although the main point ostensibly being made in this quote is that victims from black and minority ethnic groups are underrepresented because of a lack of trust in the system (which therefore is implicitly discriminatory) by members of those communities, there is a clear connotation that inappropriate beliefs within these communities prevent victims from coming forward and then protect perpetrators of child sexual abuse. It is also significant that this quote shows concern about underrepresentation rather than overrepresentation, again indicating how complex the debates around disproportionality can become.

Indeed, much of the literature in this area indicates that collectivist cultures tend to be strongly patriarchal, and children tend to be devalued in these cultures. Disclosures by children of abuse by elders are therefore treated as a betrayal of the community rather than as allegations of inappropriate or criminal conduct (Sawrikar, 2016).

These issues are further complicated in cases involving harmful traditional practices, where the actions of the parents (or other community members) towards the children are not disciplinary practices or deviant behaviour, such as child sexual abuse (which is not sanctioned by any culture or religion), but involve harmful traditional practices such as genital cutting, witchcraft, child marriage and 'honour killings'. In such cases, parents and community members are acting within the belief systems of their own cultures but are clearly breaking the law of the countries which they are living in.

Another growing area of concern is the link between child protection and radicalization. This is most developed in the United Kingdom. Recent government child protection guidance in England and Wales, which refers to the new 'prevent duty', under the Counter-Terrorism and Security Act 2015. Under the Act a range of organizations must take steps to prevent people from being drawn into terrorism. Local authorities are now required to establish 'channel panels' to assess the extent to which identified individuals are vulnerable to being drawn into terrorism and to arrange for support to be provided to those individuals (H M Government, 2015). Although not explicit, the implications are that parents are at least partly responsible for their children's radicalization and that failing to prevent their children from being radicalized constitutes a form of child abuse. Of course, these provisions are clearly aimed primarily at the Muslim community in the United Kingdom.

These developments indicate that despite strenuous efforts over decades to ensure culturally sensitive practices in social work and human services more generally, it has proved very difficult to avoid a degree of cultural deficit in the way the system interacts with 'other' families and cultures.

Poverty theories refer to the fact that indigenous and minority families have a much lower average socioeconomic status than mainstream families and that the stress of living in poverty, with the lack of resources such as adequate housing, day care or support services, leads to high levels of stress and challenging parenting contexts. There is a very extensive literature on the relationship between poverty and parenting, but still no consensus as to exactly why parents from low socioeconomic communities display more harsh and inconsistent parenting than those from more affluent families (Conger, Ge, Elder, Lorenz, & Simons, 1994; Katz, Corlyon, La Placa, & Hunter, 2007; Korbin, Coulton, Lindstrom-Ufuti, & Spilsbury, 2000; Mayer, 2002). Poverty theories do not specifically address the issue of how poverty affects families from minority and indigenous communities, although some research indicates that disadvantage has a less damaging impact on the parenting of these families than on parents from mainstream communities (Deater-Deckard, 2004). This is possibly because minority and indigenous families are poor because of discrimination and lack of opportunity, whereas many mainstream families are poor because of personal issues such as mental illness and substance abuse (Mayer, 2002). Tilbury (2009) points out that the way the child protection system is structured, in particular its focus on individual pathology and 'rescue' of abused children, fails to address the underlying risk factors for children, in particular poverty and lack of opportunity in most indigenous communities. It is important to note that there is increasing evidence that white families who live in similar circumstances to disadvantaged minority families are as likely, or indeed more likely, to become involved with child protection and some indication that those families have more complex issues (Bywaters et al., 2014b; Drake et al., 2011).

Theories of *intergenerational trauma* consider histories of trauma, sometimes over many generations, causing disruptions to traditional parenting and a consequent undermining of parental behaviour over generations. The history of most indigenous and minority groups is characterized by colonialism, occupation, attempts at cultural extermination and sometimes genocide. For refugees this also includes direct experiences of torture, conflict and displacement, as well as the culture shock of resettlement. Furthermore, the experience of children living in a community where intergenerational trauma is manifest can cause further psychological damage over and above the impact of children's experiences in their own families. Intergenerational trauma has also been linked in some theories to lateral violence, which refers to physical and psychological violence perpetrated by members of minority communities against each other but which is caused by powerlessness imposed on them by the effects of generations of colonial oppression.

While these different theories explain disproportionality, they are not mutually exclusive, and it is quite likely that they all form part of a complex picture which differs in different social and legal contexts. The challenge for service providers is compounded by the intersectionality between race/culture and the other social factors which affect vulnerable children, including gender, disability and family structure (Nadan, Spilsbury & Korbin, 2015), all of which are relevant to engaging with risk, at the policy and practice levels. A further complication for child protection practitioners and policymakers is the reflexivity of disproportionality – that is, whatever the facts of the matter, some communities respond to the involvement of child protection with the expectation that they will be discriminated against and that their children will be at greater risk of removal than children from mainstream families. This expectation can set up a conflictual dynamic between child protection workers and community members even when, from the point of view of the CPS, risk is being addressed in a purely objective fashion. The dynamic itself can then create risks (or it can be interpreted as an additional risk factor) for the children. This is because the way parents engage with CPS practitioners is one of the most important factors involved in risk assessments. Parents who are hostile or defensive are likely to be perceived as presenting a higher level of risk to their children than are parents who are compliant and accepting of help, irrespective of the 'objective' level of risk within the family. Thus the expectation of a disproportionate response from the CPS can become a self-fulfilling prophesy for parents from indigenous and minority communities.

Child protection workers are therefore forced to work with issues around disproportionality at the individual level while also having to take into account the fact that many of the facets of disproportionality arise from structural factors within society and within the child protection system and that those facets cannot be resolved by simply ensuring culturally sensitive practice.

Responding to disproportionality

Earlier in the chapter, we suggested that disproportionality may represent something basic and deep-seated about the nature of child protection itself rather than being a particular manifestation of historical circumstances, structural factors or the behaviours and attitudes of child protection workers. The problem of disproportionality is long standing, and the fact that it continues to resist change suggests that the difficulties do not rest in one – or two – domains. Weber (2010) argues that race and class are challenged at both macro and micro levels. The everyday actions of people experiencing unequal social relationships in their lives create systems of disadvantage at the macro level. At the micro level, Weber argues that 'structures of oppression provide a powerful framework, a hierarchy that persists through time and across places and that has serious consequences for social life' (2010, p. 128).

The theory of *intersectionality* opens up a broader set of risk associations within the area of child protection, but it also, importantly, offers opportunities for change and support. Within the context of intersectionality, a broader constellation of risk factors becomes the focus, both at the macro and micro levels. Intersectionality has been conceptualized as a framework 'that promotes an understanding of human beings as shaped by interacting social locations and identities (e.g., race, Indigeneity, sexuality, gender expression, migration status, age, ability, religion)' (Hunting, Grace & Hankivsky, 2015, p. 103). These writers argue that intersectionality can deepen our understandings of the related nature of micro- and macro-level issues and processes that influence and shape inclusion. Inclusion becomes a powerful means through which the impact of stigma and discrimination can be reduced (Hunting et al., 2015), and it is critical that strategies to foster greater inclusion occur at both the micro and macro levels.

Drawing upon the *intersectionality-informed model* from Hunting et al. (2015), the first step towards social inclusionary practice involves a shift in recognition that multi-level factors impact upon disadvantaged people across their lifespan:

(a) Social inclusion and exclusion are dynamic and simultaneously experienced by individuals.

(b) Experiences of social inclusion and exclusion differ and change both within and across social locations and populations according to time and place.

(c) Social inclusion and exclusion are constituted and shaped by processes and structures of power on multiple levels. (Hunting et al., 2015, p. 109)

The relationship between inclusion and exclusion is then interrogated across eight key principles that underpin the key ideas of intersectionality: multi-level analysis; intersecting categories; social justice and equity; resistance and resilience; diverse knowledges; time and space; reflexivity; and power. In examining both inclusion and exclusion across these key tenets, unintended consequences of practice can be avoided. For example,

> well-meaning inclusion initiatives can actually reify experiences of exclusion as they take the focus away from the dynamics and operation of exclusion turning it instead toward the individuals or groups deemed to be excluded. (Hunting et al., 2015, p. 110)

The multi-level domains of social inclusion and exclusion are then interrogated through questions that are both reflexive and transformative. Reflexive question may include the following:[1] What knowledge, values and experiences does the worker bring to the area of policy or practice? How have the problems been framed previously? How are groups differentially represented by this framing of the problem? What are the current policy and practice responses? Other questions, described as transformative, might include the following: What inequities actually exist in relation to the problem? How and where can interventions improve the problem? What are feasible short, medium and long-term solutions? How exactly will policy or practice responses reduce inequities, and how will implementation be assured? How will we know if inequities have been reduced? And finally, how has the analysis of intersectionality changed the way we think about relations and structures of power and equity; the nature of practice and policy development, including implementation and evaluation; and broader conceptualizations of power, exclusion and inclusion in the daily lives of service users.

Because disproportionality is so long standing, and is often seen as an intractable problem that defies solutions, there are dangers in assuming that no effort to reduce it will make a difference. In bringing ideas relating to intersectionality into the frame, we are also suggesting, however, that there are ways of influencing decision making at both the micro and macro levels and that continued efforts to both better understand and respond to disproportionality are important to the development of more responsive services.

Conclusion

Disproportionality is a deceptively simple concept which in reality involves a very complex set of phenomena affecting child protection systems around the world. There are a range of explanations for disproportionality, but none of them can fully explain its causes or consequences. There have also been many different strategies attempted to address the overrepresentation of children from particular communities in the CPS, but none of them has been particularly successful, partly because the very nature of child protection can come into conflict with other social and cultural values in minority communities. Disproportionality therefore creates risks not only for the children and families involved in the CPS but also for child protection workers as well as policymakers. In this chapter, we are suggesting that the theory of intersectionality presents child protection systems with a valuable resource for deepening understanding about the complex nature of disadvantage, inclusion and exclusion. Rather than attempting to disaggregate the ethnic/racial factors from other social factors affecting families, intersectionality views these factors as interacting and holistic. It can also open new ways of thinking about disproportionality and how to respond to it.

Notes

1 These questions have been adapted from Hunting et al. (2015), which were originally based on Hankivsky et al. (2012).

References

Australian Institute of Health and Welfare. (2015). Child protection Australia: 2013–14. Child Welfare series no. 61. Cat. no. CWS 52. Canberra: AIHW.

Bailey, R. & Brake, M. (1975). *Radical social work*. New York: Pantheon.

Bywaters, P., Brady, G., Sparks, T. & Bos, E. (2014a). Child welfare inequalities: new evidence, further questions. *Child & Family Social Work*, n/a-n/a. doi: 10.1111/cfs.12154

Bywaters, P., Brady, G., Sparks, T. & Bos, E. (2014b). Inequalities in child welfare intervention rates: the intersection of deprivation and identity. *Child & Family Social Work*, n/a-n/a. doi: 10.1111/cfs.12161

Children's Commissioner (England). (2015). Protecting children from harm: A critical assessment of child sexual abuse in the family network in England and priorities for action. London: Children's Commissioner.

Conger, R. D., Ge, X., Elder, G. H., Lorenz, F. O. & Simons, R. L. (1994). Economic Stress, Coercive Family Process, and Developmental Problems of Adolescents. *Child Development*, 65(2), 541–561. doi: 10.1111/j.1467–8624.1994.tb00768.x

Deater-Deckard, K. (2004). *Parenting stress*. New Haven, CT: Yale University Press.

Drake, B., Jolley, J. M., Lanier, P., Fluke, J., Barth, R. P. & Jonson-Reid, M. (2011). Racial Bias in Child Protection? A Comparison of Competing Explanations Using National Data. *Pediatrics*, 127(3), 471–478. doi: 10.1542/peds.2010–1710

H M Government. (2015). *Working together to safeguard children: A guide to inter-agency working to safeguard and promote the welfare of children*. London: HM Government.

Katz, I., Corlyon, J., La Placa, V. & Hunter, S. (2007). *The relationship between parenting and poverty*. York: Joseph Rowntree Foundation.

Korbin, J. E., Coulton, C. J., Lindstrom-Ufuti, H. & Spilsbury, J. (2000). Neighborhood views on the definition and etiology of child maltreatment. *Child Abuse & Neglect*, 24 (12), 1509–1527. doi: http://dx.doi.org/10.1016/S0145–2134(00)00206-4

Mayer, S. (2002). *The influence of parental income on children's outcomes*. Wellington, NZ: Ministry of Social Development, Te Manatu Whakahiato Ora.

Nadan, Y., Spilsbury, J. C. & Korbin, J. E. (2015). Culture and context in understanding child maltreatment: Contributions of intersectionality and neighborhood-based research. *Child Abuse & Neglect*, 41, 40–48. doi: http://dx.doi.org/10.1016/j.chiabu.2014.10.021

Putnam-Hornstein, E., Needell, B., King, B. & Johnson-Motoyama, M. (2013). Racial and ethnic disparities: A population-based examination of risk factors for involvement with child protective services. *Child Abuse & Neglect*, 37(1), 33–46. doi: http://dx.doi.org/10.1016/j.chiabu.2012.08.005

Sawrikar, P. (2016). *Working effectively with ethnic minorities and across cultures in Western child protection systems: A book for child welfare scholars and practitioners.* Surrey, UK: Ashgate Publishers.

Tilbury, C. (2009). The overrepresentation of indigenous children in the Australian child welfare system. *International Journal of Social Welfare*, 18(1), 57–64. doi: 10.1111/j.1468–2397.2008.00577.x

Welshman, J. (2007). *From transmitted deprivation to social exclusion: Policy, poverty, and parenting.* Bristol: Policy Press.

Wildeman, C., Emanuel, N., Leventhal, J. M., Putnam-Hornstein, E., Waldfogel, J. & Lee, H. (2014). The Prevalence of Confirmed Maltreatment Among US Children, 2004 to 2011. *JAMA Pediatrics*, 168(8).

6

SERVICE USERS AS RECEIVERS OF RISK-DOMINATED PRACTICE

Helen Buckley[*]

Introduction

Earlier chapters in this volume have outlined the development of the risk paradigm in many aspects of public life and have illustrated how child protection systems have evolved as a consequence. This chapter will also dip into that history, albeit from a slightly different perspective, in order to illustrate how the various shifts over the past three decades have directly impacted on the experience of children and families who have found themselves involved with the child welfare and protection services. While the focus of this discussion is intended to be international, the author acknowledges that the perspective is primarily Anglophone, based on research conducted in mostly English-speaking countries. Service user perspectives of child protection work will be explored, including the extent to which it is possible to reconcile traditional values about client-centred, relationship-based practice with the demands of managerial systems which are aimed at defining and responding to risk to children.

This chapter contends that a number of parallel processes, some of which are contradictory in both orientation and effect, have wittingly or unwittingly modified the experience of service users. It will argue that attempts to moderate the system and promote family participation and engagement have been losing the battle with simultaneous efforts to streamline and will also highlight how methods for quality ensure that the services have rendered the experiences of service users in the recasting of child protection as a technical process.

---

[*] Helen Buckley is an associate professor and fellow emeritus at the School of Social Work and Social Policy, Trinity College Dublin, Ireland.

The evolving relationship between the child protection system and families

It is notable that child protection literature in the decades up to the early 1990s reflected strong academic interest in the tensions and ambiguities underpinning the statutory child protection system. The issues of civil rights and protection of privacy were common themes underpinning a real concern about state intrusion into family life. Theoretical discussions on child protection at that time drew from the work of Donzelot (1980) and Foucault (1975) to explain the evolution of governmentality in respect of families and the different levels of power relations. Sociological rules were conceptualized, through which we could understand the interface between state systems and laypeople – such as 'the liberal compromise', according to which 'the family will be laid open for inspection provided that the state undertakes to make the best of what its agents find' (Dingwall et al., 1983, p. 91). At the same time, radical social work highlighted the oppressive nature of state intervention, which punished families for what Giovannoni and Billingsley (1970, p. 4) termed 'a social problem that is as much a manifestation of social and community conditions as it is of any individual parent's pathology'. This stucturalist theory was augmented by the 'sociocultural' approach (Straus, Gelles & Steinmetz, 1980), which argued that the nature of a society promoted norms which legitimated certain types of violence. These theories not only served to explain the existence of child abuse but also elucidated the gap between the experiences of children and families and the perspectives held by state agencies. Their ultimate goal was to shift the locus of culpability from individual service users to wider society and move away from individual pathology as the identified cause of child abuse. The concept of child maltreatment was described as a 'social construction' which mirrored society's concerns not just with children's safety and welfare but with gender relations, social class and deviance from an acceptable moral understanding of family life. What this early literature evidences is that as the 1970s and 1980s progressed, a growing awareness of authority in statutory social work gave rise to the recognition that child protection service users needed to have their rights protected.

Such political concerns on the part of social services, particularly in the United Kingdom, left room to manoeuvre in what was a relatively new sector of activity, whose interactions with families were described at the time as 'common sense practical reasoning' (Wise 1989). To illustrate this, Pithouse (1987), analysing the findings from ethnographic research conducted in the early 1980s in England, depicted the more flexible environment that was then occupied by frontline practitioners. He described them as operating the 'invisible trade' of child welfare, whose 'policies and philosophies ... are mediated within the work setting ... where members assert their own view of appropriate practice' (p. 7). In a similar vein, ethnographic research from Dingwall et al. (1983), conducted in the late 1970s, demonstrated a strong consciousness of the impact that intervention would have on families. Doctors, for example, were perceived as assuming honesty and competence on the part of parents and an accommodative attitude marked by surface courtesy. Social workers and health visitors drew on their perceptions of parents' characters under the rule of optimism, a rule by which 'staff are required if possible, to think the best of parents', applying flexibility to their own normative standards, accepting that inequality and cultural difference inevitably impact on the quality of parenting standards but applying tolerance if parents passed the test of loving their children.

Practitioners of the time also worried about appearing too heavy handed. Corby (1987) reported on a study which he undertook in the early 1980s in England, where he found social workers to be uncomfortable with their social control role and detected what he described as 'a certain amount of ambivalence about the benefits to be gained from close adherence to the procedural guidance'.

Literature from the late 1980s and early 1990s, however, began to reflect the different contexts and regulatory frameworks in which practice approaches were developing and showed how what were described as the 'civil libertarian concerns' of earlier years had begun to give way to a more 'routinized' response (Hallett, 1995, p. 101) as the risk paradigm gained traction. As other chapters in this volume have shown, the fallout from child abuse inquiries and scandals drove an increasingly proceduralized system. Ultimately, the unintended consequences for children and families of the more forensic approach attracted the attention of academics and researchers and became the concern of policymakers.

Disquiet about child protection systems

During the early 1990s, considerable unease began to emerge internationally about the frameworks through which frontline practitioners perceived and judged service users, the common thread linking them being the impact that an investigative, procedurally led child protection paradigm had on outcomes for children and families (Waldfogel, 1998; Kaplan & Merkel Holguin, 2008). Concepts of 'dangerousness' were used in equal measure to describe child protection services as to depict abusive families. Denis Howitt, a social psychologist, used a service user study to illustrate what he described as the 'ratcheting' effect of the child protection system – which, once initiated, inexorably progressed, finding new evidence to suit its self-fulfilling prophecies, often employing culturally relativistic, classist and gendered strategies in the process. Using his data to demonstrate the after-effects on families of child protection intervention, he went so far as to suggest that the impact made by the actual intervention of the child protection system was the 'key confounding variable' that determines the level of psychological damage that results from abuse. 'Backlash' and 'witch hunt' were terms that featured in the commentaries, when it was postulated that the system had stepped too far into the private domain of the family unit (Campbell, 1988; Myers, 1994). Services were observed to be more adult focused than child focused, rarely engaging meaningfully with children and tending to assess their situations through the constructions of adults (Buckley, 2003; Horwath & Bishop, 2003). Gendered practices were observed in relation to women (Gordon, 1988; Parton, 1990; Buckley, 1998) and in respect of men (Milner, 1996; Ryan, 2000), which impacted on their experiences of the child protection system.

Research involving service users in the United Kingdom, Ireland, the United States, Canada and Australia conducted in the 1990s and early 2000s provided further empirical evidence of the impact on carers of being investigated for suspected child abuse, which was, in the main, considered harsh and intimidating. In studies in the United Kingdom, parents reported feeling 'trapped' and powerless (Cleaver & Freeman, 1995), sensing 'shock, bewilderment, anger and the onset of profound feelings of loss' (Farmer & Owen, 1995) and 'fear and despair' (Thoburn et al., 1995). Canadian service users described their belief that the power of child protection staff could be used against them in a 'tyrannical' and 'frightening' manner (Dumbrill, 2006, p. 30). Irish service users described their feelings of embarrassment, shame, and intimidation (Buckley, 2003; Buckley, Skheill & O'Sullivan, 1997; Buckley, Whelan & Carr, 2011), and a Northern Irish study demonstrated acute and profound reactions by service users who had been referred by others to the child protection service (Spratt & Callan, 2004).

A common theme linking research in different jurisdictions was disagreement about the definition of harm to children and the factors that constituted risk. For example, in a UK study involving community members mapping risk factors, Wright (2004) found that parents and children identified the main risk factors to themselves in their locality as drug dealing, heavy traffic, burnt-out cars, the presence of paedophiles and bullying. This serves as an interesting contrast to the way risk has been constructed by child protection services, and it explains partly why parents who are subjected to risk assessment often dispute the nature or degree of maltreatment being suggested.

What might be described as a 'universal truth' emerges from these empirical studies about the hostility of service users towards child protection social workers. The 1994 film *Ladybird, Ladybird* directed by Ken

Loach[1] encapsulated a lot of the fear experienced not just by families but by social commentators about the vicious cycles in which impoverished and vulnerable parents find themselves entrapped, and it provided a valid illustration of the public image of child protection services. It was believed that the approach operating in the United Kingdom (and in many other jurisdictions) was not only causing unnecessary stigma to families but failing to assist those who were in need of assistance and support. As Gibbons et al. observed in 1995, the system resembled a 'small meshed net in which are caught a large number of minnows', a metaphor which illustrated the number of families that were brought into the system when risk was suspected, later to be discarded when it was discounted.

The start of the reform process

From the mid 1990s, a number of parallel initiatives took place in different Anglophone countries in response to the growing awareness that that the child protection system was causing a great deal of collateral damage to the families whose interests it was ultimately attempting to serve. The United States, Canada, New Zealand and Australia introduced what were termed as differential or alternative response systems, which, as the name suggests, offered a two-track response whereby families whose concerns or parenting problems did not reach the threshold for more coercive intervention were offered assessment and support services commensurate to their needs, mostly by community rather than statutory agencies. Similar approaches were developed in the United Kingdom, where the 'refocusing' initiative meant that family support and early intervention services received considerable investment. While early evaluations of the differential response model (DRM) and similar approaches were positive in terms of its impact on service users (Loman & Siegal, 2004). It has also been argued, however, that differential response, rather than reducing the adversarial nature of the relationship between service users and child protection staff, just subjects families to an alternative form of surveillance because even during assessment they are being screened for signs of maltreatment (Pelton, 2008). Despite critiques, it is ideologically popular, and different versions of this approach have been conceptualized as the solution to the unintended consequences of the one dimensional approach identified in the 1990s.

While alternative responses were being advanced, family-led practice frameworks such as Signs of Safety (Turnell & Edwards, 1999) began to be developed. The New Zealand Family Group Conference model was widely implemented. Early evaluations of this model in the United Kingdom and Ireland indicated a greater level of engagement with families (O'Brien,

2000; Holland & Rivett, 2006; Bell & Wilson, 2006), while also cautioning that the extent to which the model is actually empowering may be constrained by family members' lack of control over the outcomes of the process (Lupton, 1998) and the fact that it remains on the periphery of statutory child care services (O'Brien, 2000). Family participation in child protection conferencing also became the norm in most jurisdictions during the 1990s and early 2000s. While these processes are generally regarded as facilitative of family involvement, research over the years continues to emphasize the difference between participation and meaningful participation, cautioning that the involvement and the experiences of families depends heavily on the skills of chairpersons with service users often finding the process challenging and gruelling, tending to feel 'on trial' (Bell, 1999; Hall & Slembrouck, 2001; Buckley et al., 2008).

Child centredness in child protection work also began to be strongly promoted. Earlier inquiries including the Cleveland report (Butler Sloss, 1988) had illustrated the invisibility of children in child protection, where neither their views nor their right to participate in decision making were given due consideration. Following the ratification in a number of countries (though not the United States) of the UN Convention on the Rights of the Child and its reflection in child care legislation (for example, the 1989 Children Act in the United Kingdom), the position of the 'child' in child protection was recalibrated to a degree. The growing children's rights movement, which had started in the 1980s but began to accelerate in the 1990s had a theoretical base in the sociology of childhood, which conceptualizes children as social agents who bring about changes in their own lives as well as in society (Prout & James, 2006). While the Convention has not been directly implemented through domestic law in most of the signatory countries, it has influenced child care legislation by identifying a child's right to remain with their family and their rights to be consulted about matters concerning them (Gilbert et al., 2011). Family-led practice guidance – such as the Framework for the Assessment of Children in Need in the United Kingdom (DOH 2000) and the New Zealand practice framework (Connolly 2007), alongside a number of other similar models in other jurisdictions – were introduced with the aim of placing children's individual needs at the centre and assessing carers in terms of their parenting capacity, including strengths as well as weaknesses, rather than focusing solely on their behaviour. Tools were developed to facilitate carers and children to express their views, and consideration was given to the complex issues that affect parenting, such as culture, ethnicity, disability and health needs.

The above reforms generally aimed to divert from a forensic child protection focus towards a greater child welfare orientation provided in a manner that is less intimidating and alienating to families. As the remainder of this paper will argue, however, parallel developments in the policy world have seriously challenged the reforms' intent to be more attractive to service users.

The bureaucratization of child protection work

Although more recent studies continue to show evidence of service user unhappiness with child protection services, particularly at the initial point, mitigating factors have also emerged from research. These principally concern relationships, the strongest message from research being that the inevitable shock and distress of initial contact with the service can be diluted by a helping alliance with workers who display friendliness, respect, empathy and humour with children and families (Ruch et al., 2010; Leigh & Miller, 2006; deBoer & Cody, 2007; Lee & Ayon, 2004), where families perceive that their needs are being addressed (Ghaffar et al., 2012; Bolen, 2008) and where their strengths and the progress they have made are acknowledged (Buckley et al., 2011). The intersection of this theme with two other recent trends in child protection, however, has tended to undermine it. The two recent trends, which will be discussed below, are the effects of managerialist strategies to increase efficiency and the increase in reporting and its consequences for children and families.

Managerialism, or what is termed new public management, aims to increase the transparency, accountability and efficiency of public services, including child protection services. An implicit objective is the curtailment of risk through the implementation protocols, audit and quality standards. Apart from the general drive towards efficiency and accessibility, there are two dimensions of managerialism with relevance to service users, one positive and the other less so. The first, more positive, aspect is its function of directly addressing grievances through the creation of public redress systems which were established in order to compensate for 'democratic deficits' in civil society (Beresford & Croft, 2001). In theory, these provide an opportunity for feedback, including complaints, from service users and an opportunity to rectify errors or discrimination. Critics have nevertheless challenged the truly democratic nature of these systems as far as child protection is concerned. As Bell has argued, only the most articulate service users are likely to be included in these processes where the most marginalized families and those perceived to be problematic may achieve less participation. The downside of new public management and its impact on the quality of social work relationships with service users has been articulated by many commentators (Featherstone et al., 2014; 2012; Buckley, 2008; Munro, 2011). It has also been well illustrated in an Australian study by Harris (2012), who interviewed parents that had been subjected to assessment. He concluded that the formalistic procedures or tools used by statutory child protection agencies have led to a focus on compliance as a measure of parental ability, thereby changing the process into one that serves the agency rather than service users, some of whom in his study experienced it as intrusive, coercive, stigmatizing and ineffi-cient. As the above cited commentators have argued, efforts to streamline practices and make them more measurable have unwittingly undermined the potential for social workers to build relationships. Research with service users has also demonstrated that the qualities essential to a good helping relationship are often at odds with those required to carry out the mandated tasks of a statutory child protection worker (Drake, 1996; Yatchmenoff, 2005).

The upward spiral of reports to statutory child protection systems has also had a considerable impact on service user experiences. While prob-lems with data linkage in terms of child abuse and neglect reports make direct comparison difficult, sufficient statistical information is available to demonstrate that, first, the number of reports made in developed coun-tries has significantly increased in recent years (Canadian Incidence Study, 2003; 2008; Australian Institute for Family Studies, 2013; NCANDS, 2013) and, second, that the numbers of reported cases that are substantiated has steadily decreased (Gilbert et al., 2011). High levels of screening out in some jurisdictions, such as Ireland and Australia, have illuminated the numbers of children and families that are brought into the system only to be eliminated once an initial risk assessment is performed, replicating the fishing-net metaphor first used by Gibbons et al. in the 1990s. The increase is in large part due to the implementation of mandatory reporting laws in a number of countries, a measure that was introduced to reduce the risk of unreported abuse. Despite growing evidence that mandatory reporting is not an effective method of reducing child abuse (R. Buckley, 2014), governments seem unable to resist it, and its introduction is often only marginally related to the problem that it intends to ameliorate. For example, in Ireland it was introduced largely as a result of public anger about clerical sexual abuse, an issue that had already been robustly addressed and that constituted only a minute fraction of the harm to children, which was most often perpetrated by their parents and reported many times over (Buckley & Buckley, in press). Despite its perceived cata-strophic effect on services in some parts of Australia (Lonne et al., 2009; Scott, 2007), the number of countries adopting reporting legislation is increasing (Gilbert et al., 2011). It stands to reason that the resulting pres-sure of work compels practitioners to gate-keep and ration their responses. As a result, families who initiate contact with the services, often seeking early intervention, may be left without assistance until the risk threshold appears to have been reached. For example, a mother, interviewed in an

Irish study who had unsuccessfully sought help for her child's potentially self-harming behaviour, having been told it was 'just adolescence' made the angry observation that 'you'd need a knife in your child's back' in order to attract the attention of services (Buckley et al., 2011) A three-part study in Northern Ireland has also demonstrated over a number of years the paradoxical finding that when families are considered to be at risk, they are less likely to receive a service from statutory social workers, becoming the object of surveillance rather than the recipients of direct help (Spratt & Callan, 2004; Spratt & Hayes, 2010). Other studies elsewhere have affirmed this, with service users identifying the factors that led them to be reported to child protection to include stress, domestic violence and debt – and many found that their needs were not addressed in the process of child protection intervention (Bolen et al., 2008; Buckley et al., 2011).

When the nature of reports made to child protection systems is considered, the appropriateness of an investigative, risk-based approach again comes into question. For example, recent analysis of the Canadian Incidence Study, 2008, has indicated that neglect and emotional abuse, particularly concerning intimate partner violence, form the majority of reports made to child protection system (Trocmé et al., 2014). For several years, commentators have expressed concern about the unintended consequence of categorizing exposure to domestic violence as emotional abuse (Friend, 2008; Connolly, 2009). The resulting inflation in reporting has inevitably forced services to adopt a forensic type of screening that either leaves families without support or subjects them to punitive or unhelpful interventions. While acknowledgement and understanding of the impact of domestic violence is a positive trend, it is generally agreed that child protection services are not best placed to respond to issues of this kind. Service user research with children (Buckley et al., 2007) and with adult victims (Mullender & Hague, 2005) has reiterated this message.

Conclusion

This chapter has used service user perspectives to argue that the key mediating factor in effective child protection work, the relationship between worker and family members, has become incompatible with what is now largely utilitarian and what is described by Murphy et al. (2013) as an 'instrumental' process of service delivery. Egalitarian and respectful relationships simply do not fit with current reporting regulations, standard business processes and other administrative requirements. These measures were introduced to reduce risk but ironically increase the likelihood of poor outcomes by overwhelming service providers and alienating service users. Contrary to the aspirations of the 1990s to foster partnerships with families, the power differential between service users and service providers has grown considerably. A number of solutions have been proposed: Cooper et al., (2003) have sought a shift from the monolithic defensiveness of social services departments to a more systemic service delivered in schools, health centres and communities; Lonne et al. (2009) promote organizational restructuring that will allow staff to empower rather than intimidate service users and 'inspire to aspire' (p. 181). Following on the theme of helping alliances, Featherstone et al. (2014) have urged a reimagining of child protection work to the point where it becomes 'infrastructure light and relationship heavy' (p. 155). In the past two decades, refocusing, differential response and a definite movement to increase the visibility of children and promote community-based service user participation have all endeavoured to counterbalance the risk paradigm and have brought about some positive outcomes and experiences for families (Cameron et al., 2012). Yet, as this chapter has tried to argue, widespread acceptance and establishment of these intelligence-led and evidentially more effective models of service has been blindsided by increasing bureaucracy and legalism, including mandatory reporting. Creative, innovative and family-centred practices are as yet unable to stem to the tide of outrage, scandal and political responses. As long as reductionist, instrumental aspects of child protection work dominate, we are likely to see little change in the experience of children and families.

Note

1 *Ladybird, Ladybird* is a British film presented as a drama documentary about a British woman's dispute with social services over the care and custody of her four children (Wikipedia, accessed 23 October 2014).

References

Australian Institute of Health and Welfare 2013. Child protection Australia: 2011–12. Child Welfare series no. 55. Cat. No. CWS 43. Canberra: AIHW.

Bell, M. (1999). Working in partnership in child protection: The conflicts, *British Journal of Social Work*, 29, 437–455.

Bell, M. & Wilson, K. (2006). Research note: Children's views of family group conferences, *British Journal of Social Work*, 36, 671–681.

Beresford, P. & Croft, S. (2001). Service users' knowledges and the social construction of social work, *Journal of Social Work*, 1(3), 295–316.

Buckley, H., Skehill, C. & O'Sullivan, E. (1997). *Child Protection Practices in Ireland: A Case Study*. Dublin: Oak Tree Press.

Buckley, H. (1998). Filtering out fathers: The gendered nature of child protection practice, *Irish Social Worker*, 16, 7–11.

Buckley, H. (2003). *Child Protection Work: Beyond the Rhetoric*. London: Jessica Kingsley.

Buckley, H., Holt, S. & Whelan, S. (2007). Listen to me! Children's experience of domestic violence, *Child Abuse Review*, 16(5), 283–295.

Buckley, H., Whelan, S., Carr N. & Murphy, C. (2008). *Service Users' Perceptions of the Child Protection System*, Dublin: Office of the Minister for Children and Youth Affairs. www.dcya.gov.ie/documents/publications/CF_service_users.pdf

Buckley, H., Carr, N. & Whelan, S. (2011). 'Like walking on eggshells': Service user views and expectations of the child protection system, *Child & Family Social Work*, 16(1), 101–106.

Buckley, R. (2013). *Child Abuse Reporting in Ireland and the Socio-legal Implications of Introducing a Mandatory Reporting Law*. PhD Thesis, School of Social Work and Social Policy, Trinity College Dublin.

Butler Sloss, E. (1988). *Report of the Inquiry into Child Abuse in Cleveland 1987*. London: HMSO.

Cameron, G., DeGeer, I., Hazineh, L., Frensch, K., Smit Quosai, T. & Freymond, N. (2013). The impacts of accessible service delivery on front-line helping relationships in child welfare, *Child & Family Social Work*, 18, 253–263.

Campbell, B. (1988). *Unofficial Secrets: Child Sexual Abuse – The Cleveland Case*. London: Virago.

Canadian Incidence Study of Reported Child Abuse and Neglect 2008 (CIS 2008). Major Findings http://cwrp.ca/publications/2117 [Accessed 31 October 2014].

Cleaver, H. & Freeman, P. (1995). *Parental Perspectives in Cases of Suspected Child Abuse*. London: HMSO.

Connolly, M. (2007). Practice frameworks: Conceptual maps to guide interventions in child welfare, *British Journal of Social Work*, 37, 825–837.

Cooper, A., Hetherington, R. And Katz, I. (2003). *The Risk Factor: Making the Child Protection System Work for Children*. London: Demos Open Access www.demos.co.uk/files/The_Risk_Factor.pdf?1253012631 [Accessed 31 October 2014].

Corby, B. (1987). *Working with Child Abuse*. Milton Keynes: Open University Press.

Dale, P. (2004). 'Like a fish in a bowl': Parents' perceptions of child protection services, *Child Abuse Review*, 13, 137–157.

De Boer, C. & Cody, N. (2007). Good helping relationships in child welfare: Learning from stories of success, *Child and Family Social Work*, 12, 32–42.

Department of Health [UK] (1995). *Messages from Research*. London: Stationery Office.

Department of Health [UK] (2000). *Framework for the Assessment of Children in Need and Their Families*. London: Stationery Office.

Dingwall, R., Eekelaar, J. & Murray, T. (1983). *The Protection of Children: State Intervention and Family Life*. Oxford: Blackwell.

Donzelot, J. (1980). *The Policing of Families: Welfare Versus the State*. London: Hutchinson.

Dumbrill, G. (2006). Parental experience of child protection intervention: A qualitative study, *Child Abuse & Neglect*, 30, 27–37.

Ellet, A. (2013). Timely and needed perspectives on differential response in child protective services, *Research in Social Work Practice*, 23, 521–524.

Farmer, E. & Owen, M. (1995). *Child Protection Practice: Private Risks and Public Remedies*. London: HMSO.

Featherstone, B., White, S., & Wastell, D. (2012). Ireland's opportunity to learn from England's difficulties? Auditing uncertainty in child protection, *Irish Journal of Applied Social Studies*, 12, 28–42.

Featherstone, B., White, S., & Morris, K. (2014). *Re-imagining Child Protection*. Bristol: Policy Press.

Foucault, M. (1975). *Discipline and Punish: The Birth of the Prison*. New York: Penguin.

Gibbons, J., Conroy, S. & Bell, C. (1995). *Operating the Child Protection System*. London: HMSO.

Gilbert, N., Parton, N. & Skivenes, M. (2011). *Child Protection Systems: International Trends and Orientations*. New York: Oxford University Press.

Health & Human Services (2013). Child Maltreatment 2012. www.acf.hhs.gov/sites/default/files/cb/cm2012.pdf [Accessed 2 October 2014].

Ghaffar, W., Manby, M. & Race, T. (2012). Exploring the experiences of parents and carers whose children have been subject to child protection plans, *British Journal of Social Work*, 42, 887–905.

Giovannoni, J. & Billingsley, A. (1970). Child neglect among the poor: A study of parental adequacy in families of three ethnic groups, *Child Welfare*, 49, 196–204.

Gordon, L. (1989). *Heroes of their own Lives: The Politics and History of Family Violence*. Boston, MA (1880–1960), London: Virago.

Hall, C. & Slembrouck, S. (2001). Parent participation in social work meetings: The case of child protection meetings, *European Journal of Social Work*, 4, 143–160.

Hetherington, R. & Picquardt, R. (2001). Strategies for survival: Users' experience of child welfare in three welfare regimes, *Child and Family Social Work*, 6, 239–248.

Holland, S. & Rivett, M. (2006). Everyone started shouting: Making connections between the process of family group conferences and family therapy practice, *British Journal of Social Work*, 38, 21–38.

Hooper, C. A. (1992). *Mothers Surviving Child Sexual Abuse*. London: Routledge.

Horwath, J. & Bishop, B. (2001). *Child Neglect: Is My View Your View?* North Eastern Health Service Executive and the University of Sheffield.

Howitt, D. (1992). *Child Abuse Errors*. Hemel Hempstead: Harvester Wheatsheaf.

Kaplan, C. & Merkel-Holguin, L. (2008). Another look at the national study on differential response in child welfare, *Protecting Children*, 23, 5–21.

Lee, C. & Ayon, C. (2004). Is the client-worker relationship associated with better outcomes in mandated child abuse cases? *Research on Social Work Practice*, 14, 351–357.

Leigh, S. & Miller, C. (2004). Is the third way the best way? Social work intervention with children and families, *Journal of Social Work*, 4, 245–267.

Loman, L. & Siegal, G. (2004). *Minnesota Alternative Response Evaluation Final Report*. Institute of Applied Research, St. Louis, MO.

Lonne, B. Parton, N., Thomson, J. & Harries, M. (2009). *Reforming Child Protection.* New York: Routledge.

Lupton, C. (1998). User empowerment or family self-reliance? The Family Group Conference Model, *British Journal of Social Work,* 28, 107–128.

Milner, J. (1996). 'Men's Resistance to Social Workers' in B. Fawcett, B. Featherstone, J. Hearn & C. Toft (eds), *Violence and Gender Relations: Theories and Interventions* (pp. 115–129). London: Sage.

Mullender, A. & Hague, G. (2005). Giving a voice to women survivors of domestic violence through recognition as a service user group, *British Journal of Social Work,* 35, 1321–1341.

Murphy, D., Duggan, M. & Joseph, S. (2013). Relationship-based social work and its compatibility with the person-centred approach: Principled versus instrumental perspectives, *British Journal of Social Work,* 43, 703–719.

Myers, J. (1994).*The Backlash: Child Protection Under Fire.* Thousand Oaks: Sage.

National Child Abuse and Neglect Data System (2013). www.ndacan.cornell.edu/ datasets/datasets-list-ncands-child-file-dcdc.cfm

O'Brien, V. (2000). *Family Group Conference Pilot Project Evaluation Report.* Dublin: East Coast Area Health Board.

Parton, C. (1990). 'Women, gender oppression and child abuse', in The Violence Against Children Study Group, *Taking Child Abuse Seriously* (pp. 41–62). London: Unwin Hyman.

Pelton, L. (2008). 'Informing Child Welfare: The Promise and Limits of Empirical Research' in D. Lindsay & A. Shlonsky (eds), *Child Welfare Research: Practice and policy* (pp. 25–48). New York: Oxford University Press.

Pithouse, A. (1987). *Social Work: The Social Organisation of an Invisible Trade.* Altershot: Gower.

Prout, A. & James, A. (2006). A New Paradigm for the Sociology of Childhood? Provenance, Promise and Problems, in A. James and A. Prout (eds), *Constructing and Reconstructing Childhood* (pp. 1–33). London: Routledge Falmer.

Ruch, G. (2005). Relationship based practice and reflective practice: holistic approaches to contemporary child care social work, *Child and Family Social Work,* 10, 111–123.

Ryan, M. (2000). *Working with Fathers.* Abingdon: Radcliffe Medical Press.

Spratt, T & Callan, J. (2004). Parents' views on social work interventions in child welfare cases, *British Journal of Social Work,* 34, 199–224.

Straus, M. A., Gelles, R. J. & Steinmetz, S. K. (1980). *Behind Closed Doors: Violence in the American Family.* Garden City, NY: Anchor/Doubleday.

Thoburn, J., Lewis, A. & Shemmings, D. (1995). *Paternalism or Partnership? Family Involvement in the Child Protection Process.* London: HMSO.

Trocmé, N., Kyte, A., Sinha, V. & Fallon, B. (2014). Urgent protection versus chronic need: Clarifying the dual mandate of child welfare services across Canada, *Social Sciences,* 3, 483–498.

Turnell, A. & Edwards, S. (1999). *Signs of Safety: A Solution and Safety Oriented Approach to Child Protection Casework.* New York: Norton.

Wise, S. (1989). *Child Abuse Procedures and Social Work Practice: An Ethnographic Approach.* PhD Thesis, University of Manchester.

Waldfogel, J. (1998). *The Future of Child Protection: How to Break the Cycle of Abuse and Neglect*. Boston, MA: Harvard University Press.

Wright, S. (2004). Child protection in the community: A community development approach, *Child Abuse Review*, 6, 384–398.

Yatchmenoff, D. (2005). Measuring client engagement from the client's perspective in non-voluntary child protective services, *Research on Social Work Practice*, 15, 84–96.

7

ENGAGING FAMILIES AND MANAGING RISK IN PRACTICE

*Kate Morris and Gale Burford**

Introduction

As we can see from the preceding chapters, child protection decision making exists within an uncertain and complex environment where risk permeates the concerns of child protection professionals, managers and anyone who is charged with keeping children safe. As Jones (2008, slide 2) notes, 'whether we like it or not, management doesn't care about security. ... They care about risk'. Given the organizational messaging about risk, which creates a dominant organizational risk culture (Levy et al., 2010), it would be surprising if risk concerns did not sit at the heart of daily child protection activities. The problem within child protection organizations is that risk concern is focused not only on the child but also on the organizational risk of acting or not acting. Within a dominant risk culture, child protection systems determine who will be involved in decision making, invariably confining it to the professional system. This can mean that the potential for families, and particularly extended families, to be engaged in decision making – and thus meaningfully invested as partners in those decisions – is lost.

This chapter explores the ways in which families, and the contributions they make, are framed in the context of child protection. Building on the ideas presented by Buckley in Chapter 6, and in particular the issue of service user participation, it examines how engaging with the wider family within the decision-making processes and practices of state care and protection interventions attends to child safety and well-being and helps shape a positive view of public service providers. We consider the

* Kate Morris is a professor of social work at the Department of Sociological Studies, the University of Sheffield, UK. Gale Burford is a professor of social work at the Unviersity of Vermont, USA.

peril of states' over-reliance on technological risk assessment in child protection in ways that undercut the capabilities of families to engage with helpers and with other members of their own social and family networks. We argue that the over-reliance on risk assessment, coupled with research methodologies that take account only of well-defined interventions (Schwartz et al., 2015), serves to marginalize family engagement practices, prevents social workers from carrying out the very kind of responsive practice that families need (Featherstone et al., 2014) and contributes to negative views of public services and child protection practitioners.

We acknowledge the wide-ranging challenges faced by child protection systems in allocating resources in the service of responsively defined risks and needs. It is especially difficult for practitioners and supervisors when they find themselves in substantial agreement with family members and community partners about the 'right thing to do' but are limited to inflexible policies that hew closely to risk aversion. The constant threat of greater liability risk, blame to themselves and fear that the service system will suffer more and more cuts if they 'get it wrong' exert massive pressure on the workforce to accommodate untenable practice conditions and deeply embed a dominant risk paradigm. Fears that they are failing to protect children from trauma make risk assessment technologies appealing and serve to normalize the distancing of family members, from the immediate household of the child. It is nevertheless true that for over three decades now, this widespread reliance on professional decision making, with its singular focus on technological assessment tools, has not helped. In fact, many would argue that things have worsened, creating very real vulnerabilities for children, workers and child protection systems in English-speaking jurisdictions.

We believe it is time to stop 'tinkering around the edges', with tokenistic efforts that embrace the rhetoric of family engagement but that do not follow through with any meaningful involvement with families in child protection. We draw on various studies in the United Kingdom and from North America of family responses to welfare interventions, including family experiences of alternative approaches such as Family Group Conferences. Such models build on relational approaches to assessment that also include an assessment of risk but do so in a partnership model where families are involved in both safety planning and in crafting possibilities for those families to realize and achieve their own visions of family life and well-being for their children.

We conclude that the full infusion of strengths-based models of practice in risk-saturated systems can be accomplished only with the full engagement of significant members of the child's social network in the assessment of risk and need. We argue that assessments and interventions which are not responsive to and inclusive of the child's family system increase known risks to the child.

Families and perceptions of their contribution

Writers are increasingly describing societies that feature growing inequality (Stiglitz, 2012; Wilkinson & Pickett, 2009; Connolly, 2015). Indeed, it could be argued that there has never been a more unequal experience for families in the United Kingdom and the United States. The further down the privilege ladder you find yourself, the less access you have to decision-making processes and the more 'at risk' you are perceived to be for a wide variety of negative outcomes: the poorest in society suffer the hardest consequences of the economic and fiscal policies. Wilkinson and Pickett (2009) in their work *The Spirit Level* consider the impact of inequality on well-being. They demonstrate that inequality is linked to multiple poor outcomes: high rates of poor mental health, family violence, domestic abuse, morbidity, teenage pregnancy and drug use. The consequences of inequality are real – it materially affects the well-being of family members (Featherstone et al., 2014) and the life chances of children. As studies by groups representing the poorest families in our societies show, living with inequality and poverty places a constant strain on family life (Gupta et al., 2014).

These and other findings (Brown, 2015; Daly & Kelly, 2015; France & Utting, 2005) provoke many questions: for example, how does social work respond to poverty and deprivation in the context of growing inequalities? When set in the context of broader social and economic inequalities, families face not only a struggle to maintain day-to-day living but also an increased risk of state intervention aided by the technologies of risk assessment that negatively construct especially mothers as failing to protect their children and especially fathers either as uninvolved or as a danger to their children (Featherstone et al., 2014). And when you are poor, your contribution is perceived in a particular way.

In Chapter 5 Katz and Connolly explore the reasons why some children and families are disproportionately represented in child welfare and child protection matters. It is clear that poverty and deprivation increase the chances of your child being removed from your care, and in discussing family involvement in care and protection, these inequalities need to be carefully considered when working with disadvantaged families. When families try to do what 'is right' for their children in the face of daily practical and financial challenges, their efforts call attention to their shame and suffering, which is then depicted in assessments as further evidence of family failing. In both the United Kingdom and the United States, recognizing and taking into account such social structural issues brands one as soft on crime and neglect (Gove, 2012). Attention has increasingly returned to emphasizing individual responsibility, framing 'risk' as the potential for consumption and exploitation of scarce resources and undermining morality. The focus in practice continues to remain largely on forensic investigations aiming to prove guilt or innocence and/or pursuing child support.

But in this context of inequality and poverty it is not enough to simply seek to manage the internal risk dynamics of a family. The established (and growing) body of empirical and conceptual work clearly indicates that addressing the causes and consequences of inequality and understanding the relationship between social work practices and both poverty and deprivation has the potential to make a profound difference to our work with families. Social work must engage with what has been described (in health inequality debates) as the 'causes of the causes' (Marmot, 2010).

By their very design, compliance-driven investigation processes typically isolate family members from one another and render invisible both their individual and collective strengths and contributions for the duration of the investigation. They can also leave members reacting negatively afterwards (Braithwaite, 2014; Dumbrill, 2006; Harris, 2011; 2012; Ivec et al., 2012; Tyler, 2001; 2006) even in situations where it would be in their best interests to cooperate. The enduring impact of the incursion of adversarial and risk-averse procedural and technological responses into areas of family life, including child protection, has come to be seen as having particularly negative impacts with poor, immigrant and minority families, as reflected in rates of racial, gender and income disproportionality. Moreover, high turnover in the social work workforce continuously exposes families to discontinuity in the efforts that they make to be understood on their own terms, and it undermines belief in the state's capacity to help. One could hardly design a better blueprint for alienation and for guaranteeing failure to help families present their capacities in a favourable light.

Especially in the United Kingdom, the political positioning of families as both troublesome and resourceful presents a further difficulty (Morris and Featherstone 2010). This narrative has increasingly turned the spotlight on individual failings. Families hear and see politicians describe a feckless, failing cohort of families, families that are wilfully resistant to change, for whom the only answers are early intervention in the shape of early removal of their children:

> I want social workers to be more assertive with dysfunctional parents, courts to be less indulgent of poor parents, and the care system to expand to deal with the consequences. ... In all too many cases when we decide to leave children in need with their biological parents we are leaving them to endure a life of soiled nappies and scummy baths, chaos and hunger, hopelessness and despair. These children need to be rescued, just as much as the victims of any other natural disaster. (Michael Gove, Minister of State, 2012)

Similarly, in the United States, constructions of parents as failing and of social workers as failing to intervene for children during the important years of their brain development by leaving them with inadequate parents until it is too late to reverse the damage has fuelled anti-family rhetoric and helped further cast 'biological' families as 'risky' and to push along an agenda of adopting children by families who have the means to care for them (Bartholet, 2014; 2000). The underlying biological determinism and thinly veiled eugenics in these arguments both belie the data in rates of reunification in the United States and add fuel for race- and welfare-baiting media and political voices that call for even further cuts to family support programmes.

On the other end of the political spectrum, the state push towards kinship care means families are simultaneously found to be dysfunctional during risk assessments and yet asked to be resourceful by offering to care for children in their network. Nevertheless, results have long shown that kin and 'like family' members are willing to take action in a crisis, engage and put their own resources on the line to positive ends (Burford & Pennell, 1998; Marsh & Crow, 1998; Morris & Connolly, 2012).

Conspicuously absent in most risk assessment formulations is how the evidence that taking children into the care of the state puts the children at risk of a wide variety of negative outcomes is balanced with other risks. The case is strong enough that unless it can be shown in a particular instance that involvement of significant people from the child's social network is at odds with the safety and well-being of the child, then they should be given the opportunity to be engaged with decisions and should be supported. To ignore the harm that can come to a child by excluding people who will be, or could be, there for the child long after the professionals have all departed is ethically irresponsible in light of the evidence, and undermines the rights of families and children (Burford & Gallagher, 2015; Gal & Duramy, 2015; Pennell, Burford, Connolly & Morris, 2012). Communicating these risks and demonstrating clear efforts to engage the child's network need to be essential requirements in any situation where a child is being removed from a family, as would be expected in evidence-based practice (Fisher & Marsh, 2015).

What families think about risk interventions

Despite considerable research evidence to the contrary, fears about the risks of involving family are used to marginalize family engagement practices. Professionals worry that giving the family information will enable the abuser to better exploit the family and the child. They may be concerned that involving the family will further traumatize the child. Professionals will be mired in the family dynamics and be blinded to the risks to the child.

These fears are tenaciously held and perpetuated in risk-averse organizational cultures and in the media (Chapter 2). One of the most disturbing prices we pay for the rise of inequality is the growing distance between those needing services and those delivering services, including the increased political communication of being uncompromising. This public image conflates the notion of 'being tough' with being rigorous and precise. Too often the result is seen as authoritarian by the families even when they themselves believe that the state should be intervening. The absence of fairness and a sense of justice often turns even those who want help, and in many cases are asking for help, away from the perceived heavy-handedness of the state. In our research, this mother, for example, tried to get services that would work alongside her in her own home but got no help until her son had unexplained bruises:

> I went to them (child protective services) pleading for help with [her profoundly handicapped child,] and all the worker said was that they could 'put him in a foster home'. Then a complaint was made by [mandated reporter,] and they investigated me. ... Now the foster parents get all the respite and behavioural management services that I was asking for but could not get. ... I can take care of him but I need help. ... At the team meetings I'm made to feel like I've been a 'bad parent' and that I am the one who put the bruises on him. I've never hurt [her child,] and the police report and the investigation said they did not find any reason to think it was me, but I'm made to feel like maybe I did it. I'm afraid to complain. They cancel my visits when [her son] is 'upset'. I have cared for him by myself for 10 years and now they control my visits. I'm still his mother. (Mother in Burford, 2015)

For families facing extreme adversity, day-to-day life is grindingly difficult. They are acutely aware of being different, of being marked out and the consequences for their children. Remarkably little is known about family practices in extreme adversity and how families behave as a family in these conditions. It is a gap in research that inhibits our capacity to develop effective family support services.

Children and adults live in families, not households – the latter may be the functional arrangement, but the former is how they arrange their lives (Daly, 2015). The term 'family' is critical here as one of Morris's (2012) research participants raises: 'Do you mean who lives in this house or who is in my family?' Children are relational beings, and while we have seen the rise of notions of children as rights bearers, separated from their networks in recent child protection developments, in reality families are the primary arrangement for caring for children.

In our studies, nevertheless, even where there was explicit emphasis on seeking to test out family-minded practice, going beyond the household was unusual. In several of the larger-scale studies in the United States, researchers have not identified in reports or publications which family members were included (Ahn et al., 2013; Family Connections, n/d; Perry et al., 2013; Yoo et al., n/d), and in some cases the research sheds light on implementations that involve families very little (Pennell et al., 2010; Perry et al., 2013; Yoo et al., n/d). In limiting our engagement, we not only restrict our knowledge about safe and unsafe family members, but we also miss an opportunity to extend our understandings of a child's daily life and the knowledge and expertise within their informal networks. And there is another, particularly painful consequence. We create a legacy of guilt for some family members – aunts, grandparents who would have helped a child had they been included in the planning and decision making:

> I didn't know that he was violent. … If I'd have known that he was a violent man with that history I would have, well, done something, you know, whatever, ask me whatever, it depends on the circumstances, but I would not have tolerated that.

> … What's the point? Because they don't want to know what your side of it is, whether you be a surviving victim or a grandmother, or an uncle, they don't seem to want that angle. It's almost as though 'we are the experts; we know what should happen'.

> —Relatives of a child murdered by a boyfriend within the network
> (Morris, 2012)

In a variety of studies, the message remains the same: family-minded practice is distilled into a focus on immediate carers and mothers, with extended family relevant only where there is a request for kinship carers (Morris et al., 2015). In this sense, as noted by Shlonsky and Mildon in Chapter 8, family engagement strategies are playing at only the edges of child protection systems, and even then, often poorly.

Two further themes emerge from reading across the data from our studies of families and both care and protection interventions. First, the frequently common experience of help seeking being redefined as an indicator of risk in need of investigation, and second, the rise of assessment as a service. Both themes have a direct bearing on the use of strengths-based approaches in practice. In the following quote, a young mother describes her experience of seeking assistance with one of her children's behaviour:

> I think it was XXX had a bump on his head, and social services come out, and when they come out I told them, obviously I needed help with YYY, but they didn't want to know about YYY. They just wanted to know how this bump had come on XXX's head, so it was a bit annoying that sometimes they can come out on another matter, but they can't come and help me if I did need help ... and it like makes you want to pull your hair out, from the fact that you was asking for help, but they don't want to help you when you really need it, if you understand what I mean. (Morris, 2012)

With the rise of an authoritarian child protection project in the United Kingdom, we have become increasingly rusty in having conversations about help. We are preoccupied by models and techniques concerned with risk management and prediction, and we grow distant from discussions about worries, help and support in protecting children. Such conversations could build different relationships. The quote from the young mother above reveals the worst excesses of the current 'screen and intervene' mode of practice. But families also described repeated short-term investigations and assessments, sometimes then followed by targeted help. And this succession of interventions created a family narrative about services, a narrative of frustration, anger and at times abandonment:

> like social services for instance, like when they've been in and out of our lives for so long, they've never been allowed to stay. They've always been involved for six weeks and then cross us off, and like not one of those workers, out of all those workers in the last nine years that we've worked with, the ones like who make out that they're really close with us, and they're getting on with us and that, when they get taken off the case and never come back to see if we're coping. (Mother, in Morris, 2012)

There are interesting questions that generate critical practice dilemmas. How do we respond to the model of child protection driven by a risk-averse culture when we know families need flexible practice and workers who are confident about being creative with fluctuating degrees of concern, needs and capabilities? Social work done well is informed improvisation – it is difficult to find a fit between this and the rise of prescribed practice models and standardized technical solutions to risk. But, where practitioners had listened and sought a reciprocal relationship, the families described a real difference:

> They have turned up because they genuinely do want to help you; that's how I feel. Like when our social worker, the one we told you about, we felt that she wanted to help us. Like, it wasn't about money, it wasn't about like ... it was just things like if we didn't have something, she'd say come on let's go and take

you out somewhere. Do you know what I mean? And then when we got on our feet, we started like rewarding social services back like with XXX, for instance, she's had new buggies and stuff, and we've rung them and said can you give this to a family, and that's what it should be about, you know, they reward us, we reward them back, and...that's how I always think that's how it should be. (Mother, in Morris, 2012)

It is important to remember that it is possible to grow this kind of practice in ways that both families and professionals appreciate.

Families also perceive practice differently. In one jurisdiction in the United States where accepted reports of child abuse or neglect are assigned to either an assessment track or an investigation track, parents responded through surveys (N=444) and/or interviews (N=14) that asked about their experiences with their social workers and their views of the child protection system itself (Burford, 2015). As expected, parents assigned to assessment track were overall more likely to rate their social worker as taking a strengths-based approach with them. This positive response to the worker, however, was not confined only to the assessment track. Parents who were most likely to say that the state's interventions had helped them (as opposed to hurt them or made no difference) were those who perceived the worker to be taking a strengths-based approach; were in agreement with the legitimacy of the state's intervention; and trusted the state's intentions with them, regardless of whether it was an investigation or an assessment. Moreover, those families who had been engaged with one or more of the state's 'family' engagement offerings were more likely to report that the state's involvement had been helpful to them.

Typical of parents who did not believe that their workers were using a strengths-based approach but who agreed that there were problems that necessitated the states involvement was this mother:

They just, they don't really call you and tell you how your case is going or what's going on. For me like I wouldn't hear from my worker for months, and I wouldn't have a clue. People would be like 'So what's going on with your case'? And I'm like, 'I don't know'.

She expected that care and respect should be an important part of the way the state engaged her:

Yeah, they have a reason to be in my life, and I don't hold it against them. It's their job, but communication is just...they really definitely need to work on the communication. And even if you don't go and see your client or your person, at least give them a phone call. 'Hey how are you doing? Is there any questions you need to ask me?' (Mother, in Burford, 2015)

Because the primary purpose of an investigation is to gather information to make a finding that will stand up in court, the process is more often seen to emphasize only a parent's failings and thereby pre-empt questions that might undermine the conclusions of a report. This mother believed that the investigation should have acknowledged the efforts she had been making:

> It was basically like a one-sided report. It didn't say any of the facts that I had called previously myself. They didn't say I was willing and wanting to work with them. It really sounded like they called me numerous times, and I had not received a call back. ... I even went and got printouts of my phone records showing I had called them numerous times to no avail. So I feel like they can really twist things when they want to twist things, and that's scary. If somebody needs help and they go into that knowing there's a good chance I'm going to lose my child, it's a scary thought. (Mother, in Burford, 2015)

In the end, she was left to continue searching for services to help with her son.

Underpinning much of this discussion is a notion of care: care in practice, care practices within families, the ethic of care adopted by families. It is ironic that care is such a pivotal concept to understanding family life in adversity, and yet families and young people repeatedly talk about the careless nature of our systems and practices (The Care Inquiry, 2013).

Another mother admitted that it was her own reaction to what she perceived as an uncaring response that escalated matters during an assessment and triggered the worker to switch her to an investigation track:

> I had trusted them to a point, and then when I went in and saw it firsthand like just the shear [sic], he really just wrote me off. Like I'm sitting in this man's office literally falling apart like I was at my end. I didn't know where else to turn, who else, and I was really clear with him on that. Just kind of have it be like, 'Well, you know there's nothing I can do for you, the funding isn't there. We can't be respite.' And he didn't even refer me to any other agency. He didn't say 'Call [name of agency she ultimately found herself]'. He didn't say 'Here's a list of numbers'. He didn't say, 'Here's the screener's numbers'. He did none of that. He made one follow-up call with me, and that was it. And basically it was a threatening call. 'If you're not willing to work with me about going to court and getting custody of my son, we're going to open this case and take them [all her children] anyways'. And I was like 'What? That's not the point of my visit. My visit was to ask you for help'. (Mother, in Burford, 2015)

Other parents describe social workers and police officers who treated them with respect, were clear in raising their concerns and took the time to be supportive, including suggesting where they could get help in the mean-time. Families talked about demonstrated care in practice, in the most extraordinary of circumstances. And these experiences were building blocks for future work; their imprint on the families' perceptions of the child protection services were far greater than the scale of the practice episodes. Care as an organizing concept for our services and our practices has been much neglected, despite the evidence from multiple studies of its centrality in practice. Family Group Conferences offer us a glimpse into family prac-tices and in particular family care practices. We see how families mobilize around an ethic of care and how family practices provide emotional as well as practical care for vulnerable family members. Contemporary child pro-tection processes, however, struggle to find spaces and places for family and indeed professional care practices (Burford with Barron, 2013; Featherstone et al., 2014; Gallagher & Burford, 2015; Morris & Burford, 2009). In an increasingly structured and forensic approach to practice, the messy, shape-shifting nature of concepts such as care are pushed to one side.

Interrogating and better understanding the concept of care are miss-ing ingredients in practice, yet if we weave care into an analysis of child protection, we could arrive at some profoundly different arrangements for helping children and families to thrive. As Sevenhuijsen (2000, p. 5) notes, in so doing we also embrace rights-based practice:

> Care should be seen as a democratic practice, and democratic citizenship should guarantee everyone equal access to the giving and receiving of care.

Doing it differently: the possibilities of respectful practice

Despite these choppy waters, we have seen the development of models of practice that seek to work differently with families. Krumer-Nevo (2003, p. 274) discusses two models of help, in which she contrasts the tradi-tional model, which she characterizes as a 'coalition of despair', with an alternative that can be seen as a 'covenant of help':

> The alternative model is characterized by emphasis on the pain and strengths of the clients; on partnership and a mutual search for the most convenient ways of getting help; and on flexible and supportive organizational procedures.

Such an approach is rooted in strengths-based and rights-based narratives. These see families as having both *rights* to care, to participation and to involvement in decision making and *capabilities* to build upon in seeking to achieve change where there are concerns about harm. Models such as these do not assume all families can care safely; instead, they seek to arrive at an honest understanding of how best to meet a child's needs, including the child's protective needs. But such models demand a different conversation between practitioners and families and a different policy framework for help and support. They ask us to listen, understand, reflect and refine. They require no conversation to be out of bounds, and they demand that we intimately know the family's world.

The study of family involvement in case reviews offered critical insights into a particularly contested and challenging area of participation (Morris, Brandon & Tudor, 2015). The data from families provide examples of professionals' having the most difficult of conversations with skill and empathy, but they also describe practice that was preoccupied with procedural compliance, reputational risk and accountability to management structures rather than a focus on the child and the learning. Participation in this context is, the study established, ethically and professionally demanding. But if done well, it offers unique insights that can make a real difference to how professionals shape and deliver services. Even in this area of the most difficult and painful practice, it is possible to see how a covenant of hope can make such a difference to children and families:

> I talk about having imaginative, creative people. ... I'm thinking please, please come to the table and believe that you can do something, you know, think about it. You're being given this story of a human being who's no longer here. It's so important that you take that really seriously, and you know, it may be that you don't achieve anything, but let's give it the best possible chance. (Adult family member, in Morris, 2012)

As many families described, however, the focus on risk assessment and risk management has resulted in families receiving 'too little for too long and too much too late'. So the search is on for models that are based on a covenant of hope at a time when resources are shrinking and are increasingly focused on interventionist practices. The Care Inquiry held in the United Kingdom made explicit the critical importance of unbroken relationships between child, families and professionals. It also identified the growing trends towards creating multiple specialized services that fragment help and break relationships. Hilary Cottam and colleagues based in a small UK organization called Participle are developing a concept of *relational welfare*, a notion that we need to create new spaces and systems that have relationships at the core. They argue for the need for a truly responsive welfare state that builds the capabilities of all services that value and build on relationships – relationships that understand the devastating impact of

loneliness and that know what it is like to confront the problems of violence and depression and other complex problems that people face.

Mimi Kim (2015) recently said that 'The first responders to a violent
situation are usually friends, family, community members, and clergy. ...
Why aren't we doing more to equip them with the knowledge and the
skills to be able to intervene effectively?'

This approach recognizes that multiple changes must occur for highly
vulnerable families to thrive and that this includes changing the services
that surround them and their access to social and economic capital. The
focus needs to be on helping to strengthen relationships between and
among the immediate and long-term caretakers of the developing child.
Safety and the management of risk in this view is a product of protection
of individual rights and exercising obligations to community well-being.
Given the enormous challenges facing families, models that build on
capabilities and have respectful relationships at their core become important beacons of hope.

Family decision making and restorative approaches to care and protection have opened up new opportunities for families and for professionals. Research shows that most families have members who can and
do work to protect and care for their children, and this includes, when
given the opportunity, formal child protection situations (Burford &
Pennell, 1998; Crampton, 2006; Falck, 2008; Gunderson et al., 2003;
Harris, 2008; Huntsman, 2006; Pennell, Edwards & Burford, 2010;
Marsh & Crow, 1998; Morris, 2011; 2013; Rautkis et al., 2010; Wijnen-
Lunenburg et al., 2007). The importance of preparing people for relational engagement cannot be overstated. It is one of the most, if not
the most, time-consuming activities. Helping people step into decision
making and trusting the process and the experience that they are being
treated fairly takes time. This involves creating inclusive representation
and not forcing people to face their problems alone. The perception of
risk is to a large extent constructed around isolation, alienation and
estrangement and by judging how people deal with that instead of learning how they behave in the context of the relationships in which they
are expected to care for the child. Alone, people are unable to present
themselves as a part of an understandable, pro-social group and are easily
seen as a threat.

Conclusion

The risk of carrying out assessment, investigation, service planning and
evaluation without the knowing involvement of significant members of
the child's extended family and social network carries with it the potential

for furthering life-long disadvantage and short-term harm. In particular, when the assessments themselves rely on technology to the exclusion or minimizing of significant others, the child's future is placed at risk.

Risk assessment technology and protocols cannot supplant the need for ongoing case review, reflective supervision and relational practice. Rather, the technologies should mesh with these processes and the information they yield, including related discussion about the assessments and their implications, and they should be available to all people involved. Research is clear that these should be group discussions and not the domain of a single worker or worker and supervisor.

For more than three decades, the risk aversion in English-speaking child protection systems has dominated practice, framing families as repositories of risk and keeping them distanced from decision making, and often their children. Many have argued that things seem to be getting worse rather than better for children at risk. This worsening is happening despite very real efforts being made to reform child protection systems across international jurisdictions. Yet as we have described in this chapter, family-minded practice can and do occur, facilitated by committed, skilled and creative people who play their part in moving beyond the risk paradigm to better support vulnerable children and families. This recalibration of the risk culture might then better serve children, families and child protection systems.

References

Ahn, H., Reiman, S., O'Connor, T. S., Rushovich, B., Kolupanowich, N., Kong, J. & Moore, J. (2013). *Evaluating Family-Centered Practice in Maryland July 1, 2012 to June 30, 2013*. University of Maryland, School of Social Work. Available at http://socialwork.umaryland.edu/cwa/RYC/assets/RE-ChildWelfareResearch-201 3-Evaluating_Family_Centered_Practice.pdf [Accessed 31 July 2015].

Bartholet, E. (2014). Differential response: A dangerous Experiment in child welfare. Harvard Public Law Working Paper No. 14–31. Available at http://papers.ssrn.com/sol3/papers.cfm?abstract_id=2477089 [Accessed 1 August 2015].

Bartholet, E. (2000). *Nobody's Children: Abuse and Neglect, Foster Drift, and the Adoption Alternative*. Boston: Beacon Press.

Braithwaite, V. (2014). Defiance and motivational postures, in D. Weisburd & G. Bruinsma (eds), *Encyclopedia of Criminology and Criminal Justice* (pp. 915–925). London: Springer Verlag.

Brown, L. (2015). A lasting legacy? Sustaining innovation in a social work context. *British Journal of Social Work*, 45, 138–152. doi:10.1093/bjsw/bct107

Burford, G. (2015). Evaluation of Vermont Department for Children and Families Family Services Division Practice Transformation, Institutional Review Board CHRBS 06-115 (2014–2015).

Burford, G. with Barron, L. (2013). *Final report on the NCIC implementation project practice transformation: Department for Children & Families Family Services Division.* Burlington, VT: University of Vermont, Department of Social Work.

Burford, G. & Gallagher, S. (2015). Teen experiences of exclusion, inclusion, and participation in child protection and youth justice in Vermont, in T. Gal & B. Duramy (eds), *International Perspectives and Empirical Findings on Child Participation: From Social Exclusion to Child-Inclusive Policies* (pp. 227–255). New York: Oxford University Press.

Burford, G. & Pennell, J. (1998). *Family Group Decision Making: After the Conference —Progress in Resolving Violence and Promoting Well-being: Outcome Report (Vol I & II).* St. John's, NL: Memorial University of Newfoundland, School of Social Work.

Connolly, M. (2015). Disadvantage, equity and children's rights in twenty-first century Australasia, in E. Fernandez, A. Zeira, T. Vecchiato & C. Canali (eds), *Theoretical and Empirical Insights into Child and Family Poverty: Cross National Perspectives* (pp. 97–109). Springer: Switzerland.

Connolly, M. & Morris, K. (2012). *Understanding Child and Family Welfare: Statutory Responses to Children at Risk.* Basingstoke: Palgrave Macmillan.

Crampton, D. (2006). When do social workers and family members try family group decision making? A process evaluation. *International Journal of Child & Family Welfare,* 9(3), 131–144.

Daly, M. & Kelly, G. (2015). *Families and Poverty: Everyday Life on a Low Income.* Bristol: Policy Press.

Dumbrill, G. (2006). Parental experience of child protection intervention: A qualitative study, *Child Abuse & Neglect,* 30, 27–37.

Falck, S. (2008). *Do Family Group Conferences Lead to a Better Situation for the Children Involved?* Oslo, Norway: NOVA (Norwegian Social Research), Ministry of Education and Research.

Family Connection Grant: Family Empowerment through Family Team Conferencing Partnership for Strong Families Grant #: 90CF0021 Final Report. Available at www.pfsf.org/wp-content/uploads/Final_Report.pdf [Accessed 31 January 2016].

Featherstone, B., Morris, K. & White, S. (2014). A marriage made in hell: Early intervention meets child protection, *British Journal of Social Work,* 44, 1735–1749.

Featherstone, B., White, S. & Morris, K. (2014). *Re-Imagining Child Protection: Towards Humane Social Work with Families.* Bristol: Policy Press.

Fisher, M. & Marsh, P. (2015). The research-practice relationship and the work of Edward Mullen, in H. Soydan & W. Lorenz (eds), *Social Work Practice to the Benefit of Our Clients: Scholarly Legacy of Edward J. Mullen* (pp. 47–63). Bozen Bolzano, IT: Bolzano University Press.

France, A. & Utting, D. (2005). The paradigm of 'risk and protection-focused prevention' and its impact on services for children and families. *Children & Society,* 19(2), 177–190. doi: 10.1002/CHI.870

Gal, T. & Duramy, B. F. (2015). Enhancing capacities for child participation: Introduction, in T. Gal & B. F. Duramy (eds), *International Perspectives and Empirical Findings on Child Participation: From Social Exclusion to Child-Inclusive Policies* (pp. 1–16). New York: Oxford University Press.

Gove, M. (2012). *Speech: The Failure of Child Protection and the Need for a Fresh Start.* www.gov.uk/government/speeches/the-failure-of-child-protection-and-the-need-for-a-fresh-start

Gunderson, K., Cahn, K. & Wirth, J. (2003). The Washington State long-term outcome study. *Protecting Children*, 18(1–2), 42–47.

Gupta, A., Featherstone, B. & White, S. (2014). Reclaiming humanity: From capacities to capabilities in understanding parenting in adversity, *British Journal of Social Work*. doi: 10.1093/bjsw/bcu137

Harris, N. (2011). Does responsive regulation offer an alternative? Questioning the role of formalistic assessment in child protection investigations. *British Journal of Social Work*, 47(7), 1383–1403.

Harris, N. (2012). Assessment: When does it help and when does it hinder? Parents' experiences of the assessment process. *Child and Family Social Work*, 17(2), 180–191.

Harris, N. (2008) 'Family group conferencing in Australia 15 years on'. National Child Protection Clearinghouse, AIFS, Child Abuse Prevention Issue No. 27.

Huntsman, L. (2006). 'Family group conferencing in a child welfare context – a review of the literature'. Sydney, NSW Department of Community Services.

Ivec, M., Braithwaite, V. & Harris, N. (2012). 'Resetting the relationship' in Indigenous child protection: Public hope and private reality. *Law & Policy*, 34(1), 80–103.

Jones, J. (2008). *Risk Evolution. Risk Management Insight LLC* [PowerPoint slides]. Available at www.riskmanagementinsight.com/media/documents/Risk_Evolution.pdf [Accessed 30 July 2015].

Kim, M. (2014). Converge: Reimagining the movement to end gender violence, 7–8 February, University of Miami School of Law. Available at http://mediaforchange.org/reimagine [Accessed 31 January 2016].

Krumer-Nevo, M. (2003). From a 'Coalition of Despair' to 'a Covenant of Help' in Social Work with Families in Distress. *European Journal of Social Work*, 6(3), 273–282.

Levy, C., Lamarre, E. & Twining, J. (February 2010). Taking control of organizational risk culture. McKinsey Working Papers on Risk, #16. Available at www.mckinsey.com/client_service/risk/latest_thinking/working_papers_on_risk [Accessed 31 December 2015].

Marmot, M. (2010). *Fair Society, Healthy Lives: The Marmot Review. Strategic Review of Health Inequalities in England post-2010.* www.instituteofhealthequity.org/projects/fair-society-healthy-lives-the-marmot-review

Marsh, P. & Crow, G. (1998). *Family Group Conferences in Child Welfare.* Oxford: Blackwell Science.

Morris, K. (2011). *Family Experience of Multiple Service Use.* Nottingham City Council: Nottingham.

Morris, K. (2012). Thinking family? The complexities of family engagement in care and protection, *British Journal of Social Work*, 42(5), 906–920.

Morris, K. (2013). Troubled families: Vulnerable families' experiences of multiple service use. *Child & Family Social Work*, 18(2), 198–206.

Morris, K. & Burford, G. (2009). Family decision making: New spaces for participation and resistance, in M. Barnes & D. Prior (eds), *Subversive Citizens: Power, Agency and Resistance in Public Services* (pp. 129–135). Bristol: The Policy Press.

Morris, K. & Featherstone, B. (2010). Investing in children, regulating parents, thinking family: A decade of tensions and contradictions. *Social Policy & Society*, 9(4), 557–566.

Morris, K., Brandon, M. & Tudor, P. (2015). Rights, responsibilities and pragmatic practice: Family participation in case reviews. *Child Abuse Review*, 24, 198–209.

Morris, K., White, S., Doherty, P. & Warwick, L. (2015). Out of time: Theorizing family in social work practice, *Child & Family Social Work*. doi: 10.1111/cfs.12257

Pennell, J., Edwards, M. & Burford, G. (2010). Expedited family group engagement and child permanency. *Children and Youth Services Review*, 32(7), 1012–1019.

Pennell, J. with Allen-Eckard, K., King, J. & Latz, M. (2010). Annual report to the North Carolina Division of Social Services, Fiscal Year 2009, Summary. North Carolina Family-Centered Meetings Project. Center for Family and Community Engagement, North Carolina State University. Available at www.cfface.org/documents/09-10_NCFCMP_Summary_report-web.pdf [Accessed 2 August 2015].

Pennell, J., Burford, G., Morris, K. & Connolly, M. (2011). Introduction – Taking child and family rights seriously: Family engagement and its evidence in child welfare. *Child Welfare*, 90(4), 9–18.

Perry, R., Yoo, J., Spoliansky, T. & Edelman, P. (2013). Family team conferencing: Results and implications from an experimental study in Florida, *Child Welfare*, 92(6), 63–96.

Rauktis, M. E., McCarthy, S., Krackhardt, D. & Cahalane, H. (2010). Innovation in child welfare: The adoption and implementation of family group decision making in Pennsylvania. *Children and Youth Services Review*, 32, 732–739. doi:10.1016/j.childyouth.2010.01.010

Schwartz, S., Prins, S. J., Campbell, U. B. & Gatto, N. C. (2015). Is the 'well-defined intervention assumption' politically conservative? *Social Science & Medicine*. Available at http://dx.doi.org/10.1016/j.socscimed.2015.10.054

Sevenhuijsen, S. (2000). Caring in the third way: The relation between obligation, responsibility and care in Third Way discourse, *Critical Social Policy*, 20(1), 5–27.

The Care Inquiry (2013). *Making not Breaking: Buildings Relationships for Our Most Vulnerable Children*. London: FRG www.frg.org.uk/images/Policy_Papers/care-inquiry-full-report-april-2013.pdf

Tyler, T. R. (2006). *Why People Obey the Law*. Princeton, NJ: Princeton University Press.

Tyler, Tom R. (August 2001). Trust and law abidingness: A proactive model of social regulation. The Australian National University, Australian Taxation Office, Centre of Tax System Integrity, Canberra, AU. Working Paper No 16.

Wilkinson, R. & Pickett, K. (2010) *The Spirit Level: Why Equality is Better for Everyone*. London: Penguin Books.

Yoo, J. & Perry, R. (Undated). Family Connection Grant: Family Empowerment through Family Team Conferencing Partnership for Strong Families Grant #90CF0021 Final Report. Available at www.pfsf.org/wp-content/uploads/Final_Report.pdf [Accessed 3 August 2015].

Wijnen-Lunenburg, P., Beek, F. & van Gramberg, P. (2007). *'It is the family's move': The effects of Eigen Kracht conferences within the context of youth protection and with respect to safety, social cohesion and control.* Amsterdam, Vrije Universiteit/Voorhout, WESP.

PART 2

INNOVATIVE PRACTICES IN CHILD PROTECTION

8

ASSESSMENT AND DECISION MAKING TO IMPROVE OUTCOMES IN CHILD PROTECTION

*Aron Shlonsky and Robyn Mildon**

Introduction

The decision to place children in out-of-home care is but one of the many decisions made by child protection workers and the systems in which they are embedded. Every day, potential reporters of child maltreatment (mandated or otherwise) are faced with the decision of whether to call child protection services. Phone screeners must decide whether a report is sufficiently severe and meets the legal requirements in their jurisdiction to take further action. Professionals who investigate the report must assess and make numerous decisions about whether children are safe in their homes. And professionals who have an ongoing role with the family must continually assess safety, permanency planning and the services that will best provide for the needs and interests of the child. Within all of these (and other) major decisions are countless smaller decisions that potentially influence outcomes, such as when, where and how to interview children and parents; how much their opinions and preferences should be weighted towards key decisions; how often visits should be made; and what statements and actions are recorded in those visits. These decisions are made in the context of other components of the system that are constantly tasked with making judgements, and their decisions are influenced (but not entirely contingent upon) the determinations of caseworkers. Supervisors and managers in agencies authorize actions based on

---

* Aron Shlonsky is a professor in social work at the University of Melbourne, Australia. Robyn Mildon is the head of the Centre for Evidence and Implementation, Victoria, Australia and an associate professor at the University of Melbourne, Australia.

information provided by caseworkers. Courts make legal decisions about plans, their merit and their enforcement. Related systems such as adult and child social services, health, education and criminal justice make numerous decisions – all about the very same child and family.

Each decision contains a degree of uncertainty and corresponding error, and these errors are compounded with each decision and across decision makers in child-protection-involved systems. One would be hard pressed to find a more complex decision-making environment. Uncertainty is generally characterized in the child protection literature as risk, and this risk tends to exist between two opposing pathways that extend down the entire continuum of child protection services: taking no action (leaving children and families in their current state) and taking some action (i.e. increasing involvement in the system; decreasing involvement in the system). Perception of risk involves more than risk of maltreatment harm to children at the hands of their parents. It also involves the risk of making a poor decision that impacts the life of a child in other ways that may be profound. Removing children from their parents, for instance, may expose children to future harm across a range of outcomes (Doyle, 2007), such as unknown and potentially poor foster care placement experiences (Aarons et al., 2010; Biehal, 2014; James, Landsverk & Slymen, 2004; Newton, Litrownik & Landsverk, 2000), and may also result in the breakdown of sibling relationships when they are placed in different homes (Hegar, 2005; Shlonsky, Webster & Needell; Webster, Shlonsky, Shaw & Brookhart, 2005). In other words, child protection workers do not function in a singular-risk environment; they function in a competing-risk environment. Where one risk is potentially mitigated (further parental harm to children), another may become a major concern (risk that being involved in the 'system' will be harmful), and these competing concerns are weighed, consciously or otherwise, by the professionals involved.

In this chapter, we explore emerging frameworks for assessing risk that move beyond dominant discourses around risk decision making towards better-integrated frameworks that specifically focus on decision making that improves outcomes for vulnerable children. This requires attention to systemic decision-making ecologies that consider the impact of broader systems and the ways in which focused response might make a difference.

The Decision-Making Ecology (DME)

The series of decisions described above, and many more just like it, are made in the context of uncertainty and are expressed as risk by child protection systems. These decisions have begun to be explored by scholars and an emerging framework for understanding them has been introduced and its elements tested. The Decision-Making Ecology (Baumann, Fluke, Dalgleisch & Kern, 2011; Baumann, Fluke, Dalgleisch & Kern, 2014) draws upon an ecological framework that describes influences on decisions in child protection.

The DME's four main influences are categorized as follows:

1 **case factors** (characteristics of the maltreatment, such as maltreatment type; or characteristics of the family, such as income, age of children, family resources);

2 **organizational factors** (agency culture/climate, policies and procedures that dictate certain behaviour, supervision structure, training and service resources);

3 **external factors** (relevant laws, community resources and attitudes, dispersion of poverty in the population);

4 **decision-maker factors** (personal experience and attendant biases, level of training achieved, level of skill).

These factors combine in potentially predictable ways, at various decision points in the child protection system, to produce decisions that vary for children and families, even when they might be similar in many ways. In truth, the four factors are not independent of one another. For example, case factors (e.g. a policy to always investigate allegations of child sexual abuse) may dictate certain organizational responses and external factors (e.g. the vivid publication of a child death within the organization's jurisdiction) may drive both short- and medium-term individual and organizational behaviour (Jagannathan & Camasso, 2013). The outcomes of each decision may or may not be explicitly stated or even measured, but they are theoretically and empirically linked back to these four key influences in a reciprocal dance that continues over time and as children progress through (and return to) the child protection system.

Baumann et al. (2011; 2014) go further and describe how these influences may be interpreted and acted upon differently by individual actors who have the same information. That is, a decision is based, at least in part, on an individual's assessment of risk. But each person's conceptualization of what the risk is, and how risky it might be, varies according to their own background, experience and a host of other factors. On an assessment of risk ranging from low to high, individuals both interpret information from their assessment and set it against a threshold for action (i.e. the point at which action is taken). In other words, not only does the assessment of risk vary between people, but the point at which different people will take action (and perhaps even the action they would take) is also very likely to be different when there is uncertainty about either assessment or outcome.

To further explain, assessments can be prognostic (Will you get 'it'? Will 'it' happen), diagnostic (Do you have 'it'? Did 'it' happen?), or contextual (What are the circumstances in which 'it' is occurring?). These types of assessment can be confused both in terms of what is being focused upon in the decision and the level and type of information needed to come to a reasonable conclusion. Baumann et al. (2011; 2014) use the example of a social worker and doctor coming into contact with the same family and an assessment is being made about whether to report the family for alleged maltreatment. These two 'actors' are trying to respond to the risk that a child has been maltreated or may be maltreated in the future by their parent if nothing is done. Even given the same information and agreement about what is being observed (case factors), their threshold for action may well differ based on the organizational, external and individual influences unique to each actor. On the caseworker end, the caseworker may be under pressure to report and investigate families when there is even a slight possibility that a child has been or will be harmed by their parent in the future. Better safe than sorry. On the physician end, the doctor might see many similar cases in the clinic and perceives (and has maybe experienced) that reporting families for maltreatment risks the doctor's relationship with the family. While this example uses actors from two different disciplines and systems, the reliability of decisions can vary even between actors in the same discipline based on their interpretation of assessments and where they personally set their threshold for action, and there is a history of evidence to suggest that there are substantial reliability issues in child protection services (CPS) (Camasso & Jagannathan, 2000, 2013; Lindsey, 1992; Ruscio, 1998). That is, when the answer is not obvious to all (which is often the case), variation in response will inevitably emerge (see, for example, statistical modelling by Doyle, 2007). Unfortunately, one of the primary axioms of measurement is that if a process is unreliable (different decision made by different actors who share the same information) it cannot be valid. This means that, even if there are valid decisions to be made, if the level of reliability of decisions is low enough, then there will be an unacceptable number of false positives (predicting something will happen when it will not) and/or false negatives (predicting something will not happen and it does).

Research to date on the utility of the DME for understanding how decisions are made is in the early stages, but it has already yielded some important tools and findings. Many of these advances are described in a 2015 special issue of *Child Abuse and Neglect* (López, Fluke, Benbenishty

& Knorth, 2015). At the very least, the DME offers a structure to test the relationship between influences and decisions made and how these may link to outcomes over time. For instance, Spratt, Devaney & Hayes, (2015) discussed and then tested whether one of the major cognitive or heuristic biases, confirmation bias (preferring information that confirms or supports one's beliefs rather than objectively evaluating all information available), was in operation in cases of child neglect, and the authors found that this bias was present at different stages of interaction within the child protection system.

Key to considering how decisions are made is a reliable and valid way to measure bias and influences that might exist among individual decision makers. To this end, there has been substantial work on the development (Dettlaff, Christopher Graham, Holzman, Baumann & Fluke, 2015) and use (Graham, Dettlaff, Baumann & Fluke, 2015) of an instrument that measures caseworker and organizational factors known to influence child protection decisions. These and other tools have been combined with survey and information from electronic case files to move beyond the identification of influences to statistically testing the magnitude of their effect on important outcomes. Studies of this type are beginning to find that, despite the presence of individual bias, the broader contextual and organizational factors, not the personal factors, have the greatest influence on casework decisions across decision points along the continuum of child protection services (Shlonsky, 2015). In particular, Graham (2015) controlled for a wide range of such factors to test their influence on the decision to place a child in out-of-home care, finding that case level factors (such as individual child/family risk factors and poverty) and organizational factors (such as perceived decision support and caseload) were far more influential than individual caseworker factors such as ethnic background. In the same special issue, Fallon et al. (2015) and Font & Maguire-Jack (2015) found that factors external to the caseworker influenced placement of children in out-of-home care, and this even extends to the reunification of children with their parents (Wittenstrom, Baumann, Fluke, Graham & James, 2015). Indeed, these studies indicate that simply looking at the ethnic background of either caseworkers or children absent the broader context may be insufficient to explain important phenomena such as the overrepresentation of African American children in the United States and indigenous children in the United States, Canada, Australia and New Zealand in out-of-home care (Shlonsky, 2015).

Perhaps the most important influence on the types of decisions made is the range of options available. If services are available, they appear to have a major influence on the types of choices made (Font & Maguire-Jack, 2015). Difficult decisions are often made in uncertain circumstances.

If a viable alternative to placing a child in care is available, such as providing services that are effective at eliminating or at least minimizing abusive behaviour, they are more likely to be chosen. In the context of uncertainty and high risk, conservative decisions (e.g. child placement) are more likely to be made than more risky decisions (leaving the child in the home). On the other hand, if that risk can be minimized through the provision of effective services, the difficult choice to place a child is less likely to be made before attempting the alternative.

Risk assessment and its misuse as a framework

Given that there is substantial variability in decision making based on factors both internal and external to the parties involved in each decision, an argument that supports the use of valid and reliable risk assessment measures can be made. The title of this book, however, 'Moving beyond the risk paradigm', implies that there is something wrong with staying exclusively focused on the assessment of risk in child protection. And there is. To date, risk assessment has tended to dominate the discourse around decision making in the United States, particularly on the development, testing and use of risk assessment tools (see, for example, Baird & Wagner, 2000; Camasso & Jagannathan, 2013; Gambrill & Shlonsky, 2000; Schwalbe, 2004; Shlonsky & Wagner, 2005). This singular focus has, in some ways, detracted from the broader objectives of child protection (the safety, permanence and well-being of children) for two reasons: (1) the risk tools themselves are measuring risk as defined by the system rather than measuring actual safety or progress towards functional goals; (2) the opportunity cost of doing something different, something better, is never explored, because once risk for an individual is established, the system itself is put at risk if it does not respond in a way that is highly protective.

As illustrated in the DME, risk assessment is a process that all decision makers go through at each decision point. Sometimes, this risk is translated into a quantifiable form that is actionable with clear thresholds (i.e. risk assessment tools with varying reliability and validity). From a methodological point of view, perhaps the use of risk assessment tools is inevitable. The major concerns about the reliability and validity of potentially life-changing decisions are substantial, making the use of reliable and valid tools for specific decisions highly defensible (Shlonsky & Wagner, 2005). From an outcomes perspective, however, the view may be somewhat different. Risk assessment tools have a history of being poorly used, or at least poorly interpreted, as a decision-making framework rather than as one part of an overarching framework that is focused on individual outcomes. In the absence of a method, risk will prevail, and all of its attendant problems will manifest.

Take Structured Decision Making (SDM) as an example. This decision-making 'system' is built around the known decision points that a 'case' (child and/or family) encounters as the child and/or family proceeds through the system (i.e. initial screening, safety assessment, risk assessment, risk reassessment, reunification assessment, etc.). The centrepiece of SDM is an actuarial tool that reliably and validly predicts the likelihood of recurrence of reported maltreatment, which is then used to inform the intensity of services, lending support for the imposition of a level of intrusiveness if conditions are exceptionally dangerous or families are uncooperative (e.g. child placement in out-of-home care). All of the other SDM tools have been informed by findings in the existing research literature, but they have not been psychometrically validated. Seen within the context of the system, this approach is viable. There is a scarcity of funds, and the resources at our disposal should be allocated to those who are most at risk.

But seen through an outcomes-based lens, the sole focus on system-defined outcomes (rather than individually defined outcomes) is problematic. The assessment of risk is only valuable if it *improves decisions*, and decisions are based on so much more than risk of a new indicated or substantiated maltreatment finding. Children who are placed in out-of-home care tend to be highly vulnerable to a wide range of poor outcomes (Courtney et al., 2011; Doyle, 2007), and the focus on safety (as defined by the system) ignores a host of other risks, including the risk that the system itself poses to the child and family (Gambrill & Shlonsky, 2001). Starting with risk or prognosis, rather than diagnosis, ignores both the causes of behaviour as well as the range of things that might be done to change behaviour. It is simply an estimate of how the system will likely respond to this family if nothing is done. This may be valuable information, but it is woefully inadequate for validly assessing behaviour and measuring change over time. There is a movement in the field of corrections towards a hybrid approach to risk assessment that includes dynamic or changeable factors related to systems-level outcomes, such as recidivism (Schwalbe, 2008). However, the functioning of these tools in terms of predictive capacity may not measure up to instruments that use more static or fixed elements (Baird et al., 2013), and the tools themselves appear to be based more on risk than on the causes and consequences of specific, changeable behaviours.

While the DME incorporates outcomes in its model, its application to date has tended to be limited to system-level outcomes such as recurrence of maltreatment and placement in out-of-home care as opposed to improvements in parental and/or child functioning. A broader outcomes-driven framework (rather than a risk framework) that includes consideration of child well-being at all points of the system would regard a new substantiated maltreatment allegation as a potential indicator of child safety but not as a meaningful outcome. The overlap between substantiation and functioning is not complete, and substantiation, which is driven by law as much as it is by behaviour and is primarily focused on safety concerns as defined by the system, does a poor job of describing specific behaviours that can be changed to improve child and family functioning. Moreover, assessment alone is insufficient without considering how this assessment will be used (Gambrill & Shlonsky, 2001; Shlonsky, 2015).

In all fairness, the DME is a model for understanding the influence of various internal and external factors on decisions made within the bounds of the current system. It is not a framework geared towards achieving outcomes, nor does it tell us how to make decisions that lead to better outcomes. Outcomes-based frameworks do nevertheless exist that can incorporate the DME and, along with an approach to selecting services that have a better chance of being effective, can be used to improve individual outcomes for vulnerable children and families. The rest of this chapter is devoted to one such outcomes-based framework.

Focusing on outcomes

It may be that the singular focus on risk is based on the difficulty we have in expanding our thinking about the existing child protection system. Outcomes can be difficult to define; adequate and timely measurement may not be easily achieved; and rarely is there only one hoped-for outcome for children growing up in complex familial and social circumstances (Shlonsky, 2015).There has been movement in the United States towards an outcomes-based framework to maximize child safety, permanence and well-being in out-of-home care that incorporates a developmental perspective (U.S. Department of Health and Human Services, Administration for Children and Families, 2012). This type of thinking (moving the system towards developmentally focused, child-specific outcomes) is universal in its application and can be adapted across jurisdictions and junctures in the child protection and child welfare systems. For example, the US model and the associated Framework for Well-Being for Older Youth in Foster Care (Hanson Langford & Badeau, 2013) has been adapted for use in New South Wales, Australia (Table 8.1), as part of its transition of out-of-home care services to the non-governmental sector (Mildon, Shlonsky, Michaux & Parolini, 2015).

A quality assurance framework (QAF) that defines specific, measurable outcomes to be achieved is a long way from simply measuring risk. It also requires a rethinking of the child protection system itself. Several initiatives, including the movement to differential response and, to some extent, the use of family group conferencing, have played at the edges of system transformation. In a sense, they envision a more responsive, family-driven child protection system that works to meet the needs of families rather than the system imposing its more coercive strategies for minimizing risk. Without properly specified outcomes to work towards, however, these approaches are likely to falter at anything beyond better engagement.

The New South Wales Quality Assessment Framework (Mildon et al., 2015) covers the three overarching goals of most modern-day child welfare systems (child safety, permanency and well-being), and within these are arrayed seven more detailed domains: safety; permanency; cognitive functioning; physical health and development; mental health; social functioning; and cultural and spiritual identity. Each domain is further broken down into child developmental stages (infancy; early childhood, middle childhood; adolescence) to reflect the fact that the inputs, outputs and outcomes within each domain are dependent upon the changing needs of children as they mature.

The domains are defined as follows:

Safety

Children and young people have the opportunity and support needed to ensure that they are physically and psychologically safe and free from maltreatment.

Permanency

Children and young people have permanency and stability in their living situations, and the continuity of family relationships and connections is preserved.

Cognitive functioning

Children and young people have the opportunity and support needed to maximize their intellectual ability and functioning and to achieve educational success to their fullest potential.

Physical health and development

Children and young people have the opportunity and support needed to maximize their physical health, strength and functioning.

Mental health

Children and young people have the opportunity and support needed to manage their mental health and wellness.

Social functioning

Children and young people have the opportunity and support needed to cultivate a strong and resilient self-identity, to develop supportive and nurturing relationships and to feel hopeful about life and the future.

Cultural and spiritual identity

Children and young people have the opportunity, encouragement and support needed to engage with, and develop, their own cultural, ethnic and spiritual identity. It is critically important that components of this domain are developed through culturally specific processes that are cognizant of the child's cultural system.

Each of these developmental strata can then be linked to reliable and valid tools that measure progress over time. In this instance, the approach was to suggest measures that were low or no cost and could be administered with minimal training. While this QAF is geared towards children in out-of-home care, this approach can be applied at any juncture within the child welfare and child protection systems, adding a layer of information to the DME that not only measures how decisions are made but also prompts potentially different decisions based on transparent objectives. In this way, the measurement of child functioning and progress is not defined by the system in which children are located. Rather, *the system has to adjust to the needs of children* by focusing on outcomes that match individual need.

The space between: using evidence-informed practice (EIP) to make decisions that lead to improved outcomes

The inputs to decision making are numerous and occur at many different levels. One of the major findings when evaluating the causal pathway towards individual decisions is the availability of services (Font & Maguire-Jack, 2015). That is, the range of possible decisions is influenced by the set of service choices available at a given decision point. Perhaps inevitably, however, all services are not created equal with respect to their level of effectiveness. Some services have far more evidence than others with respect to certain outcomes, and all else being equal, using such services will more often lead to improvement (Shlonsky & Mildon, 2014). That said, simply making available a random set of potentially effective services is unlikely to result in better outcomes and would not represent an evidence-informed approach. The articulation of such an approach

Table 8.1 New South Wales Quality Assurance Framework for Out-of-Home Care

Developmental Phase	Intermediate Outcome Domains		Well-Being Outcome Domains				
	Safety	Permanency	Cognitive Functioning	Physical Health and Development	Mental Health	Social Functioning	Cultural and Spiritual Identity
Prenatal infancy (birth to age 2)	Maltreatment occurrence in OOHC, maltreatment recurrence post restoration, accidental injury.	Timely and lasting legal permanence (restoration, guardianship, adoption), residential stability, least restrictive living environment, maintenance of family and other key relationships (birth patents, siblings, extended kin)	Language development	Normative standards for growth and development, gross motor and fine motor skills, overall health, BMI	Self-control emotional management and expression, Internalizing and externalizing behaviors, trauma symptoms	Social competencies, attachment and caregiver relationship, adaptive behavior	To be developed with approapriate stakeholders with expertise in this domain
Early Childhood (3–5)	Maltreatment Occurrence in OOHC, Maltreatment recurrence post restoration, accidental Injury, feelings of personal safety and security, presence of relationships that facilitate disclosure of risk and/or harm	Timely and lasting legal permanence (restoration guardianship, adoption), residential stability, least restrictive living environment, maintenance of family and other key relationships (birth parents siblings, extended kin)	Language development, pre-academic skills (e.g., numeracy) approaches to learning, problem-solving skills	Normative standards for growth and development, gross motor and fine motor skills, overall health, BMI	Self-control, self-esteem, emotional management and expression, internalizing and externalizing behavior, trauma symptoms	Social competencies, attachment and caregiver relationships, adaptive behavior	To be developed with approapriate stakeholders with expertise in this domain

(Continued)

Age group	Safety	Permanence	Cognitive/Academic	Physical Health	Emotional	Social	(To be developed)
Middle Childhood (6-12)	Maltreatment occurrence in OOHC, maltreatment recurrence, post restoration, accidental injury, feelings of personal safety and security, presence of relationships that facilitie disclosure of risk and /or harm, risk-taking behavior	Timely and lasting legal permanence (restoration, guardianship, adoption), residential stability least restrictive living environment, maintenance of family and other key relationships (birth parents, siblings, extended kin)	Academic achievement, school engagement, school attachment, problem-solving skill, decision-making	Normative standards for growth and development, overall health, BMI, risk-avoidance behavior related to health	Emotional intelligence, self-efficacy, motivation, self-control, prosocial behavior, positive outlook, coping, internalizing and externalizing behaviors, trauma symptoms	Social competencies, social connections and relationships, social skills, adaptive behavior	To be developed with appropriate stakeholders with expertise in this domain
Adolescence (13-18)	Maltreatment occurrence in OOHC, maltreatment recurrence, post restoration, accidental injury, feelings of personal safety and security, presence of relationships that facilitie disclosure of risk and /or harm, risk-taking behavior	Timely and lasting legal permanence (restoration, guardianship, adoption), residential stability least restrictive living environment, maintenance of family and other key relationships (birth parents, siblings, extended kin), planning for transaction to adulthood	Academic achievement, school engagement, school attachment, problem-solving skills, decision-making	Overall health, BMI, risk-avoidance behavior related to health	Emotional intelligence, self-efficacy, motivation, self-control, prosocial behavior, positive outlook, coping, internalizing and externalizing behaviors, trauma symptoms	Social competence, social connections and relationships, social skills, adaptive behavior	To be developed with appropriate stakeholders with expertise in this domain

1. U.S. Department of Health and Human Services (DHHS), Administration for Children Families, Administration on Children, Youth and Families, Children's Bureau. (2012). Information memorandum (Log No: ACYF-CB-IM-12-04). Retrieved on 11 January 2015 from www.acf.hhs.gov/programs/cb/resource/im1204.

2. Hanson Langford, B. & Badeau, S. (2013). Connected by 25: A plan for Investing in the Social, Emotional and Physical Well-Being of Older Youth in Foster Care. USA: Youth Transition Funders Group. Retrieved from http://yftg.org/wp-content/uploads/2015/02/FCWG_Well-Being_Investment_Agenda_Exec_Summary.pdf

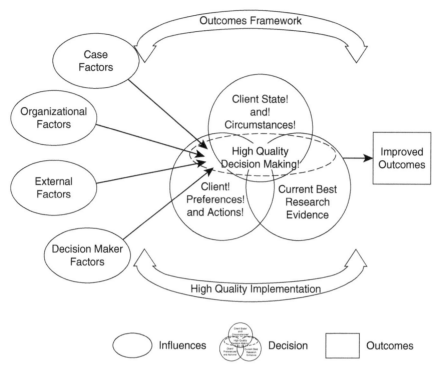

Figure 8.1 An evidence-informed decision-making process
Note that this figure incorporates elements of the DME (Baumann et al., 2011) and
evidence based medicine as articulated by Haynes, Devereaux and Guyatt (2002).

is complex and time-consuming, and it would require clear and critical thinking at each decision-making juncture in the child protection system. But this is what is required if we are to be responsive to individual needs within current system constraints. An example of such an approach that combines an evidence-informed decision-making process with the DME is provided in Figure 8.1.

At each decision juncture case, organizational, external and decision-maker factors are considered and responded to as part of high-quality decision making. Also considered, though, is current best evidence about the specific issues facing the child(ren) and family, the individual context in which the issue is occurring (clinical state and circumstances) and client preferences and their individual behaviours. This entire process occurs within an overarching outcomes framework that guides decisions towards specific outcomes (such as found in the out-of-home care QAF described above) and high-quality implementation of both the decision-making process and the resulting services that are chosen.

A system that makes effective services available to its caseworkers and managers must do so in a way that facilitates the delivery of services that best meets the needs of individual children/families, rather than providing barriers to this. At the same time, a system can make informed choices about the range of services it makes available at each decision point, based on the distribution of demographic characteristics, individual difficulties and logistic challenges faced by children/families who encounter each decision juncture. Within an outcomes framework, effective services that generally meet the needs of existing children/families will most often be chosen over those with little evidence that they can deliver hoped-for outcomes. But the opportunity for a different choice, based on child/family need, is there, and the assumption is never made that any service will be effective 100 per cent of the time. In such instances, innovative thinking and substantial clinical expertise may be required to bring about improved outcomes.

Underpinning the outcomes framework and the evidence-informed process is high-quality implementation. While the DME is helpful in understanding which decision points to focus on and the types of pressures that influence each juncture, the outcomes framework focuses individual and systemic efforts on specific areas of change and measures progress. Importantly, evidence-informed practice facilitates the selection of potentially effective services and facilitates the proper delivery of services within a complex child welfare service environment (Shlonsky, 2015; Mildon, Dickenson & Shlonsky 2014). Yet, having evidence, an outcomes framework and a process of selecting services is insufficient for ensuring that children/families actually receive an effective and practical service or set of services. Quality implementation is critical, which is why the entire process is underpinned by high-quality implementation. Although our understanding of what it takes to effectively implement services within existing health and social care systems has grown over the last two decades, the documented evidence of systems-level influences on key decisions in child welfare continues to accumulate (Fallon et al., 2015; Font & Maguire-Jack, 2015; Graham et al., 2015; Wulczyn, Gibbons, Snowden & Lery, 2013). It will do little good to offer services without ensuring that they will actually be delivered to children/families (Mildon & Shlonsky, 2011), and failure to deliver is likely to occur in systems that are not aligned with the interventions needed to deliver individual outcomes.

Services that incorporate high-quality implementation strategies aimed at working within, and ultimately altering, the existing service delivery system have the greatest likelihood of being delivered well and used widely within systems (Aarons et al., 2012; Aarons, Hurlburt & Horwitz, 2011; Mildon, Dickinson & Shlonsky, 2014). Yet the impediments to system reform are substantial. As we have seen in earlier chapters, the actual delivery of services will be influenced by the clinical needs of highly vulnerable children and families facing numerous, complex and co-occurring challenges and the myriad of organizational barriers to the uptake and maintenance of change (i.e. the hierarchical and bureaucratic structure of child welfare systems; lack of resources and training; and staff turnover and resistance) (Mildon et al., 2014; Mildon & Shlonsky, 2011; Shlonsky, 2015). If these are not dealt with properly as part of an overall approach to making sure that services are delivered as intended, to the right people and in the right dose and at the right time, there is little chance that better outcomes will be achieved (Shlonsky, 2015).

Within implementation science as a discipline, there are a number of individual strategies (Powell et al., 2015), many of them nested in existing frameworks, that have been identified and utilized in healthcare and social care settings. There is substantial work remaining, however, in terms of testing which elements, in which combinations, ordering and intensity, are most effective (Albers, Mildon, Lyon & Shlonsky, forthcoming). Nonetheless, there is evidence to suggest that even modestly effective services, implemented well, have a larger treatment effect than highly effective services that are delivered poorly (Lipsey, 2009). The best and most logical step, going forward, is to undergird all changes in service delivery with a comprehensive, ongoing implementation framework that incorporates a range of strategies relevant to the service context. As outcomes improve and the range of potentially effective services are expanded, these will begin to change the system and the decision-making processes of individual actors within the system.

Conclusion

The risk paradigm, while valid in some ways, is nevertheless a reactive lens for a system that is not geared to achieve nuanced understandings of individual outcomes for children and families with complex needs. The system itself is built on concerns for child safety, which is an indispensable component of any child welfare system. But in and of itself, it is insufficient for describing the range of needs that must be met if we are to maximize the life chances of vulnerable children. In order to move beyond the risk paradigm, the system needs to support individual decision making that considers a range of outcomes, and this will require wholesale system changes that include the identification of key, developmentally sensitive outcomes and the use of effective services to achieve them.

References

Aarons, G. A., Green, A. E., Palinkas, L. A., Self-Brown, S., Whitaker, D. J., Lutzker, J. R., ... Chaffin, M. J. (2012). Dynamic adaptation process to implement an evidence-based child maltreatment intervention. *Implementation Science*, 7(1), 32. http://doi.org/10.1186/1748-5908-7-32

Aarons, G. A., Hurlburt, M. & Horwitz, S. M. (2011). Advancing a conceptual model of evidence-based practice implementation in public service sectors. *Administration and Policy in Mental Health and Mental Health Services Research*, 38(1), 4–23.

Aarons, G. A., James, S., Monn, A. R., Raghavan, R., Wells, R. S. & Leslie, L. K. (2010). Behavior problems and placement change in a national child welfare sample: A prospective study. *Journal of the American Academy of Child & Adolescent Psychiatry*, 49(1), 70–80. http://doi.org/10.1016/j.jaac.2009.09.005

Albers, B., Mildon, R., Lyon, A. & Shlonsky, A. (forthcoming). *Implementation Frameworks in Child, Youth and Family Services: Results from a Scoping Review*.

Baird, C., Healy, T., Johnson, K., Bogie, A., Wicke Dankert, E. & Scharenbroch, C. (2013). *A Comparison of Risk Assessment Instruments in Juvenile Justice (No. 244477)*. Washington, DC: US Department of Justice.

Baird, C. & Wagner, D. (2000). The relative validity of actuarial and consensus-based risk assessment systems, *Children and Youth Services Review*, 22(11/12), 839–871.

Baumann, D. J., Dalgleish, L., Fluke, J. & Kern, H. (2011). *The Decision-Making Ecology*. Washington, DC: American Humane Association.

Baumann, D. J., Fluke, J., Dalgleisch, L. & Kern, H. (2014). The Decision-Making Ecology, in *From Evidence to Outcomes in Child Welfare: An International Reader* (pp. 24–40). New York: Oxford University Press.

Biehal, N. (2014). Maltreatment in foster care: A review of the evidence, *Child Abuse Review*, 23(1), 48–60. http://doi.org/10.1002/car.2249

Camasso, M. J. & Jagannathan, R. (2000). Modeling the reliability and predictive validity of risk assessment in child protective services, *Children and Youth Services Review*, 22(11/12), 873–895.

Camasso, M. J. & Jagannathan, R. (2013). Decision making in child protective services: A risky business? *Risk Analysis*, 33(9), 1636–1649. http://doi.org/10.1111/j.1539-6924.2012.01931.x

Courtney, M. E., Dworsky, A., Brown, A., Cary, C., Love, K., Vorhies, V. & Hall, C. (2011). *Midwest Evaluation of the Adult Functioning of Former Foster Youth: Outcomes at Age 26*. Chapin Hall Center for Children at the University of Chicago.

Dettlaff, A. J., Christopher Graham, J., Holzman, J., Baumann, D. J. & Fluke, J. D. (2015). Development of an instrument to understand the child protective services decision-making process, with a focus on placement decisions, *Child Abuse & Neglect*, 49, 24–34. http://doi.org/10.1016/j.chiabu.2015.04.007

Doyle, J. J., Jr (2007). Child protection and child outcomes: Measuring the effects of foster care, *American Economic Review*, 97(5), 1583–1610. http://doi.org/10.1257/aer.97.5.1583

Fallon, B., Chabot, M., Fluke, J., Blackstock, C., Sinha, V., Allan, K. & MacLaurin, B. (2015). Exploring alternate specifications to explain agency-level effects in placement decisions regarding Aboriginal children: Further analysis of the Canadian Incidence Study of Reported Child Abuse and Neglect Part C, *Child Abuse & Neglect*, 49, 97–106. http://doi.org/10.1016/j.chiabu.2015.04.012

Font, S. A. & Maguire-Jack, K. (2015). Reprint of 'Decision-making in child protective services: Influences at multiple levels of the social ecology', *Child Abuse & Neglect*, 49, 50–62. http://doi.org/10.1016/j.chiabu.2015.10.011

Gambrill, E. (1999). Evidence-based practice: An alternative to authority-based practice, *Families in Society – the Journal of Contemporary Human Services*, 80(4), 341–350.

Gambrill, E. (2012). *Critical Thinking in Clinical Practice: Improving the Quality of Judgements and Decisions*. John Wiley & Sons.

Gambrill, E. & Shlonsky, A. (2000). Risk assessment in context, *Children and Youth Services Review*, 22(11–12), 813–837.

Gambrill, E. & Shlonsky, A. (2001). The need for comprehensive risk management systems in child welfare, *Children and Youth Services Review*, 23(1), 79–107.

Gibbs, L. E. (2003). *Evidence-Based Practice for the Helping Professions: A Practical Guide with Integrated Multimedia*. Pacific Grove, CA: Brooks/Cole-Thomson Learning.

Graham, J. C., Dettlaff, A. J., Baumann, D. J. & Fluke, J. D. (2015). The decision making ecology of placing a child into foster care: A structural equation model, *Child Abuse & Neglect*, 49, 12–23. http://doi.org/10.1016/j.chiabu.2015.02.020

Hanson Langford, B. & Badeau, S. (2013). Connected by 25: A plan for investing in the social, emotional and physical well-being of older youth in foster care. USA: Youth Transition Funders Group. Retrieved from www.fostercareworkgroup.org/media/resources/FCWG_Well-Being_Investment_Agenda.pdf

Hegar, R. L. (2005). Sibling placement in foster care and adoption: An overview of international research, *Children and Youth Services Review*, 27(7), 717–739. http://doi.org/10.1016/j.childyouth.2004.12.018

Jagannathan, R. & Camasso, M. J. (2013). *Protecting Children in the Age of Outrage*. New York: Oxford University Press.

James, S., Landsverk, J. & Slymen, D. J. (2004). Placement movement in out-of-home care: patterns and predictors, *Children and Youth Services Review*, 26(2), 185–206. http://doi.org/10.1016/j.childyouth.2004.01.008

Lewin, S., Glenton, C., Munthe-Kaas, H., Carlsen, B., Colvin, C. J., Gülmezoglu, M., ... Rashidian, A. (2015). Using Qualitative Evidence in Decision Making for Health and Social Interventions: An Approach to Assess Confidence in Findings from Qualitative Evidence Syntheses (GRADE-CERQual), *PLOS Medicine*, 12(10), e1001895. http://doi.org/10.1371/journal.pmed.1001895

Lindsey, D. (1992). Reliability of the foster care placement decision: A review, *Research on Social Work Practice*, 2(1), 65–80.

Lipsey, M. (2009). The primary factors that characterize effective interventions with juvenile offenders: A meta-analytic overview, *Victims and Offenders*, 4, 124–147.

López, M., Fluke, J. D., Benbenishty, R. & Knorth, E. J. (2015). Commentary on decision-making and judgements in child maltreatment prevention and response: An overview, *Child Abuse & Neglect*, 49, 1–11. http://doi.org/10.1016/j.chiabu.2015.08.013

Mildon, R., Dickinson, N. & Shlonsky, A. (2014). Using Implementation Science to Improve Service and Practice in Child Welfare: Actions and essential elements, in *From Evidence to Outcomes in Child Welfare: An International Reader*. New York: Oxford University Press.

Mildon, R. & Shlonsky, A. (2011). Bridge over troubled water: using implementation science to facilitate effective services in child welfare, *Child Abuse & Neglect*, 35(9), 753–756. http://doi.org/10.1016/j.chiabu.2011.07.001

Mildon, R., Shlonsky, A., Michaux, A. & Parolini, A. (2015). *The NSW Statutory Out-of-Home Care Quality Assurance Framework*. Melbourne: Parenting Research Centre and University of Melbourne.

Newton, R. R., Litrownik, A. J. & Landsverk, J. A. (2000). Children and youth in foster care: disentangling the relationship between problem behaviors and number of placements, *Child Abuse & Neglect*, 24(10), 1363–1374. http://doi.org/10.1016/S0145–2134(00)00189–7

Powell, B. J., Waltz, T. J., Chinman, M. J., Damschroder, L. J., Smith, J. L., Matthieu, M. M., ... Kirchner, J. E. (2015). A refined compilation of implementation strategies: results from the Expert Recommendations for Implementing Change (ERIC) project, *Implementation Science*, 10(1), 21. http://doi.org/10.1186/s13012–015–0209–1

Regehr, C., Stern, S. & Shlonsky, A. (2007). Operationalizing evidence-based practice: The development of an institute for evidence-based social work, *Research on Social Work Practice*, 17(3), 408–416. http://doi.org/10.1177/1049731506293561

Robling, M., Bekkers, M.-J., Bell, K., Butler, C. C., Cannings-John, R., Channon, S., ... Torgerson, D. (2016). Effectiveness of a nurse-led intensive home-visitation programme for first-time teenage mothers (Building Blocks): a pragmatic randomised controlled trial, *The Lancet*, 387(10014), 146–155. http://doi.org/10.1016/S0140–6736(15)00392-X

Ruscio, J. (1998). Information integration in child welfare cases: An introduction to statistical decision making, *Child Maltreatment: Journal of the American Professional Society on the Abuse of Children*, 3(2), 143–156.

Sackett, D. L., Richardson, W. S., Rosenberg, W. & Haynes, R. B. (1997). *Evidence-Based Medicine: How to Practice and Teach EBM*. New York: Churchill Livingstone.

Sackett, D. L., Rosenberg, W. M., Gray, J. A., Haynes, R. B. & Richardson, W. S. (1996). Evidence based medicine: what it is and what it isn't, *BMJ: British Medical Journal*, 312(7023), 71.

Sackett, D. L., Straus, S. E., Richardson, W. S., Rosenberg, W. & Haynes, R. B. (2000). *Evidence-Based Medicine: How to Practice and Teach EBM* (Vol. 2). New York: Churchill Livingstone.

Schwalbe, C. (2004). Re-visioning risk assessment for human service decision making, *Children and Youth Services Review*, 26(6), 561–576. http://doi.org/10.1016/j.childyouth.2004.02.011

Schwalbe, C. S. (2008). Strengthening the integration of actuarial risk assessment with clinical judgment in an evidence based practice framework, *Children and Youth Services Review*, 30(12), 1458–1464. http://doi.org/10.1016/j.childyouth.2007.11.021

Shlonsky, A. (2015). Current status and prospects for improving decision making research in child protection: A commentary, *Child Abuse and Neglect, the International Journal*, 49, 154–162. doi:10.1016/j.chiabu.2015.09.006

Shlonsky, A. & Gibbs, L. (2004). Will the real evidence-based practice please stand up? Teaching the process of evidence-based practice to the helping professions, *Brief Treatment and Crisis Intervention*, 4(2), 137. http://doi.org/10.1093/brief-treatment/mhh011

Shlonsky, A. & Mildon, R. (2014). Methodological pluralism in the age of evidence-informed practice and policy, *Scandinavian Journal of Public Health*, 42(13 Suppl.), 18–27. http://doi.org/10.1177/1403494813516716

Shlonsky, A., Noonan, E., Littell, J. H. & Montgomery, P. (2011). The role of systematic reviews and the Campbell collaboration in the realization of evidence-informed practice, *Clinical Social Work Journal*, 39(4), 362–368. http://doi.org/10.1007/s10615-010-0307-0

Shlonsky, A., Needell, B. & Webster, D. (2003). The ties that bind: A cross-sectional analysis of siblings in foster care, *Journal of Social Service Research*, 29(3), 27–52.

Shlonsky, A. & Wagner, D. (2005). The next step: Integrating actuarial risk assessment and clinical judgment into an evidence-based practice framework in CPS case management, *Children and Youth Services Review*, 27(4), 409–427.

Spratt, T., Devaney, J. & Hayes, D. (2015). In and out of home care decisions: The influence of confirmation bias in developing decision supportive reasoning, *Child Abuse & Neglect*, 49, 76–85. http://doi.org/10.1016/j.chiabu.2015.01.015

US Department of Health and Human Services, Administration for Children and Families (2012). ACYF-CB-IM-12-04-im1204.pdf. Retrieved from www.acf.hhs.gov/sites/default/files/cb/im1204.pdf

Webster, D., Shlonsky, A., Shaw, T. & Brookhart, M. A. (2005). The ties that bind II: Reunification for siblings in out-of-home care using a statistical technique for examining non-independent observations, *Children and Youth Services Review*, 27(7), 765–782. http://doi.org/10.1016/j.childyouth.2004.12.016

Wittenstrom, K., Baumann, D. J., Fluke, J., Graham, J. C. & James, J. (2015). The impact of drugs, infants, single mothers, and relatives on reunification: A Decision-Making Ecology approach, *Child Abuse & Neglect*, 49, 86–96. http://doi.org/10.1016/j.chiabu.2015.06.010

Wulczyn, F., Gibbons, R., Snowden, L. & Lery, B. (2013). Poverty, social disadvantage, and the black/white placement gap, *Children and Youth Services Review*, 35(1), 65–74. http://doi.org/10.1016/j.childyouth.2012.10.005

9

SIGNS OF SAFETY: REORIENTING WORK WITH CHILDREN, FAMILIES AND COMMUNITIES

Andrew Turnell, Peter J. Pecora, Yvonne H. Roberts, Mike Caslor and Dan Koziolek[*]

Introduction: safety and risk assessment as challenging areas of child welfare policy and practice

This book began with cautions from Nigel Parton that in many child protection services (CPS) systems, 'a culture of blame' dominates where policies and procedures have been introduced to make practice so transparent that 'any negative outcome can be defended', thereby shifting the concern 'from trying to make the *right* decision to making a *defensible* decision' (p. 6). Parton noted some of the important reform perspectives in the 1990s:

> Rather than simply be concerned with a narrow, forensically-driven focus on child protection, it was argued there needed to be a 'rebalancing' or 'refocusing' of the work, such that the essential principles of a broader child welfare approach could dominate. Policy and practice should be driven by an emphasis on partnership, participation, prevention and family support. The priority should be on *helping* parents and children in the community in a supportive way and should keep notions of policing and coercive intervention to a minimum. (p. 9)

[*] Andrew Turnell is the Signs of Safety co-creator and director of Resolutions Consultancy, Australia. Peter Pecora is the managing director of research services for Casey Family Programs and a professor at the School of Social Work, the University of Washington, USA. Yvonne Roberts is a senior research associate at Casey Family Programs, USA. Mike Caslor is a licensed Signs of Safety trainer and consultant and is the owner of Building Capacity Consulting Ltd in Manitoba, Canada. Dan Koziolek is a licensed Signs of Safety trainer and consultant in Minnesota, USA.

In Chapter 7 Morris and Burford state that 'it is time to stop "tinkering around the edges", with tokenistic efforts that embrace the rhetoric of family engagement but don't follow through with any meaningful involvement with families in child protection' (p. 92).

In Chapter 8, Shlonsky and Mildon highlight the value of taking a more comprehensive view of competing risks as these risks and other factors interact in a 'decision-making ecology' across key decision points in child welfare that has been researched by Baumann, Fluke, Dalgleisch and Kern (2014). And it is important to be as transparent as possible about the pressure points, organizational supports (e.g. caseload size, values towards preserving families) and other factors that influence decision making. They call for a less narrow approach that does *not* detract from the broader objectives of child protection (child safety, permanence and well-being) and that takes into account the risks that the system itself poses to the child by avoiding the following key problems:

(1) the risk tools themselves are measuring risk as defined by the system rather than measuring actual safety or progress towards functional goals; (2) the opportunity cost of doing something different, something better, is never explored because once risk for an individual is established, the system itself is put at risk if it does not respond in a way that is highly protective. (p. 116)

We agree that child welfare organizations cannot act as mainly 'risk management' agencies, because most societies expect them to view children and their families more holistically:

The 'child rescue' orientation/framework continues to serve as the basis for public child protection policy and practice in this country. Currently, the media, policy makers and the public continue to equate child removals with child safety, especially when responding to child maltreatment deaths. This fundamental belief drives child welfare funding, public policy, and practice. Protecting children from maltreatment cannot be achieved without a fundamental paradigm shift away from 'child rescue' as the primary societal response. Children need strong healthy families and families need strong healthy communities for children to be safe and to thrive. This change would set the stage for a broader framework that child maltreatment is a public health problem that requires the active involvement of multi-systems and communities to promote child safety and wellbeing, and to prevent maltreatment from occurring in the first place. Improving the safety, permanency and wellbeing of children requires multiple systems and community partners to address the underlying issues that impact families and communities. (Pecora & Chahine, 2016, p. 11)

We believe that there are also a large number of approaches and worker skills that can help avoid these problems and achieve the improved functioning that these authors are calling for, including family finding, family group conferencing, motivational interviewing, strengths-based assessment and solution-focused practice – to name just a few.

In the area of child protective services and child welfare, many states and counties in the United States are refining how they approach safety and risk assessment to make the process more transparent, more comprehensive *and* more child/family centred. Despite a steady set of setbacks due to leadership turnover, child deaths and swings in funding availability (among others), in some communities there is evidence that clinical decision making can be improved, unnecessary foster care placements are being reduced and children are achieving legal permanence without large increases in child maltreatment recurrence rates or foster care re-entry (e.g. Casey Family Programs, 2013; Ellis et al., 2013; Marts et al., 2008; McCroskey et al., 2010).

The issues of safety and risk assessment are central to effective child welfare practice, and yet the field continues to struggle in this area (Pecora, Chahine & Graham, 2013). (For a review of how difficult of a challenge this is, see Munro, 2010; Turnell, Munro & Murphy, 2013). One of the more recent efforts to reform child welfare work with families is Signs of Safety – a strengths-based, safety-focused approach to child protective services. This chapter summarizes some of the key aspects of Signs of Safety that help agencies and practitioners' revision of risk assessment as a rigorous, participatory and more hopeful process and practice rather than being overwhelmed in anxiety and risk aversion, and the chapter then presents some of the evaluation work that is supporting the development of the approach.

The Signs of Safety approach

The Signs of Safety approach was created by Andrew Turnell, social worker and brief family therapist, and Steve Edwards, child protection practitioner, in partnership with over 150 child protection caseworkers in Western Australia during the 1990s. The approach has continued to evolve over time since that initial work, based on the experiences and feedback of child protection practitioners and agencies that use the Signs of Safety. The approach is currently being implemented in hundreds of jurisdictions in 15 countries around the world (www.signsofsafety.net/signs-of-safety-2/). The Signs of Safety approach was designed to give CPS practitioners a framework for engaging all persons involved in a case, including professionals, family members and children. A participatory risk assessment framework is at the heart of the approach, and Signs of Safety draws on a range of practitioner-designed practice tools, all targeted at building the safety of children in their everyday lives.

The Signs of Safety approach draws upon the participatory thinking and techniques of solution-focused (brief) therapy (SFBT) and strengths-based practices while always maintaining a rigorous focus on danger and harm (Turnell, 2007). The approach aims always to work in partnership with families and children to conduct risk assessments and produce safety plans together. It reduces danger by building from and deepening the strengths, existing success, resources and networks that the family may already have. This is done by sustaining a rigorous focus on demonstrating and growing safety for children throughout the work.

Signs of Safety also seeks to create a more constructive culture around child protection organization and practice. Central to this are the three core framework principles:

> ➤ establishing constructive working relationships and partnerships between professionals and family members, and between professionals themselves

> ➤ engaging in critical thinking and maintaining a position of inquiry

> ➤ staying grounded in the everyday work of child protection practitioners. (Turnell, 2012)

Revisioning risk assessment as a constructive practice

The issue of risk is the defining motif of child protection practice, so for child protection practice to be genuinely participatory and constructive rather than adversarial and to go beyond 'tinkering around the edges', the Signs of Safety approach has pursued an agenda of revisioning the framing and practice of risk assessment.

One of the key reasons that more hopeful, relationally grounded approaches such as solution- focused or strengths-based approaches have often failed to make significant headway within the child protection field is that they have failed to engage seriously with the risk assessment task. Child protection risk assessment is often dismissed as too judgemental, too forensic and too intrusive by proponents of strengths-based and solution-focused practice (see, for example, Berg & Kelly, 2000; Ryburn, 1991). This usually leaves the frontline practitioner who hopes to practise collaboratively caught between strengths-based, support-focused aspirations and the harsh, problem-saturated, forensic reality that they have ultimate responsibility for child safety. In this situation a risk-averse interpretation of the forensic child protection imperative consistently leads to defensive intervention and the escalation of a defensive case culture (Barber, 2005).

Risk does not just define child protection work in isolation. It is in fact an increasingly defining motif of the social life of Western countries in the late twentieth and early twenty-first centuries (Beck, 1992; Giddens, 1994; Wilkinson, 2001). The problem in all this is that risk is almost always constructed in the negative. Risk is framed as something that must be avoided because everyone is worried about being blamed and sued for something, and institutions have become increasingly risk-averse to the point of risk-phobia. Risk is almost always only seen in terms of the BIG loss or the BIG failure, almost never in terms of the BIG win.

If we change the lens to focus on sports, it is easier to consider risk differently. Usain Bolt does not hide from the world championships; Serena Williams does not avoid Wimbledon. These players champ at the bit to get to these places because while they may fail spectacularly, on the biggest stage, in front of millions, it is actually very possible they will succeed gloriously. The analogy is not exact, particularly because people rarely die at Wimbledon, the Olympics or World Championships, and no matter how successful, the outcomes in a high-risk child abuse case are rarely glorious. But in sports we can clearly see the vision of the BIG win, and this win is most likely to occur when the athlete can focus on the win while having strategies for overcoming assessed weakness.

In child protection work, that vision, the possibility of success, is often extinguished or envisioned only faintly. With the erasure of a vision of success within the risk equation, a professional's only hope is to avoid failure; and the practitioner and agency's key motivation then readily defaults to an oft-repeated child protection maxim: 'protect your backside'.

The Signs of Safety approach seeks to revision this territory and reclaim the risk assessment task as a constructive solution-building undertaking, a process that incorporates the idea of a win as well as a loss. Signs of Safety does not set problems in opposition to strengths and solution focus, nor does it set forensic, rigorous professional inquiry off against collaborative practice. Quite simply, the best child protection practice is always both forensic and collaborative, and it demands that professionals are sensitive to and draw upon every scintilla of strength, hope and human capacity they can find within the ugly circumstances where children are abused.

Comprehensive risk assessment and the Signs of Safety

Within its practice framework, the Signs of Safety approach seeks to move from solely a problem focus to both a problem and solution focus by utilizing a comprehensive approach to risk that

> is simultaneously forensically exploring harm and danger and, with the same rigour, eliciting and inquiring into strengths and safety (see Figure 9.1.);

> brings forward clearly articulated professional knowledge while also equally eliciting and drawing upon family knowledge and wisdom;

> is designed to always undertake the risk assessment process with the full involvement of all stakeholders, both professional and family, from the judge to the child, from the child protection worker to the parents and grandparents;

> is naturally holistic since it brings everyone (both professional and family member) to the assessment table. (Some assessment frameworks trumpet their holistic credentials but often do so by slavishly and obsessively gathering vast amounts of information about every aspect of a family and child's life that then swamps the assessment process and everyone involved with too much information.)

Figure 9.1 The Signs of Safety Conceptual Framework for Assessment

The Signs of Safety grounds these aspirations in a one-page assessment and planning protocol. The protocol or framework maps harm, danger, complicating factors, strengths, existing and required safety and a safety judgement in situations where children are vulnerable or have been maltreated. The Signs of Safety Assessment and Planning Protocol, and the questioning processes and inquiring stance that underpins it, is designed to be the organizing map for child protection intervention from case commencement to closure.

At its simplest, this framework can be understood as containing four domains for inquiry:

1 What are we worried about? (Past harm, future danger and complicating factors)

2 What's working well? (Existing strengths and safety)

3 What needs to happen? (Future safety goal and next steps)

4 Where are we on a scale of zero to ten, where ten means there is enough safety for child protection authorities to close the case and zero means it is certain that the child will be (re)abused (Judgement). (Zero on this safety scale is often also described as meaning the situation is so dangerous that the child must be permanently removed.)

The four domains operating in the Signs of Safety assessment and planning are simply and clearly identified in the 'three columns' Signs of Safety Assessment and Planning Protocol in Figure 9.2. as follows.

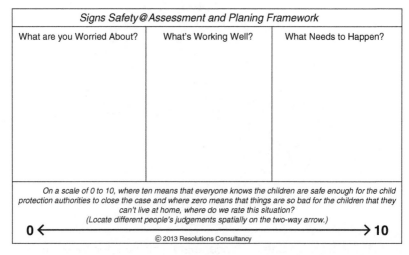

Figure 9.2 The Signs of Safety Assessment and Planning Framework

Evaluation domains and indicators

Evaluation: what child and family services organizations are striving to accomplish

More and more countries are moving to careful use of performance-based contracting with the real-time measurement of quality, fidelity and outcomes – with a strengthened, authentic use of parent and child feedback. In this world, non-randomly selected parent surveys with 20 per cent response rates or 'parent satisfaction surveys' that use general or non-respectful questions are seen as invalid.

In these systems, programme theories of change are expected to be both well-grounded in client-centred practice and very specific about which family needs will be met and how – and with what proximal, intermediate and distal outcomes. But the evaluations must also be cognizant of the larger systems dynamics that affect the implementation of Signs of Safety and related services. Law enforcement, medical, education, mental health/substance abuse treatment, employment, housing, public/income assistance and other systems play key roles and need to be taken into account.

Reflecting the realities of their communities, these systems embrace theories of change, logic models, quality parameters and performance targets **that evolve over time** – with intervention strategies and measurement approaches that also evolve as part of a continuous quality improvement approach to services and developing staff members. The goal is to truly become a 'Learning Organization' (Senge, 1999), where finger pointing and blame are replaced with shared ownership and a dedication to improvement over time (Turnell, Munro & Murphy, 2013).

As more and more evidence-based assessment approaches, practice models and interventions are being created in the human services, policymakers, key constituents and the organizations implementing the model are interested in measuring the quality, fidelity and outcomes (including the proximal, intermediate and distal results). With respect to fidelity, model developers and researchers are interested in identifying the core aspects of the model that need to be implemented well to achieve certain levels of quality and positive outcomes.

Signs of Safety is enabling child protection staff to use solution-focused therapy techniques within a safety, strengths and risk assessment context. But the evidence base is modest and needs to be increased across a range of domains. We illustrate the domains and performance indicators in Table 9.1, drawing from some of the research that has been conducted related to Signs of Safety. Note that a more comprehensive review is being undertaken by Andrew Turnell as part of an upcoming book and other papers (Munro, Turnell and Murphy 2016). Many of the research questions in Table 9.1 are drawn from the Theory of Change/Results Logic manuscript and workshop presented to the Signs of Safety Steering Group in December 2013 (Salveron & Bromfield, 2014). This table has been constructed to highlight (but not exhaustively catalogue) evaluation domains and performance indicators related to key research questions.

Table 9.1 Research domains and questions for Signs of Safety[1]

QUALITY AND FIDELITY

1. **Context fidelity** refers to the structural aspects that encompass the framework for service delivery. Contextual aspects of fidelity might include
 	
   a. professional development activities (e.g. occurrence and quality of pre-service and in-service training),
 	
   b. ongoing supervisor and staff coaching,
 	
   c. organizational climate,
 	
   d. administrative practices,
 	
   e. qualifications of staff,
 	
   f. supervisor/staff ratio and staff/client ratio.
 	
Note that contextual aspects of fidelity are different from compliance or competence in that they are not related to direct service delivery or the interaction between the practitioner and the client.[2]

2. **Compliance fidelity** refers to the extent to which the practitioner uses the core programme components as intended by the developer. Is there evidence to suggest that Signs of Safety is being routinely used in practice?
 	
 Compliance aspects of fidelity assess dosage and content of service delivery and capture the interaction between the practitioner and the client. Compliance aspects of fidelity might include the following: frequency of service, intensity of service, service duration and delivery of prescribed activities and/or curriculum.[3] Raters can be supervisors, parents, peers or the workers themselves. Sample indicators rated by the supervisor or the parent for the worker include the following:
 	
   a. Is there evidence to suggest that Signs of Safety is routinely used in practice?
 	
   b. Uses three column conversations with families to gather information.
 	
   c. Uses three houses to gather information when interviewing children.
 	
   d. A risk assessment map exists for each case.
 	
   e. A Words and Pictures document exists for each case.
 	
   f. Safety houses include the children's ideas about what would make them safe.
 	
   g. Safety networks are involved and meeting together with professionals.
 	
   h. A safety plan exists.

i. Do children participate in the Signs of Safety assessment and safety planning process?

j. Do children feel heard, valued, respected and included in the process?

k. Does safety planning involve parents and other family members?

l. Are safety networks established, when needed and feasible?

m. Are safety networks maintained once child protection service has closed the case? What factors contribute to that?

n. Do parents feel heard, valued, respected and included in the process?

o. Are there age, gender, race and other differences in how children and parents experience Signs of Safety?

Does worker adherence to compliance with service standards change?

3. **Competence fidelity** refers to the level of skill shown by the practitioner and the 'way in which the service is delivered'. Competency aspects of fidelity assess the quality of service delivery and capture the interaction between practitioner and client. Competency aspects of fidelity might include the following:

a. the type of strategies used by the practitioner (e.g. verbal, active, modelling),

    i. reflective practice,

    ii. relational work,

    iii. trauma-informed work,

    iv. participant responsiveness (e.g. client report of their level of engagement or motivation).[4]

b. The parents and family feel heard and understood, and their views about the situation and ideas are important.

c. The children feel heard and understood, and their views about the situation and ideas are important.

d. The professionals have a common vision for how the CPS work with the family will unfold.

e. Everyone involved understands why CPS is involved or the children are in the care, including the children.

f. Everyone involved understands what it would take for CPS to get out of their life, including the children.

g. Everyone involved knows in detail who needs to do what to ensure that

    i. the children are always safe, including the children;

    ii. everyone was involved in developing, practicing, reviewing and improving on the plan over time so that everyone can feel confident it will keep the child safe into the future.

4. **Fidelity-related predictive validity:**

a. Is worker fidelity to Signs of Safety associated with parents feeling engaged and perceiving their children as safe?

b. Does fidelity predict child outcomes?

(Continued)

Table 9.1 (Continued)

5. **Worker safety:** Are there fewer caseworker assaults by clients because staff use practice skills in appreciative inquiry, client-centred practice and other Signs of Safety strategies?

OUTCOMES

6. **Child safety:** Has there been a significant change in children's safety since the implementation of Signs of Safety?[5] For example,   a. CPS re-referrals,   b. rates of CPS substantiated re-reports,   c. if repeat maltreatment occurs, the severity of the CAN is less,   d. rates of severe child injuries due to child abuse or neglect,   e. rates of child fatalities during or immediately after child welfare services   Are there age, gender, race and other differences in how children and parents experience Signs of Safety?
7. **Child functioning:** As a result of the case plans that are put in place with Signs of Safety, does child emotional and social functioning improve?
8. **TPRs:** Are there fewer involuntary terminations of parental rights?
9. **Other Outcomes:** Because of better worker–family relationships, well-designed safety plans[6] and other factors, are these outcomes affected? Some of these outcomes may include   a. rates of out-of-home placement,   b. court diversions,   c. rates of family reunification or achievement of some other kind of permanency, such as adoption or legal guardianship,   d. length of stay in out-of-home care,   e. foster care re-entry rates decrease as safety plans and networks are more effective,   f. case openings for services (non-foster care).

ORGANIZATIONAL CULTURE AND CLIMATE, WORKER MORALE AND RETENSION

10. **Organizational Culture and Climate:**[7] Some examples include   a. clarity of mission,   b. sense of congruence among staff and mid-management and senior management,   c. changes in middle management and senior management attitudes or behaviour.
11. **Staff experiences:** What are the experiences of practitioners/caseworkers with the Signs of Safety approach? Does the implementation of Signs of Safety affect   a. worker perceptions of job satisfaction, professional identity, burnout and stress;   b. worker retention rates;   c. the use of sick leave or other forms of staff leave;   d. feelings of being valued, respected and engaged in the process;   e. the ability of practitioners to work together?

12. Caseworker time and other workload issues
a. Is caseworker time less, the same or more to accomplish the case tasks?
b. Do other aspects of worker caseload lessen, stay the same or increase?

Assessing fidelity as a specialty area

As the Signs of Safety approach has been implemented by more and more jurisdictions, it is typical that agencies and managers ask questions of fidelity or about the degree to which the delivery of a practice adheres to the programme model as intended. In consultation with the international Signs of Safety community of practitioners, Casey Family Programs and Sacramento County Child Protective Services, the Fidelity Research Project is now well underway. The project was established to create a series of assessment tools that will enable agencies to assess the fidelity of Signs of Safety practice of workers, supervisors, leaders and agencies. Measuring how well and to what degree practices are implemented is critical to facilitating change and improvements in the quality and effectiveness of services and organizational supports for distributing accountability and ownership across the organization. Fidelity assessment can help reflect progress towards an organizational culture of partnership, participation for the purpose of safety, permanency and well-being for children.

The Supervisor Assessment part of the project began in 2012 with a working group of over 100 Signs of Safety practitioners/trainers/consultants from eight different countries. Members articulated key elements of the Signs of Safety practice approach, as well as the key attributes and behaviours that best represent a skilled Signs of Safety practitioner. Responses were collated and distilled into a core list of attributes and behaviours relevant to Signs of Safety fidelity. The identified core list of items were then distributed back to international stakeholders for review, confirmation and feedback on supervisor and parent fidelity assessment items drafted based on the information provided by the group. The initial pilot of the 'Signs of Safety Supervisor Practice Fidelity Assessment' was undertaken with a small number of supervisors from the international working group. Feedback from the initial pilot was used to refine the assessment tool. The current international pilot tests the first complete version of the Supervisor Assessment, which included 35 items rated on an 11-point Likert-type scale, ranging from 0 (Never) to 10 (Always), to assess worker fidelity to the Signs of Safety model.

Factor analyses revealed a final 28-item tool, yielding the above proposed four factors, or sub-scales: Indicators of Good Child Protective

Services practice, Signs of Safety Mapping, Signs of Safety Family/Support Network Engagement in Safety Planning, and Signs of Safety Engagement with Children. Advanced Item Response Theory analyses confirmed this proposed tool and found that items provided good fit to the measurement model and no pronounced patterns in ratings. Qualitative information from supervisors revealed that, overall, the checklist was an opportunity to reflect on both individual- and group-level practice in Signs of Safety, to identify areas of strength and areas in need of further development and to clarify what good practice looks like, specific to Signs of Safety.

Conclusions

This chapter has summarized Signs of Safety and highlights research questions, along with their accompanying evaluation domains and performance indicators. There has been only one randomized control study of one aspect of Signs of Safety, but many more other kinds of studies have begun to address a wide variety of implementation, fidelity and outcome areas, including studies that directly gathered the perceptions of parents who were served by this model. Much more work is needed to address the research questions listed in Table 9.1. But an impressive amount of research is underway.

Important opportunities exist to help jurisdictions document the effects of implementing Signs of Safety. But there are challenges as well: care must be taken to avoid the use of poorly matched comparison groups, the attribution of causal effect with study designs that are not suitable for making those conclusions and obtaining low survey response rates because of designs that are vulnerable to that problem versus using in-person data collection or phone interviews with a small but random sample of participants. All of these research problems undermine confidence in a study's findings. In contrast, there is much to build on based on prior risk assessment research and new evaluations of the approach. Signs of Safety is a promising approach aspiring towards meaningful child protection reform through a balanced risk assessment, ongoing planning rooted in partnerships and a focus on safety as well as alignment of the whole organization around these priorities.

Notes

1 Research questions were adapted from Salveron & Bromfield (2014), and then research highlights of findings have been added.

2 For Signs of Safety, this concept could be broadened to include the organization's community environment. To what extent is the agency's Signs of Safety child protection framework understood by key stakeholders, including non-government organizations, other government agencies and the wider community? What evidence is there that these community stakeholders use the Signs of Safety framework to inform key areas of *their* practice including the following:

> ➢ exchange of information

> ➢ influencing decisions in individual safety planning

> ➢ shaping their agency's response to their core business.

3 Note that Sedlar et al. (2015) uses a different definition of compliance than what Rubien (2014) uses in that they emphasize activities to establish fidelity:

Compliance refers to whether a provider followed through with the necessary activities to establish fidelity. For example, if the fidelity protocol requires an expert rater to review session videotapes, the provider needs to supply the tapes to be coded. If the fidelity protocol includes an expert consultant verifying that a provider discusses their therapeutic interventions in a model-consistent way, the provider needs to attend the consultation calls on which these discussions occur. Without participation in these activities, it is unknown the extent to which a given provider is operating with fidelity to the model. (p. 7)

4 Rubien (2014), pp. 4–5. See also Sedlar, G., Bruns, E. J., Kerns, S. E. & Walker, S. E. (2015).
5 Are there particular features of cases or types of harm that have an impact on the following?

> ➢ the confidence of child protection workers

> ➢ the willingness of family members to be part of a safety network

> ➢ the willingness of stakeholder agencies to be part of a safety network.

6 Is there an optimum number of people who should be involved in a safety network? Does this vary depending on the type of harm suffered/likely to be suffered by the child/children? How do workers assess that the safety network has been effective and is no longer needed? Which tools do practitioners use and what evidence do they use (and record and share with the family) to inform their decision making?
7 See the programme of research by Glisson for information about how changes in organizational culture or climate can affect service outcomes in mental health and child welfare. See, for example, Glisson & Hemmelgarn (1998); Glisson (2007).

References

Barber, N. (2005). Risking optimism: practitioner adaptions of strengths-based practice in child protection work. *Child Abuse Protection Newsletter*, 13(2), pp. 10–15.

Beck, U. (1992). *Risk Society: Towards a New Modernity*. London: Sage.

Berg, I. K. & Kelly, S. (2000). *Building Solutions in Child Protective Services*. New York: W. W. Norton.

Baumann, D. J., Fluke, J., Dalgleisch, L. & Kern, H. (2014). The Decision-Making Ecology, in *From Evidence to Outcomes in Child Welfare: An International Reader* (pp. 24–40). New York: Oxford University Press.

Bromfield, L., Salveron, M., Turnell, A., Simmons, J., Lee, A. & Lewig, K. (2014). *Signs of Safety: Articulating the Theory of Change*. Adelaide, South Australia: Australian Centre for child protection, Hawke Research Institute, University of South Australia.

Casey Family Programs (2013). Traditions Renewed: The Mill Lacs Band of Ojibwe Improves Its Indian Child Welfare Programs by Incorporating Tribal Family Values. Seattle, WA: Author. Available at www.casey.org/Resources/Publications/MilleLacs.htm

Ellis, M. L., Eskenazi, S., Bonnell, R. & Pecora, P. J. (2013). *Taking a Closer Look at the Reduction in Entry Rates for Children in Sacramento County with an Emphasis on African American Children: A Spotlight on Practice*. Seattle, WA: Casey Family Programs.

Fluke, J. & Hollinshead, D. (2003). *Child Abuse Recurrence: A Leadership Initiative of the National Resource Center on Child Maltreatment*. Duluth: National Resource Center on Child Maltreatment. Available at www.nrccps.org/PDF/MaltreatmentRecurrence.pdf

Giddens, A. (1994). *Beyond Left and Right: The Future of Radical Politics*. Cambridge: Polity.

Glisson, C. & Hemmelgarn, A. (1998). The effects of organizational climate and interorganizational coordination on the quality and outcomes of children's service systems, *Child Abuse and Neglect*, 22(5), 401–421.

Glisson, C. (2007). Assessing and changing culture and climate for effective services, *Research on Social Work Practice*, 17(6), 736–747.

Marts, E. J., Lee, R., McCroy, R. & McCroskey, J. (2008). Point of engagement: Reducing disproportionality and improving child and family outcomes, *Child Welfare*, 87(2), 335–358.

McCroskey, J., Franke, T., Christie, T., Pecora, P. J., Lorthridge, J., Fleischer, D. & Rosenthal, E. (2010). *Prevention Initiative Demonstration Project (PIDP): Year Two Evaluation Summary Report*. Los Angeles: LA County Department of Children and Family Services and Seattle: Casey Family Programs. www.casey.org

McKeigue, B. & Beckett, C. (2004). Care proceedings under the 1989 Children Act: rhetoric and reality, *British Journal of Social Work*, 34(6): 831–849.

Morris, K. & Burford, G. (2017). Engaging families and managing risk in practice, from Chapter 7 in M. Connolly (ed.), *Beyond the Risk Paradigm in Child Protection*. London: Palgrave.

Munro, E. (2010). *The Munro Review of Child Protection Part One: A Systems Analysis*. London: Secretary of State, Department of Education. Product Reference: DFE-00548–2010. Available at www.education.gov.uk

Munro, E., Turnell, A. & Murphy, T. (2016). You can't grow roses in concrete: Organisational reform to support high quality Signs of Safety practice. Action research final report. Signs of Safety English Innovations Project. Perth: Resolutions. Available at www.signsofsafety.net

Parton, N. (2017). Concerns about risk as a major driver of professional practice, from Chapter 1 in M. Connolly (ed.), *Beyond the Risk Paradigm in Child Protection*. London: Palgrave.

Pecora, P. J. & Chahine, Z. (2016). Catalysts for child protection reform. *CW360 – Child Welfare Reform*. (A publication of the University of Minnesota), page 11. Retrieved from http://cascw.umn.edu/wp-content/uploads/2016/05/CW360_Spring2016_WEB.pdf

Pecora, P. J., Chahine, Z. & Graham, C. (2013). Safety and risk assessment frameworks: Overview and implications for child maltreatment fatalities, *Child Welfare*, 92(2), 139–156.

Rubien, D. (2014). *Fidelity of Preventive Service Models: Desk Guide*. New York: NYC Administration for Children's Services, p. 4.

Ryburn, M. (1991). The myth of assessment, *Adoption and Fostering*, 15(1), 20–27.

Salveron, M. & Bromfield, L. (2014). *Signs of Safety Program of Research Discussion Paper*. Adelaide, South Australia: Australian Centre for child protection, Hawke Research Institute, University of South Australia

Sedlar, G., Bruns, E. J., Kerns, S. E. & Walker, S. E. (2015). Developing a quality assurance system for multiple evidence based practices in a statewide service improvement initiative, *Administration and Policy in Mental Health and Mental Health Services Research*, Published online June 2015: doi: 10.1007/s10488–015–0663–8

Senge, P., Kleiner, A., Roberts, C., Ross, R., Roth, G. & Smith, B. (1999). *The Dance of Change: The Challenges of Sustaining Momentum in Learning Organizations*. New York: Doubleday/Currency. See also http://infed.org/mobi/peter-senge-and-the-learning-organization/

Shlonsky, A. & Mildon, R. (2017). Decision making and outcomes in child protection, from Chapter 8 in M. Connolly (ed.), *Beyond the Risk Paradigm in Child Protection*. London: Palgrave.

Turnell, A. (in press). *Building Safety in Child Protection Practice: Working with a Strengths and Solution-Focus in an Environment of Risk*. New York: Palgrave Macmillan.

Turnell A. (2007). Solution-focused brief therapy: Thinking and practicing beyond the therapy room, in F. Thomas & T. Nelson (eds), *Clinical Applications of Solution-focused Brief Therapy*. Bimmington: Haworth Press.

Turnell, A. (2012). *The Signs of Safety: A Comprehensive Briefing Paper*. Retrieved from www.signsofsSigns of Safetyafety.net

Turnell, A, Murphy, T. & Munro, E. (2013). Soft is hardest: Leading for learning in child protection services following a child fatality, *Child Welfare*, 92(2), 199–216.

Wilkinson, I. (2001). *Anxiety in a Risk Society*. London: Routledge.

10

SHIFTING THE FOCUS: WORKING DIFFERENTLY WITH DOMESTIC VIOLENCE

Cathy Humphreys and Nicky Stanley[*]

Introduction

Risk assessment undertaken with families is often confused in its focus and fails to distinguish clearly where in the family risks reside and which family members pose a threat to other family members. The use of non-specific terms such as 'parenting' or 'family' can obscure the power relations that underpin and shape levels of risk. There is, however, widespread recognition of the gendered nature of domestic violence. Analyses that have highlighted how risks in families experiencing domestic violence are gendered (Scourfield, 2003; Mandel, 2014) have argued the case for risk assessment and management to differentiate between the risks posed by mothers and fathers to children's safety and well-being. This chapter describes how a conceptual shift away from the risks located in mothers' living with domestic violence to address those found in violent fathers has generated new approaches to risk assessment as well as innovations in service provision.

The response to domestic violence has been primarily developed by advocates working on behalf of women to secure safety and a greater sense of well-being. The response was closely tied to the women's movement, which provided active, long-term support. Over many decades it has shone a light on the prevalence, risks and severity of violence experienced by women in their own homes or when separating from violent and abusive partners. It has also arguably been the women's movement aligned with women's refuges which surfaced the needs and the risks to children living

[*] Cathy Humphreys is a professor of social work at the University of Melbourne, Australia. Nicky Stanley is a professor at the School of Social Work, Care and Community, the University of Central Lancashire, UK.

with domestic violence. Children were accompanying their mothers to refuges, and their needs were palpable. They were as distressed, fearful and disturbed as their mothers by the violence and abuse they were living with. The researchers followed, drawing attention to the needs of these children (Jaffe, Wolfe & Wilson, 1990; Mullender & Morely, 1994).

Attention to children living with domestic violence has shifted the focus of domestic violence intervention. The specialist domestic violence services have in some sense been co-opted to address a different task: the needs of children living with domestic violence. In many jurisdictions, the attention to children fell firmly into the statutory arena and became 'hitched to the child protection juggernaut' (Featherstone & Trinder, 1997, p. 149). While it can be argued that the specialist women's sector was not designed to meet the needs of children, the statutory child protection response was equally poorly equipped to respond appropriately to the needs of children living with domestic violence. A number of problems have emerged consistently and provide ongoing challenges to the statutory safeguarding services (Humphreys & Absler, 2011; Shlonsky, Friend & Lambert, 2007; Stanley et al., 2011a).

In this chapter, we will explore an area where the strains within the service system are most evident, and where new practices are being developed, including in the area of risk assessment and risk management. The areas for innovation lie in the re-focusing of domestic violence intervention, particularly in the human services sector to address the perpetrator of domestic violence. This has resulted in attention swinging over to men rather than women, who have been the traditional target of child protection intervention.

Background

The focus on interventions to address the perpetrator of domestic violence has a substantial history. Much of the work has centred, however, on legal and court remedies to ensure that both the criminal (Hester, 2006) and the civil (Laing, 2012) justice systems provide effective consequences for men who use violence. Attention has also been given to developing and commissioning Domestic Violence Perpetrator Programs (DVPPs), known as men's behaviour change (MBC) programmes in Australia and batterer programmes in the United States (for the purposes of this chapter, we will refer to DVPPs). These group programmes provide interventions for abusive men and also provide partner support services (increasingly known as women's support services).

These programmes have traditionally focused on assisting men to understand the circumstances in which they resort to violence towards their partners, the methods they use for control and domination, their attitudes to women and gender equality and the encouragement of positive alternatives to their behaviours (Shepard & Pence, 1999). Consideration of the relationship between men's abuse of their partners and their role as fathers has been slower to emerge. Programmes have struggled to incorporate a dual focus on violence and abuse that attends to both the effects on children as well as the impact on women. The background to this chapter traverses a short history of the work which initially focuses on the perpetrator of violence to provide the context for the emerging innovations and practices in risk assessment and management which are currently developing. It will also look 'beyond risk' to explore the creative responses in programme responses for men who use violence.

There have been a number of significant outcome evaluations, both single site evaluations and meta-analyses, on the efficacy of DVPPs (Buttell & Carney, 2008; Costello, 2006; Gondolf, 2002; Miller, Drake & Nafziger, 2013; Kelly & Westmarland, 2015). These evaluations investigate the impact of attendance, full programme completion versus partial completion, programme length, counsellor qualities, mandatory attendance, female partner involvement, women's assessment of good outcomes and completion rates. The efficacy of differing programme approaches is also being explored, including psychoeducational approaches (Gondolf, 2002), the restorative-strengths perspective (Van Wormer & Bednar, 2002), narrative approaches (Jenkins, 2009) and constructivist approaches (Laming, 2005).

There are a number of important considerations when assessing the merit of the research into DVPPs. Many of the studies have no control group, so results cannot be definitively attributed to the intervention (Silvergleid & Mankowski, 2006). There is little agreement regarding how perpetrator characteristics, typologies and demographics impact on programme effectiveness (Buttell & Carney, 2008; Huss, 2008). Most studies are plagued by low response rates. Many have short-term follow-up with high and selective attrition. These issues distort findings as those who are most likely to drop out are also those who are least likely to change their behaviour (Gondolf, 1997; Laing, 2002).

A finding from an interesting strand of research within the DVPP literature suggests that programmes appear to be more effective the more tightly they are aligned and supported by other parts of the domestic violence and justice intervention systems (Edleson, 2012; Gondolf, 2002; 2011). To illustrate this point, Gondolf (2002) has coined a phrase, 'the system matters', meaning that the retention and accountability participants in a programme increases as DVPPs become more integrated within the wider system, involving the police, courts, child protection, women's services and drug and alcohol counselling. This approach draws from the Duluth approach, which consistently emphasizes that DVPPs need to go beyond risk management in order to be part of a coordinated community response (Shepard & Pence, 1999), contributing not only to men's accountability but also to community building and safety more generally (Gondolf, 2011; Diemer, Humphreys, Laming & Smith, 2015).

This development, which broadens the intervention with perpetrators of domestic violence to encompass the wider multi-agency system, brings with it a range of new practice initiatives. The notion that all work in the human services landscape which relates to perpetrators can be 'hived off' to the specialist DVPPs is being challenged. While these programmes are increasingly perceived as essential to an integrated domestic violence response, the high attrition rates from the programmes (even when men are court mandated), the lack of suitability or access for significant groups of men and the equivocal evaluation results have provided an opportunity for innovation and for alternative interventions.

A broader range of organizations are now engaging in, and developing work to support the accountability of perpetrators of domestic violence. For example, Maternal and Child Health Services are exploring primary prevention interventions with first time fathers as part of their early parenting support programmes (Flynn, 2011). In Victoria, Australia, this is known as the Baby Makes 3 programme, and it is currently in the early stages of development and exploration of the engagement of men with these programmes (Pfizner, Humphreys & Hegarty, 2015). Primary healthcare services are also exploring the role they have to play in the identification of and interventions with men in their GP practices who are disclosing their involvement in domestic violence perpetration (Feder et al., 2011). Drug and alcohol services and DVPPs are taking incremental steps to explore the ways in which men on their programmes, who are both perpetrating domestic violence and misusing alcohol and other drugs, can be engaged in addressing their problematic behaviours and attitudes (Wilson, Graham & Taft, 2014).

Of particular interest has been the shifting focus of child protection workers. The lack of attention by child protection workers to the perpetrator of domestic violence has been a long standing criticism of statutory child care intervention (Featherstone & Peckover, 2007; Humphreys & Absler, 2011). A focus on the mother's ability to protect the children, rather than interventions which target the perpetrator of domestic violence directly, has proven hard to defend in the face of criticisms of both mothers themselves and other professionals, contributing to multi-agency domestic violence interventions. Both have described child protection workers as involved in 'mother-blaming' (Lapierre, 2010; Douglas & Walsh, 2010).

Risk assessment is a key area where the differences in inter-agency practice are most apparent. Different organizations working with families who experience domestic violence are using different risk assessments and coming to different decisions about where the risks to children lie (Radford, Blacklock & Iwi, 2006). Most organizations derive their risk assessment in the domestic violence arena from the actuarial tools which have developed on the basis of serious crimes and domestic homicides towards primarily female partners. There is no actuarial tool to assess the domestic violence risk to children, although Jaffe et al. (2014) argue that the severity of the risk to the mother is the closest indicator of the severity of risk to the child. Nevertheless, child protection has continued to prioritize the assessment of the protectiveness of the child's mother rather than the abuse from the perpetrator. This is therefore an area ripe for change where new practices are beginning to emerge (Stanley & Humphreys, 2014).

The shift from the assessment of the mother and her protectiveness in relation to her violent partner (or ex-partner) to the perpetrator of that violence, however, requires a major cultural change. Child protection workers have a long history of providing the 'separation ultimatum'. The entrenched nature of this practice (in spite of decades of criticism) suggests that it may have organizational imperatives such as the management of overwhelming caseload demand. Alternatively, it may represent a means of defending practitioners themselves against the professional risks of child injury or death that they encounter. As long as the woman separates from the violent partner, the case can be closed because it is deemed that protective action has been taken. Unfortunately, state sanctioned separations have a long history of failure, and these families continue to be re-referred to child protection (Stanley et al., 2011).

Violent and abusive fathers do not just go away. Many children, thrust into homelessness, isolated from their cultural communities, plunged into poverty, 'forced' into extensive unsupervised contact with abusive fathers, exposed to post-separation violence and abuse which often occurs at handover, are no safer when their parents separate (see Holt, 2015). For women whose residency status is dependent upon their partners, the consequences of separation are dire for both themselves and their children (Thiara & Gill, 2009). Forced state separation is an arid practice which belies the work which needs to be undertaken to ensure that children's safety and well-being are actually addressed.

Work is now developing to enable child protection workers to take a more skilled, sensitive and effective response to perpetrators of domestic violence. The 'Safe and Together' model developed by David Mandel and colleagues (Mandel, 2014) points to the complexity of the change process which may be required. While essentially a model of training and development, it also provides coaching of workers through ongoing supervision or joint working, case reading to assist workers to reflect on the focus of their work and its outcomes and a theoretical approach which identifies the need to strengthen the mother–child relationship alongside the focused work with perpetrators of abuse. Promising evaluations in Florida, Ohio and Connecticut suggest that this may be an intervention which is shifting the historically poor practice in child protection intervention in domestic violence (Jones & Steinman, 2014). The innovative work undertaken by the London-based Domestic Violence Intervention Program (DVIP), described later in this chapter, echoes a similar focus in Hackney, London. However given the contrasting contexts, the practices which have emerged differ.

The shift in focus to perpetrators of domestic violence has identified a broader range of risks that impact upon women and their children. Comparatively little attention has been given to research on the attitudes and behaviour of family violence perpetrators towards their children (Guille, 2004; Bromfield et al., 2010). What research there is suggests cause for concern. Qualitative research studies and evaluations point to a significant group of family violence perpetrators who have poor parenting skills resulting from their sense of entitlement, self-centred attitudes and over-controlling behaviour (Scott & Crooks, 2007; Bancroft & Silverman, 2002) and over-use of physical forms of discipline (smacking) when compared with other fathers (Fox & Benson, 2004). The evaluation of a Canadian/UK programme, the Caring Dads programme (discussed further below) also highlighted a subgroup of family violence perpetrators who had developed a relatively responsive relationship with their children and were in touch with their children's lives (for example, health and education needs) but who actively manipulated and undermined the mother–child relationship (Scott & Crooks, 2004). However, while poor fathering highlights particular risks to children, it is also emerging as a potential point of change for men, and for programmes, it is an opportunity for innovation. Studies are indicating that for men who are accessing men's behaviour change programmes, maintaining contact with their children and being better fathers are important factors contributing to their motivation to change (Stanley et al., 2012).

The evidence base for the shifting focus to intervention with perpetrators of domestic violence is in the early stages of development. The principle of developing perpetrator accountability is a stronger driver of the change process than the current knowledge base at this stage. Nevertheless, a suite of reforms in this area are worth exploring as new practices develop and lend themselves to evaluation and possible wider implementation.

Interventions to reduce the risks of men's violence

Below we provide examples of interventions for abusive men that illustrate new models for assessing and managing the risks posed by domestic violence perpetrators. These interventions are tasked with tackling the simultaneous risks of harm to both women and children while delivering programmes that aim to change men's abusive behaviour. We draw on a number of examples to examine the impact of varying referral routes, differing patterns of collaboration with children's social services, varying service mechanisms or components and theories and models of change. The relationship between child protection services and these programmes is developing and appears central to the way in which risks are conceptualized and managed. In considering the findings from relevant evaluations of such interventions, we highlight the variety of risks to be managed which are apparent in the range of outcomes measured.

Strength to Change (STC) is an innovative programme for men who perpetrate domestic violence delivered in Hull in North-East England. This intervention is not unique in its requiring men to self-refer, but staff argue that this approach is crucial to building men's motivation from the outset (Stanley et al., 2011b). To this end, a social marketing campaign was delivered across the city, which aimed to enable men to recognize their own behaviour as abusive and to seek help to change it (Thomson et al., 2012). STC is a lengthy programme consisting of individual assessments and ten individual sessions for participants that are followed by a 40-week group-work programme. A range of therapeutic techniques that include cognitive approaches and some elements of the mindfulness approach are utilized in the individual and group sessions. The evaluation (Stanley et al., 2011b), undertaken over the first 18 months of the service's life, described the programme as 'empowering', and the requirement for men to self-refer was identified as a factor that assisted in building motivation. However, the evaluation also argued that engagement with the programme was assisted by extrinsic factors such as involvement with child protection services (Stanley et al., 2012). Over half the female partners interviewed reported feeling safer since their partner had been using the STC service, and most reported positive change in the partner's behaviour. There was a reduction in both domestic violence incidents and other offences while men were on the programme in comparison to the two years prior to joining it. Unfortunately, follow-up beyond programme completion was not possible within the time frame of the evaluation. The programme succeeded in promoting men's capacity for self-reflection and sensitivity to the feelings of others. One woman summed up this shift thus: 'it's made him realise that it's not all about him' (Emily, Stanley et al., 2012, p. 270).

The Mirabel Project showed similar findings concerning men's increased ability to acknowledge and respect their partner's views, leaving the women with increased 'space for action' (Kelly & Westmarland, 2015). This evaluation of 12 UK community Domestic Violence Perpetrator Programs (DVPPs) employed six measures of success: improved and respectful relationships; increased 'space for action' for female partners; safety for women and children; safe and shared parenting; enhanced awareness of self and others in men; and safer, healthier childhoods for participants' children. Kelly and Westmarland (2015) argue that these indicators are more 'nuanced' than those of earlier studies, which tended to use either reconviction rates or women's accounts as measures of success. However, while these measures may be sensitive, they are also numerous and require DVPPs to act to reduce risk by impacting on a number of different spheres: men's capacity for self-reflection and sensitivity to others; non-coercive communication and behaviour in interpersonal relationships; increased autonomy for women; improved shared parenting; and increased safety and well-being for children.

These last two outcomes reflect the increasing part played by child protection and private/family law services as a source of both referrals and funding for DVPPs. Kelly and Westmarland found that over two-thirds of the referral sources for men on the programmes in their study were identified as children's services or CAFCASS; they argue that men who enter programmes with the aim of gaining access to their children or under pressure from child protection services will have a purely instrumental approach to programme participation. However, the research did not examine outcomes by referral pathway. The four programmes selected as case studies for the evaluation (1) operated from within local authorities' children's services or (2) were co-located with them or had staff seconded from local authority children's services, indicating how close this relationship has become.

Only three of the 12 DVPPs studied by Kelly and Westmarland were providing direct services to perpetrators' children in addition to providing programmes for men and a support service for women. For most children, therefore, the benefits of the programme would be mediated through improvements in their fathers' parenting. While Alderson et al.'s (2015) qualitative interviews with 13 children who reported on their perceptions of their father's parenting before and after participation in a DVPP found improvements in their feelings towards and relationships with their father after the programme, the quantitative outcome measures utilized in the main evaluation (which relied on mothers' reports) showed variable results in respect to changes in men's parenting. Improvements were evident in children's fear of the perpetrator and worries about their mother's safety and such measures represent a means of assessing the level of risk for children. However, there were fewer changes found in measures relating to their behaviour, health and well-being, indicating the long-term impact of living with domestic abuse (Kelly & Westmarland, 2015).

Caring Dads is a programme for abusive men that focuses explicitly on their parenting. Based on a Canadian model (Scott & Lishak, 2012), the programme comprises weekly group-work sessions over 17 weeks and is delivered in five UK sites. Programme staff make contact with participants' partners and children to monitor any risks and measure progress. The original goals for the intervention articulated by Scott et al. (2014) all concerned building trust and increasing men's understanding of positive fathering. However, UK evaluations to date have also examined the extent to which the programme impacts on women's and children's safety. McConnell et al.'s (2014) evaluation measured reduced risk from abusive behaviour for children and partners, as well as feelings of safety and well-being and the quality of the parents' relationship. The evaluation reported a decrease in parenting stress among participating fathers, as well as a reduction in their use of controlling behaviours, particularly emotional abuse. However, the researchers were not able to provide evidence of significant improvements in children's well-being and found mixed results with regard to children's accounts of change in their fathers' behaviour. McCracken and Deave's (2012) evaluation of the Caring Dads service in Wales found that the intervention was more successful in improving men's attitudes towards their children and their parenting than it was in shifting their appreciation of their partners' needs for safety.

London's **Domestic Violence Intervention Project (DVIP)** initiatives have included a range of pilot projects, which are developing innovations which bring their expertise in working with perpetrators of domestic violence into a range of different programme areas. As with other developments mentioned above, they are developing work to strengthen both the mothering and fathering of children where there has been domestic violence (The Jacana Project). The evaluation of the programme (Coy et al., no date) pointed to both strengths and weaknesses in the interface between the community sector organization and the child protection social workers, the case audit bringing to light the difficulties and the reluctance of statutory workers to leverage the power that they have to engage the perpetrator of violence. However, there were some initial, very positive results from the perspectives of women, men and workers.

A further initiative from DVIP that has a long history of providing risk assessments on abusive men to inform child protection decisions (see Radford et al., 2006) involves the London Borough of Hackney. The project aims to transfer expertise in the risk assessment of fathers who perpetrate domestic violence. In addition to delivering a local DVPP and producing risk assessments of perpetrators and safety plans for victims, the DVIP staff provide training for child protection workers and ongoing consultation to inform child protection interventions with families experiencing domestic violence (Blacklock & Phillips, 2015). Phillips' (2012) process evaluation of this initiative suggests that social workers' confidence and readiness to engage with perpetrators may have increased as a result of this initiative but does not include any evidence on the quality of risk assessments or on outcomes for families.

The future for risk assessment and management in domestic violence

The accounts above give an indication of the range of risks practitioners working in both men's behaviour change programmes and in statutory services are being asked to assess and manage. These include the risks to the child from poor fathering, the risks involved in contact with abusive fathers, the risks to the child who witnesses direct violence, the risks to the mother–child relationship and the risks of violence and abuse for mothers. Most of these risks involve emotional harm for the child and will therefore not be readily discerned or assessed. Practitioners who lack expertise in talking to and assessing children may be required to identify and manage threats to children's health and development that are unfamiliar to them. There is a danger that expertise will be lost, particularly in the context of austerity, where commissioners may argue for developing men's behaviour change programmes that are required to manage risks for all family members.

The research base in the field of men's behaviour change programmes is still developing. We need to know more about how the involvement of children's protection services' impacts on men's engagement and motivation or if it affects outcomes. We also need to understand more about how these interventions work, in particular the key mechanisms of change. Most interventions use psychoeducational approaches, but the therapeutic bond with facilitators may be equally important (Rees & Rivett, 2005). Outcome measures appear to be becoming broader and less focused on risk. This approach may deliver measures that are more closely aligned with the changes that children, mothers and men themselves would like interventions to deliver. Alderson et al.'s (2015) use of children's accounts as a means of evaluating perpetrator programmes represents a new approach to expanding the evidence base for these interventions.

A key trend evident in the case studies above is the closer interaction between men's behaviour change programmes and child protection services. This is generally to be welcomed as child protection services have traditionally failed to engage with abusive fathers with the consequence that mothers have been left to take sole responsibility for managing the risks that men pose to children. The child protection agenda has also been successful in unlocking funding for perpetrator services at a time when restrictions in public spending have impacted on the domestic violence sector. However, there is a possibility that services for female victims may 'lose out' to perpetrator programmes in the competition for resources. There is also the potential for risk assessment to become confused, with risks for victims being reframed as risks to parenting of children. Those assessing and managing risk in relation to domestic violence need to rec-ognize the different positions and needs of different family members and avoid the temptation to use a single approach to risk assessment and man-agement for victims, children and perpetrators. In the United Kingdom, the CAADA-Dash risk assessment tool (Richards et al., 2008) has been widely used for assessing domestic violence risks for both victims and children. Its evidence base is now being questioned, and the relevance of a tool based on a review of domestic homicide cases for assessing risk to other groups of victims has been challenged.

Risk assessment also needs to be dynamic and to pay attention to time. The harm inflicted on children by domestic violence is known to accu-mulate over time (Stanley, 2011), and children's needs for safety may not coincide with the time required for behavioural change in perpetrators. Similarly, the time immediately after separation when men's feelings of abandonment and fear are high is when they present a particularly acute risk of harm for the adult victim and children (Richards, 2004), and risks need to be carefully monitored in this period. Furthermore, the hope engendered in both perpetrators and victims at the point where a man enters a programme may produce very positive feedback from him and his family, which will need to be re-evaluated over time.

Conclusion

The field of domestic violence intervention is evolving, and new policies and practices are continually emerging. A stronger focus on perpetrators of domestic violence brings both risks and opportunities. Engaging with men who use violence is skilled work, where simplistic and naïve approaches can have the unintended consequence of escalating violence, risk and danger to women, children and workers. On the other hand, shifting from a focus on the women's capacity to protect to one which addresses the perpetrator of the violence is long overdue. The programmes and initiatives discussed in this chapter point to promising changes. Stronger attention to the evidence base for these new approaches will be required if the work is to be both credible and sustained.

References

Alderson, S., Kelly, L. & Westmarland, N. (2015). Expanding understandings of success: Domestic Violence Perpetrator Programmes, children and fathering, in Stanley, N. & Humphreys. C. (eds), *Domestic Violence and Protecting Children: New thinking and approaches*. London: Jessica Kingsley.

Bancroft, L. & Silverman, J. G. (2002). *The Batterer as Parent*. Thousand Oaks: Sage.

Bromfield, L., Lamont, A., Parker, R. & Horsfall, B. (2010). *Issues for the Safety and Wellbeing for Children in Families with Multiple and Complex Problems*. National Child Protection Clearinghouse, Issues Paper no.33 1–23.

Blacklock, N. & Phillips, R. (2015). Reshaping the Child Protection Response to Domestic Violence through Collaborative Working, in Stanley, N. & Humphreys. C. (eds), *Domestic Violence and Protecting Children: New thinking and approaches*. London: Jessica Kingsley.

Buttell, F. & Carney, M. M. (2008). A large sample investigation of batterer intervention program attrition: Evaluating the impact of state program standards, *Research on Social Work Practice*, 18(3), 177–188.

Costello, S. (2006). Invitations to collusion: A case for greater scrutiny of men's behaviour change programs, *Australian & New Zealand Journal of Family Therapy*, 27(1), 38–47.

Diemer, K., Humphreys, C., Laming, C. & Smith, J. (2015). Continuous improvement practice principles for men's behaviour change programs in Victoria, *Journal of Social Work*, 15, 65–85.

Douglas, H. & Walsh, T. (2010). Mothers, domestic violence & child protection, *Violence Against Women*, 16, 489–508.

Featherstone B. & Peckover S. (2007). Letting them get away with it: Fathers, domestic violence and child welfare, *Critical Social Policy*, 27(2), 181–202.

Feder, G., Davies, R. A., Baird, K., Dunne, D., Eldridge, S., Griffiths, C., Gregory, A., Howell, A., Johnson, M., Ramsay, J., Rutterford, C. & Sharp, D. (2011). Identification and referral to improve safety (IRIS) of women experiencing domestic violence with a primary care training and support programme: a cluster randomised controlled trial, *Lancet*, 378, 1788–1795.

Featherstone, B. & Trinder, L. (1997). Familiar subjects: Domestic violence and child welfare, *Child and Family Social Work*, 2, 147–160.

Fox, G. & Benson, M. (2004). Violent men, bad dads? Fathering profiles of men involved in intimate partner violence, in R. Day & M. Lamb (eds), *Conceptualizing and measuring father involvement*. Mahwah, NJ: Lawrence Erlbaum Associates Publishers

Flynn, D. (2011). *Baby Makes 3: Project Report: Whitehorse Community Health Service*. Melbourne: VicHealth.

Gondolf, E. (1997). Batterer programs: What we know and need to know, *Journal of Interpersonal Violence*, 12, 83–98.

Gondolf, E. W. (2002). *Batterer Intervention Systems: Issues, Outcomes and Recommendations*. Thousand Oaks, CA: Sage.

Gondolf, E. (2011). The weak evidence for batterer program alternatives, *Aggression and Violent Behavior*, 16, 347–353.

Guille, L. (2004). Men who batter and their children: An integrated review, *Aggression and Violent Behaviour*, 9, 129–163.

Hester, M. (2006). Making it through the Criminal Justice system: Attrition and domestic violence, *Social Policy and Society*, 5, 79–90.

Holt, S. (2015). Focusing on Fathering in the Context of Domestic Abuse: Children's and Fathers' Perspectives, in Stanley, N. & Humphreys. C. (eds), *Domestic Violence and Protecting Children: New Thinking and Approaches*. London: Jessica Kingsley.

Humphreys, C. & Absler, D. (2011). History repeating: Child protection responses to domestic violence, *Child and Family Social Work*, 16, 464–473.

Huss, M. & Ralston, A. (2008). Do batterer subtypes actually matter? Treatment completion, treatment response, and recidivism across a batterer typology, *International Association for Correctional and Forensic Psychology*, 35, 710–724.

Jaffe, P. G., Wolfe, D. & Wilson, S. (1990). *Children of Battered Women*. Thousand Oaks, CA: Sage.

Jenkins, A. (2009). *Becoming Ethical: A Parallel Political Journey with Men Who Have Abused*. Lyme Regis: Russell House.

Jones, S. & Steinman, K. (2014). *Ohio intimate partner violence collaboration: final evaluation report of the Safe and Together training program*. http://endingviolence. com/wp-content/uploads/2014/04/Ohio-Safe-and-Together-Model-Training-F inal-Evaluation-Report-March-2014.pdf

Kelly, L. & Westmarland, N. (2015). *Domestic Violence Perpetrator Programmes: Steps Towards Change*. London and Durham, NC: London Metropolitan University and Durham University. www.dur.ac.uk/criva/projectmirabal

Laing, L. (2012). *'It's Like this Maze': Women's Experiences of Seeking an ADVO in NSW*, Sydney: NSW Law and Justice Foundation.

Laming, C. (2008). *Challenging Men's Violence Against Women. A Constructivist Approach* (Vol. PhD). VDM Verlag: Saarbruchen.

Lapierre S. (2010). More responsibilities, less control: Understanding the challenges and difficulties involved in mothering in the context of domestic violence, *British Journal of Social Work*, 40, 1434–1451.

Mandel, D. (2014). *Safe and Together Model: Overview and Evaluation Draft Briefing*. https://endingviolence.com/wp-content/uploads/2013/01/2015Overview-and-Evidence-Briefing-October-2014.pdf [Accessed 30 June 2015].

McConnell, N., Barnard, M., Holdsworth, T. & Taylor, J. (2014). *Caring Dads: Safer children. Interim Evaluation Report*. London: NSPCC.

McCracken, K. & Deave, T. (2012). *Evaluation of the Caring Dads Cymru Programme*. Wales: Welsh Assembly Government.

Miller, M., Drake, E. & Nafziger, M. (2013). What works to reduce recidivism by domestic violence offenders? (Document No. 13-01-1201). Olympia, WA: Washington State Institute for Public Policy.

Mullender, A. & Morley, S. (eds) (1994). *Children Living with Domestic Violence*. London: Whiting and Birch.

Pfitzner, N., Humphreys, C. & Hegarty, K. (2015). Engaging men: A multi-level model to support father engagement, *Child and Family Social Work*. Early access doi:10.1111/cfs.12250

Phillips, R. (2012). *DVIP's Co- Location in Hackney Children's Services: A Process Evaluation*. London: Child & Woman Abuse Studies Unit, London Metropolitan University.

Radford, L., Blacklock, N. & Iwi, K. (2006). Domestic violence risk assessment and safety planning in child protection –Assessing perpetrators, in Humphreys, C. & Stanley, N. (eds), *Domestic Violence and Child Protection: Directions for Good Practice* (pp. 171–189). London: Jessica Kingsley Publications.

Rees, A, Rivett, M. (2005). 'Let a hundred flowers bloom, let a hundred schools of thought contend': Towards a variety in programmes for perpetrators of domestic violence, *Probation Journal*, 52, 277–288.

Richards, L. (2004). *'Getting Away With It': A Strategic Overview of Domestic Violence Sexual Assault and 'Serious' Incident Analysis*. London: Metropolitan Police Service.

Richards, L., Letchford, S. & Stratton, S. (2008). *Policing Domestic Violence*. Oxford: Oxford University Press.

Scott, K. L. & Crooks, C. V. (2007). Preliminary evaluation of an intervention program for maltreating fathers, *Brief Treatment and Crisis Intervention*, 7, 224–238.

Scott, K., Kelly, T., Crooks, C. V. & Francis, K. (2014). *Caring Dads: Helping Fathers Value their Children* (2nd edn). Charleston, SC: Createspace Publishers.

Scott, K. L. & Lishak, V. (2012). Intervention for maltreating fathers: Statistically and clinically significant change, *Child Abuse and Neglect*, 36(9), 680–684.

Scourfield, J. (2003). *Gender and Child Protection*. Basingstoke: Palgrave Macmillan.

Shepard, M. & Pence, E. (eds) (1999). *Coordinating Community Responses to Domestic Violence: Lessons from Duluth and Beyond*. Thousand Oaks, CA: Sage.

Silvergleid, C. & Mankowski, E. (2006). How batterer intervention programs work: Participant and facilitator accounts of processes of change. *Journal of Family Violence*, 21, 139–159.

Shlonsky, A., Friend, C. & Lambert, L. (2007). From culture clash to new possibilities: A harm reduction approach to family violence and child protection services. *Brief Treatment and Crisis Intervention*, 7, 345–363.

Stanley, N. (2011). *Children Experiencing Domestic Violence: A Research Review*. Dartington: RIP.

Stanley, N., Graham-Kevan, N. & Borthwick, R. (2012). Fathers and domestic violence: Building motivation for change through perpetrator programmes, *Child Abuse Review*, 4, 264–274.

Stanley, N. & Humphreys, C. (2014). Multi-agency risk assessment and management for children and families experiencing domestic violence, *Children and Youth Services Review*, 47(1), 78–85.

Stanley, N., Borthwick, R., Graham-Kevan, N. & Chamberlain, R. (2011b). *Strength to Change: Report of the Evaluation of a New Initiative for Perpetrators of Domestic Violence*. Preston: University of Central Lancashire.

Stanley, N., Miller, P., Richardson-Foster, H. & Thomson, G. (2011a). A stop-start response: Social services' interventions with children and families notified following domestic violence incidents, *British Journal of Social Work*, 41(2), 296–313.

Thiara, R. K. & Gill, A. (2009). *Violence Against Women in South Asian Communities: Issues for Policy and Practice*. London: Jessica Kingsley Publications.

Thomson, G., Stanley, N. & Miller, P. (2013). Give me 'strength to change': Insights into a social marketing campaign in the North of England, *Primary Health Care Research and Development*, 14, 350–359.

Van Wormer, K. & Bednar, S. (2002). Abuse interventions working with male batterers: A restorative-strengths perspective. *Families in Society: The Journal of Contemporary Human Services*, 83(5/6), 557–565.

Wilson, I., Graham, K. & Taft, A. (2014). Alcohol interventions, alcohol policy and intimate partner violence: a systematic review, *BMC Public Health*, 14, 881. Available at: http://bmcpublichealth.biomedcentral.com/articles/10.1186/147 1-2458-14-881

11

FAMILY RISK AND RESPONSIVE REGULATION

*Joan Pennell**

Introduction

Narrowing risk assessment to the judgement of workers closes out the insights of children and their families and local communities. Stories from the US state of North Carolina propose a viable alternative of collectively identifying concerns and determining solutions that safeguard children and their families. To support this enlarged input, child welfare systems have adopted inclusionary decision-making practices such as family group conferencing and, in North Carolina, child and family team meetings. The term 'child and family teams' (CFTs) originated in child mental health but in North Carolina is also used in child welfare. Child and family teams are seen as integral to wrapping services around children and their families in a manner that creates a responsive and unified system of care (Burchard & Burchard, 2000).

Across types of forums, the intent is to bring together the immediate family with their informal and formal networks to make plans in which all participants can invest their caring and resources to reach resolutions. Two important groups often excluded from these forums are youth and fathers. Workers may worry that young people who are already traumatized will be overloaded by the subject matter under deliberation and that fathers who have committed domestic violence will intimidate their children's mother and other family group members (Hayden et al., 2014; Ptacek, 2010). It is clear that precautionary steps are warranted so that participation is respectful and productive.

Drawing on experiences from the field, this chapter reviews two strategies for supporting family engagement in assessing and managing risks. The first is preparing foster youth for participating in decision making with their families

---

* Joan Pennell is a professor of social work at North Carolina State University, USA.

and service providers. The second is educating men who have a history of committing domestic violence about responsible fatherhood. Both strategies are placed within a framework of *restorative regulation*. A restorative regulatory system responds flexibly to risk, and when safe and feasible, it engages key stakeholders in preventing future harm. The affirming process and resulting actions have the potential of restoring relationships. The conclusions reflect on the contributions that restorative regulation can make to attenuating risk and expanding democratic practice.

Restorative regulation

The term 'restorative regulation' references two, often intersecting, theoretical frameworks: restorative justice and responsive regulation. Restorative justice starts from the premise that people, not the state, own their conflicts (Christie, 1977). Accordingly, people should be brought together to determine and enact collaborative solutions to their shared concerns. This approach is not new and is rooted in indigenous and faith-based traditions from around the globe (Sullivan & Tifft, 2006), and as one Guatemalan practitioner reflected, 'We are already doing a lot of this work without a name' (Roby et al., 2014, p. 9).

Today, a range of models are available in different countries to put restorative justice into practice, such as family group conferencing and healing circles (van Wormer & Walker, 2013; Zinsstag & Vanfraechem, 2012). These democratizing practices can for participants of different ages affirm their sense of moral agency (Calhoun & Pelech, 2010), strengthen their family and community networks (Pennell & Anderson, 2005), develop their problem-solving skills transferrable to other situations (Gal, 2011) and provide a base from which to develop more collaborative relationships with service providers (van Pagée, van Lieshout & Wolthuis, 2012).

Involving people in resolving their issues, however, does not mean leaving them to their own devices. State intervention is called for when families do not provide adequate care and protection for their children and when people abuse their intimate partners. Here the framework of responsive regulation serves as a means of combining, in conceptual and practical terms, state regulatory functions and restorative justice.

Responsive regulation, initially developed to address infractions in the private sector, presents an alternative to rule-bound procedures to enforce compliance by punishing offenders (Ayres & Braithwaite, 1992). Such top-down approaches are likely to provoke court action and become quite costly to government regulators in time and resources. Rather than simply applying sanctions, responsive regulators gauge the level of risk and respond flexibly to the situation. Responsive regulators may first engage the business in collaboratively identifying and implementing remedies. Only when this restorative justice approach fails does the regulator advance up what has been conceived as a 'regulatory pyramid' to methods of deterrence such as inspections and fines or incapacitation such as criminal penalties and revoking licences (Braithwaite, 2002).

It must be emphasized that the assessment of risk does not in itself determine the regulatory response. The risk may be high, but if the company is taking appropriate corrective measures, escalating up the regulatory pyramid may discourage the company and impede progress. Nevertheless, the clear possibility of recourse to disciplinary measures at the narrow apex of the pyramid may in itself prompt participation in deliberations at its broad base and prevent upward escalation. Moreover, changing circumstances may mean that the regulator can de-escalate and return to less expensive and often more effective self-regulation by firms. As John Braithwaite (2011) observes, 'The job of responsive regulators is to treat offenders as worthy of trust, because the evidence is that when they do this, regulation more often achieves its objectives' (para. 23).

More recently, the applicability of responsive regulation in different fields, including child welfare and domestic violence, has been identified (Adams, 2004). If there is immediate risk of serious harm, the involved authorities may need to remove children from their home or arrest violent partners. Even if these interventions are taken, workers can move down the regulatory pyramid to restorative practices, or better yet, with sufficient safeguards in place, they can begin with inclusionary processes. An early Canadian study of family group conferencing found no violence occurring at the deliberations and found post-conference reductions in family violence as reported by family group members, child protection and police (Pennell & Burford, 2000).

The available evidence points either to positive effects or to no harm resulting from restorative practices in criminal justice. Strang and colleagues (2013) conducted a meta-analysis of ten trials, in which cases were randomly assigned to restorative justice conferencing or to prosecution. They report that conferencing has a small but significant effect (Cohen's $d = -.155$; $p = .001$) on reducing rates of conviction or arrest two years later. A literature review by Weatherburn and Macadam (2013) of only post-2007 studies concludes that restorative justice offending has little impact on reoffending rates. Contrary to fears that victims will be harmed by contact with offenders, both reviews report victim satisfaction with restorative justice proceedings.

Randomized controlled trials in child protection are limited in number. Nevertheless, comparative studies of families with and without conferencing yield a persistent finding. Involving the family group in deliberations increases the likelihood that children will be reunified with their families or placed with kin (Ottolini, 2011; Pennell, Edwards & Burford, 2010). These effects are particularly pronounced for African American and Latinx children (Wang et al., 2012).

Conferencing also reduces the anxiety of children in care, possibly because they see tangible evidence of their families continued active involvement in their lives, and conference participation increases the satisfaction of parents and relatives with the decision-making process and its comprehensiveness in addressing issues (Sheets et al., 2009). Another notable effect of conferencing in child welfare is providing an initial boost to families receiving needed services, particularly parenting services, children's counselling and mental health treatment for parents (Weigensberg, Barth & Guo, 2009). Although this effect tapers off over time, it is important to consider how early uptake may improve families' relationship with child welfare, build parenting capacity and address children's behavioural health issues.

Rather than comparing families with and without meetings, researchers may instead analyse the relationship between outcomes and fidelity to the wider efforts towards change in which the meetings take place. This is the approach used for child and family teams embedded in systems of care. A North Carolina study (Graves, 2005) measured caregiver and young people's perceptions of adherence to system-of-care principles, including child and family teams. The study found a statistically significant and positive association between fidelity and increases in caregiver satisfaction and decreases in children's behaviours that are internalizing (e.g. depression) or externalizing (e.g. aggression).

Participant satisfaction with the deliberations and their follow through on the action steps point to the pivotal role of conferencing in improving plans. As John Braithwaite (2014) identifies, restorative justice and responsive regulation are each a 'meta-strategy' to select strategies to address the areas of concern. Given their short duration and their demarcated function, even modest effects from restorative processes, he notes, are remarkable. Accordingly, he proposes that research be devoted less to the effects of restorative justice and responsive regulation and more to enhancing the process of selecting beneficial strategies. It is the latter charge that this chapter addresses.

The examples from North Carolina each offer distinct means of improving the selection of strategies to assess and manage risk. From different vantage points, they contribute to understanding restorative processes within the regulatory system of public child welfare. These vantage points are those of youth who are in care and fathers who abuse their intimate partners.

The importance of being important

The adverse and long-term consequences of trauma on children's physical, emotional, cognitive, and social development have been well documented (Centers for Disease Control and Prevention, 2014), and these effects are certainly apparent for many youth in care. Foster youth have faced both trauma in the home and trauma resulting from displacement from their families and often as well displacement from their schools and communities (Smithgall, Jarpe-Ratner & Walker, 2010). These experiences disrupt relationships and generate a sense of helplessness. Compared to youth not in care, foster youth have lower educational attainment (National Working Group on Foster Care and Education, 2014) and higher rates of substance use (Braciszewski & Stout, 2012), behavioural disorder, post-traumatic stress disorder and attention deficit hyperactivity disorder (Havlicek, Garcia & Smith, 2013). Not surprisingly, children and youth in care pose a risk to themselves, having above normal levels of suicide and attempted suicide (Katz et al., 2011).

Regaining a sense of mattering is crucial for foster youth. One mechanism for doing so is participating in decision-making forums about their own affairs. A survey of foster youth in North Carolina, developed in consultation with a youth advisory council, asked whether respondents had taken part in a CFT and if they 'feel important' at these deliberations. The youth who participated in their CFT overwhelmingly affirmed feeling important at their CFT (Hall, Pennell & Rikard, 2015). Furthermore, matched school-child welfare data from 347 meetings found that if youth were present at their meetings, they were less likely to change their placements, creating more stability in their lives (Pennell & Rikard, 2013). Far too often, though, foster youth are not in attendance at the meetings (Hall et al., 2015), and their absence is indicative of a pattern in many places (Crampton & Pennell, 2009).

In response, practice guidance for family meetings urges the inclusion of all family members and their preparation, with special attention devoted to children and youth who have experienced maltreatment (American Humane Association, 2010; Burford, Pennell & MacLeod, 1995). To support inclusionary approaches, the North Carolina Division of Social Services adopted the definition for child and family teams endorsed by a state-wide collaborative of youth and family organizations and public agencies: 'Child and family teams are family members and their community supports that come together to ***create, implement and update*** a plan ***with*** the child, youth/student and family' (North Carolina Collaborative, 2007, p. 1, emphasis in original). The policy manual of the North Carolina Division of Social Services (NC DHHS, 2009) iterates, 'It is not a question about **whether** the children/youth should be involved in the process, but rather **how** they should be involved in the process' (p. 13, emphasis in original). The manual further stresses that in determining the extent and type of the young people's participation, their 'own wishes shall be the first consideration' (p. 13). The manual particularly recommends that young people have the opportunity to select a support person or mentor to stay by them during the meeting and, with their permission, speak on their behalf.

Validation of inclusionary approaches by the state collaborative and public child welfare system helps to promote a regulatory context that supports restorative practices. Stopping here, though, is insufficient. Given the extensive variability in including young people, reinforcement from multiple directions is necessary. This means having an integrated strategy with clear performance standards (Connolly & Smith, 2010) and a series of implementation drivers (Kaye, DePanfilis, Bright & Fisher, 2012). One strategy is making it mandatory for workers to invite youth to meetings or to follow strict protocols in requesting a waiver from this requirement (Crampton & Pennell, 2009). Such agency policies, however, do not necessarily result in young people feeling welcomed and included.

It is incumbent on agencies to seek feedback from a range of participants, including young people, about whether key practices for promoting family empowerment actually occurred – that is, measuring model fidelity (Pennell, 2004; Rauktis, Bishop-Fitzpatrick, Jung & Pennell, 2013). A Pennsylvania study reports significantly higher levels of perceived model fidelity by White participants as compared to African Americans and by professionals as compared to family group members (Rauktis, Huefner & Cahalane, 2011). Such feedback can then be used to take corrective action to improve the process, to link delivery of the intended model to the outcomes for children and their families and fundamentally to acknowledge that the participants' views are valued.

A frequently used strategy is training service providers. The trainings are enriched by involving youth in curricular development and delivery, and as long as adults are assisted in engaging their youth partners in a respectful manner, the process helps to build youth's sense of efficacy and self-worth (Clay, Amodeo & Collins, 2010). The co-training model is applied by the Center for Family and Community Engagement at North Carolina State University. This means pairing trainers who have received services (family or youth partners) with those who have delivered services (agency partners). It also means creating a supportive context by establishing a cross-system collaborative to recruit, train and network the training partners.

Follow-up surveys of co-trained sessions found that the large majority of participants took away insights that benefited to the youth and families with whom they worked. Giving examples, participants wrote that as a result of the co-trained sessions, they were arranging CFT meetings to 'help [youth] construct realistic goals for themselves', 'allowing them to have more input' and to have 'more sensitivity in addressing issues of [the] teen during the meet[ing]' (Pennell, 2013, p. 30).

All too often, youth are not clear about what CFT meetings are and what the youth's role is in them. In response, the centre conducted focus groups with foster youth about their experiences in care and what they needed in order to plan for their futures. From this foundation were developed two mutually supportive and well-received curricula, one directed to workers and the other directed to youth. The first, for workers, is intended to assist participants in engaging youth in CFT meetings as they prepare for leaving care. The second, for youth, helps the participants understand how to make good use of the meetings. An especially appreciated exercise asks youth to identify possible support persons for their CFT meetings. Having a youth partner in the training room provides a reassuring person with whom the youth participants can connect. Behind the scenes, agency coordinators work with the trainers on the arrangements for youth attending the sessions and, if it became necessary, supporting the youth afterwards.

Robust preparation for participating in decision making is essential to effective restorative practices at the base of the responsive regulatory pyramid. For foster youth who so often feel marginalized, being invited to and welcomed at CFT meetings is vital to their gaining a positive sense of identity and learning how to work with others in setting constructive goals and action steps. At heart, these same principles apply to men who abuse their intimate partners.

Learning patience

Abuse of women is widespread globally (Garcia-Moreno et al., 2005). It negatively affects its victims physically, psychologically and economically (Black et al., 2011), and it poses a threat to their children. Exposure to domestic violence increases children's risk of maltreatment and fatality in the United States (USDHHS, 2013) and elsewhere (Chan, 2011; Krug, Dahlberg, Mercy, Zwi & Lozano, 2002) and can lead to children's placement in foster care. Fathers who abuse may estrange children from their mothers or may estrange themselves from their children and partners and then move on to new households and perpetrate further abuse (Bancroft, Silverman & Ritchie, 2012). This means that children miss out on positive co-parenting that promotes their healthy development (Lamb, 2010; Lee, Bellamy & Guterman, 2009) and may lead to their exhibiting externalizing and internalizing behaviours (Herrenkohl, Sousa, Tajima, Herrenkohl & Moylan, 2008). It also means that men lose out on the opportunity to grow into responsible fathers and partners.

Child protection workers invest far more in working with mothers than with fathers, who are commonly viewed as having limited skills as parents, as hard to contact and as potentially dangerous, especially if they have a history of domestic violence (Gordon, Oliveros, Hawes, Iwamoto & Rayford, 2012). Quite often workers are unaware of the contact that young Black fathers maintain with the children and their mother, something encouraged by the extended family network (Roy & Vesely, 2010). Restorative practices offer a means of countering workers' omission or exclusion of fathers by engaging them and their side of the family in decision making (Gunderson et al., 2003).

According to a North Carolina study by Francis (2008), child protection workers and women's advocates identified a number of positive outcomes of CFT meetings for abused women. A domestic violence advocate stated that CFTs brought the family members and the involved organizations together to figure out plans to help them through crises. According to a child protection worker, the CFT meetings served as a forum in which to let the perpetrator know that domestic violence was 'flat out unacceptable' (Francis, 2008, p. 112). A domestic violence advocate referring to abusive husbands and fathers iterated, 'You can't hold them accountable without engaging them with their children—safely and in a productive way' (Francis, 2008, p. 120).

A recurring question about family group conferences, CFT meetings and family-involvement meetings in general is whether they should be held if the family had a history of domestic violence. To address this quite legitimate question, consultations in North Carolina were held with women's groups about safety measures. These groups included the North Carolina Coalition Against Domestic Violence, shelter staff, former shelter residents (Pennell & Francis, 2005) and female participants, both workers and family members (Pennell & Koss, 2011). Much of their advice reflected good practice for any family group meeting, such as clarifying purpose; conferring on invitees and arrangements; preparing participants; building commitment to respectful and safe ways of taking part in the meetings; and assessing and monitoring for safety (see American Humane Association, 2010; Burford et al., 1995).

Survivors should be encouraged to identify a support person to stay by them during the meetings and to monitor their safety. Likewise, men who abuse should be assisted in identifying support persons who will help them maintain self-control. Inviting women's advocates to speak about the dynamics and impact of family violence can help with enlarging the family groups' understanding and can enrich the planning. Workers should check on whether a no-contact order is in place and make sure that its terms are upheld. This may mean holding staggered meetings with the mother present in the first half and the father in the second half (Pennell & Kim, 2010).

Another way of preparing men who abuse for taking part in CFTs is by helping them to gain a greater understanding of the impact of domestic violence on their children and to learn positive communication and parenting approaches. These are the focus of Strong Fathers, a fathering programme for men who abuse that has been developed and tested in North Carolina. Over the course of the group sessions, the men come to acknowledge their lack of patience with their children, push themselves to acquire parenting skills, develop non-confrontational ways of relating to their partners and children and redefine masculinity as a responsible family leader (Pennell, Sanders, Rikard, Shepherd & Starsoneck, 2013).

The pre-/post-assessments by the child protection workers show a substantial drop in findings that children are in need of protection and that domestic violence is occurring in the household (Pennell, Rikard & Sanders, 2014). Focus groups and interviews held with child protection workers and representatives from different community groups further testify to the men's growth. For instance, a worker commented, 'I saw a huge difference in the father midway through the programme. At the end, he was a different person.' In addition, they point to the men transferring learning from the group to how they participate in CFTs. One example that was provided concerns a father who walked out of the CFT meeting, but with the assistance of his support person, he returned, apologized and was able to explain why he had become so frustrated. Engaging in the CFT meeting for this father built on his prior learning in Strong Fathers and provided new learning about the importance of patience in emotionally charged deliberations.

Restorative regulation and risk

As the case with other restorative practices, CFT meetings are not intended to be therapeutic treatments but often have therapeutic impacts. The process is self-affirming as reported by the foster youth, and it places demands on adults to act responsibly as found by the men enrolled in Strong Fathers. These positive results mitigate the likelihood of harm to self or others at a time when participants are experiencing considerable uncertainty about their futures. For foster youth, it may be facing the imminence of transitions out of care; for Strong Father participants, it may be facing the permanency of separations from partners and children.

Besides the benefits from participation itself, restorative practices are a meta-strategy for selecting constructive and comprehensive strategies (Braithwaite, 2014). As reported earlier, the available evidence indicates that family groups understand the needs of their relatives, formulate sound plans and are generous in offering their own resources, including their homes. Studies show that family-involvement meetings in child welfare reunify children with their families or place them with relatives, give an initial boost to the utilization of an array of needed services and lessen the anxiety of children about losing their family connections.

The ensuing benefits would likely be greater if children and youth were consistently at their meetings. For instance, as previously discussed, a North Carolina study found an association between children's presence at their CFT meeting and a decreased likelihood of changing placements. To alter practice requires multiple implementation drivers, including CFT policy, training by paired agency and youth partner trainers, directing the training to both workers and the youth and seeking out participants' perspectives of the extent to which the practice is in keeping with principles of empowerment. Including men who abuse also requires attention to safety measures and to educating them on communication and engagement with their families. All this not only supports restorative practices but also a responsive system attuned to the people they are intended to serve.

The restorative impact of the meetings is enhanced by their placement at the base of a regulatory pyramid. The meetings offer an opportunity for family members to have a significant role in the decision making. At the same time, the participants know that with or without their involvement, plans need to be set in place as to where children will live or what family services are required. This awareness may have motivated the return of the frustrated father who walked out of the CFT meeting. More broadly, though, the value of taking part in CFT meetings is felt by child and adult participants precisely because they know that the restorative practice is connected to the regulatory structure of the agency and to its capacity to approve services and authorize expenditures on these services.

'The most important way we improve regulation, according to the responsive approach, is by conceiving of regulatory culture not as a rulebook but as a storybook and helping one another to get better at sharing instructive stories' (Braithwaite, 2011, para. 67). In this spirit, the chapter offered some stories from the field that may be instructive for others in developing their own restorative practices within responsive systems. The overarching moral of the North Carolina tales is that a culture of restorative regulation instils norms that encourage agencies to involve families in decision making and that support families in making wise decisions over their affairs. This generates a virtuous circle of learning that diminishes the risks that family members face in their lives or pose to others. Fundamentally, restorative regulation moves beyond a paradigm focusing on risk to enlarging the space for democratic engagement.

References

Adams, P. (ed.) (2004). Restorative justice and responsive regulation, Special issue of *Journal of Sociology and Social Welfare*, 31(1).

American Humane Association and the FGDM Guidelines Committee (2010). *Guidelines for family group decision making in child welfare.* Englewood, CO: Author. Retrieved from www.ucdenver.edu/academics/colleges/medicalschool/departments/pediatrics/subs/can/FGDM/Pages/FGDM.aspx

Ayres, I. & Braithwaite, J. (1992). *Responsive regulation: Transcending the deregulation debate.* New York: Oxford University Press.

Bancroft, L., Silverman, J. G. & Ritchie, D. (2012). *The batterer as parent: Addressing the impact of domestic violence on family dynamics* (2nd edn). Los Angeles, CA: Sage.

Black, M. C., Basile, K. C., Breiding, M. J., Smith, S. G., Walters, M. L., Merrick, M. T., Chen, J. & Stevens, M. R. (2011). *The national intimate partner and sexual violence survey: 2010 Summary report.* Atlanta, GA: National Center for Injury Prevention and Control, Centers for Disease Control and Prevention. Retrieved from www.cdc.gov/ViolencePrevention/pdf/NISVS_Report2010-a.pdf

Braciszewski, J. M. & Stout, R. L. (2012). Substance use among current and former foster youth: A systematic review. *Children and Youth Services Review*, 34, 2337–2344. http://dx.doi.org/10.1016/j.childyouth.2012.08.011

Braithwaite, J. (2002). *Restorative justice and responsive regulation.* New York: Oxford University Press.

Braithwaite, J. (2011). The essence of responsive regulation. *UBC Law Review*, 44, 475–520.

Braithwaite, J. (2014). Restorative justice and responsive regulation: The question of evidence. Plenary presentation at *Responsive Regulation, Restorative Justice, and Complex Problems Conference*, University of Vermont, Burlington, VT.

Burchard, J. D. & Burchard, S. N. (2000). The wraparound process with children and families, in G. Burford & J. Hudson (eds), *Family group conferencing: New directions in community-centered child and family practice* (pp. 140–152). Hawthorne, NY: Aldine de Gruyter.

Burford, G., Pennell, J. & MacLeod, S. (August 1995). *Manual for coordinators and communities: The organization and practice of family group decision making* (revised). St. John's, NL: Memorial University of Newfoundland, School of Social Work. Retrieved from http://faculty.chass.ncsu.edu/pennell//fgdm/manual

Calhoun, A. & Pelech, W. (2010). Responding to young people responsible for harm: A comparative study of restorative and conventional approaches, *Criminal Justice Review*, 13, 287–306. doi:10.1080/10282580.2010.498238

Centers for Disease Control and Prevention (2014). *Injury prevention & control: Adverse childhood experiences (ACE) study.* Retrieved from www.cdc.gov/violenceprevention/acestudy/

Chan, K. (2011). Co-occurrence of intimate partner violence and child abuse in Hong Kong Chinese families, *Journal of Interpersonal Violence*, 26(7), 1322–1342.

Christie, N. (1977). Conflicts as property, *British Journal of Criminology*, 17, 1–14.

Clay, C., Amodeo, M. & Collins, M. E. (2010). Youth as partners in curriculum development and training delivery: Roles, challenges, benefits, and recommendations, *Families in Society*, 91(2), 135–141. doi:10.1606/1044-3894.3071

Connolly, M. & Smith, R. (2010). Reforming child welfare: An integrated approach, *Child Welfare*, 89(3), 9–31.

Crampton, D. S. & Pennell, J. (2009). Family-involvement meetings with older children in foster care: Intuitive appeal, promising practices and the challenge of child welfare reform, in B. Kerman, M. Freundlich & A. N. Maluccio (eds), *Achieving permanence for older children and youth in foster care* (pp. 266–290). New York: Columbia University Press.

Francis, S. L. (2008). *Current interventions in co-occurring child maltreatment and domestic violence: A qualitative study of changing policy, practice and collaboration in North Carolina*. Doctoral thesis, University of North Carolina at Chapel Hill.

Gal, T. (2011). *Child victims and restorative justice: A needs-rights model.* New York: Oxford University Press.

Garcia-Moreno, C., Jansen, H., Ellsberg, M., Heise, L. & Watts, C. (2005). *WHO multi-country study on women's health and domestic violence against women.* Geneva: World Health Organization. Retrieved from www.who.int/gender/violence/who_multicountry_study/summary_report/en/index.html

Gordon, D. M., Oliveros, A., Hawes, S. W., Iwamoto, D. K. & Rayford, B. S. (2012). Engaging fathers in child protection services: A review of factors and strategies across ecological systems, *Children and Youth Services Review*, 34, 1399–1417. doi:10.1016/j.childyouth.2012.03.021

Graves, K. N. (2005). The links among perceived adherence to the system of care philosophy, consumer satisfaction, and improvements in child functioning, *Journal of Child and Family Studies*, 14(3), 403–415.

Hall, J., Pennell, J. & Rikard, R. V. (2015). Child and family team meetings: The need for youth participation in educational success, in T. Gal & B. Faedi Duramy (eds), *International perspectives and empirical findings on child participation: From social exclusion to child-inclusive policies* (pp. 207–226). Oxford: Oxford University Press.

Hayden, A., Gelsthorpe, L., Kingi, V. & Morris, A. (eds) (2014). *A restorative approach to family violence: Changing tack.* Surrey, UK: Ashgate.

Herrenkohl, T., Sousa, C., Tajima, E., Herrenkohl, R. & Moylan, C. (2008). Intersection of child abuse and children's exposure to domestic violence, *Trauma, Violence & Abuse*, 9(2), 84–99.

Katz, L. Y., Au, W., Singal, D., Brownell, M., Roos, N., Marten, P. J., Chateau, D., Enns, M. W., Kozyrskyj, A. L. & Sareen, J. (2011). Suicide and suicide attempts in children and adolescents in the child welfare system, *CMAJ*, 183(17), 1977–1981.

Kaye, S., DePanfilis, D., Bright, C. L. & Fisher, C. (2012). Applying implementation drivers to child welfare systems change: Examples from the field, *Journal of Public Child Welfare*, 6(4), 512–530. doi:10.1080/15548732.2012.701841

Krug, E., Dahlberg, L., Mercy, J., Zwi, A. & Lozano, R. (eds) (2002). *World report on violence and health.* Geneva: World Health Organization. Retrieved from http://whqlibdoc.who.int/publications/2002/9241545615_eng.pdf

Lamb, M. (Ed.). (2010). *The role of the father in child development* (5th edn). Hoboken, NJ: John Wiley & Sons.

Lee, S., Bellamy, J. & Guterman, N. (2009). Fathers, physical child abuse, and neglect: Advancing the knowledge base, *Child Maltreatment*, 14(3), 227–231.

National Working Group on Foster Care and Education (2014). *Fostering success in education: National factsheet on the educational outcomes of children in foster care.* Retrieved from www.fostercareandeducation.org/NationalWorkGroup.aspx

North Carolina Collaborative for Children, Youth and Families (2007). *Child and family teams.* Retrieved from http://nccollaborative.poweredbyeden.com/files/647/27508.pdf

North Carolina Department of Health and Human Services, Division of Social Services [NC DHHS] (2009). *Family Services manual*, Vol. I: Children's Services, Chapter VII: Child and Family Team Meetings. Raleigh, NC: Author. Retrieved from http://info.dhhs.state.nc.us/olm/manuals/dss/csm-55/man/CSVII.pdf

Ottolini, D. (2011). *The family conferencing: A ground-breaking practice for community based child protection in Kenya.* Limuru, Kenya: Franciscan Kolbe Press. Retrieved from http://resourcecentre.savethechildren.se/sites/default/files/documents/the_family_conferencing_-_diego_ottolini1.pdf

Pennell, J. (2004). Family group conferencing in child welfare: Responsive and regulatory interfaces, *Journal of Sociology and Social Welfare*, 31(1), 117–135.

Pennell, J. (with Allen-Eckard, K., King, J. & Latz, M.) (September 2013). *Family-Centered Practice Project: Annual report to the North Carolina Division of Social Services, fiscal year 2012–2013: Summary report.* Raleigh, NC: North Carolina State University, Center for Family & Community Engagement. Retrieved from http://cfface.chass.ncsu.edu/documents/2012_2013_FCPP_Summary_of_Annual_Report-Final.pdf

Pennell, J. & Anderson, G. (eds) (2005). *Widening the circle: The practice and evaluation of family group conferencing with children, youths, and their families.* Washington, DC: NASW Press.

Pennell, J. & Burford, G. (2000). Family group decision making: Protecting children and women, *Child Welfare*, 79(2), 131–158.

Pennell, J., Edwards, M. & Burford, G. (2010). Expedited family group engagement and child permanency, *Children and Youth Services Review*, 32, 1012–1019. doi: 10.1016/j.childyouth.2010.03.029

Pennell, J. & Francis, S. (2005). Safety conferencing: Toward a coordinated and inclusive response to safeguard women and children, *Violence Against Women*, 11(5), 666–692. doi:10.1177/1077801205274569

Pennell, J. & Kim, M. (2010). Opening conversations across cultural, gender, and generational divides: Family and community engagement to stop violence against women and children, in J. Ptacek (ed.), *Restorative justice and violence against women* (pp. 177–192). New York: Oxford University Press.

Pennell, J. & Koss, M. P. (2011). Feminist perspectives on family rights: Social work and restorative justice processes to stop women abuse, in E. Beck, N. P. Kropf & P. B. Leonard (eds), *Social work and restorative justice: Skills for dialogue, peacemaking, and reconciliation* (pp. 195–219). New York: Oxford University Press.

Pennell, J. & Rikard, R. V. (June 2013). *Fostering Youth Educational Success: Final evaluation report.* Grant Number 90CO1075/01, U.S. Department of Health and Human Services, Administration for Child and Families, Children's Bureau. Retrieved from http://cfface.chass.ncsu.edu/documents/Fostering_YES_Final_Report_June_2013_edited_v3.pdf

Pennell, J., Rikard, R. V. & Sanders, T. (2014). Family violence: Fathers assessing and managing their risk to children and women, *Children and Youth Services Review,* 47, 36–45. doi: 10.1016/j.childyouth.2013.11.004

Pennell, J., Sanders, T., Rikard, R. V., Shepherd, J. & Starsoneck, L. (2013). Family violence, fathers, and restoring personhood, *Restorative Justice,* 1(2), 268–289. doi: 10.5235/2050472.1.1.2.1

Ptacek, J. (Ed.). (2010). *Restorative justice and violence against women.* New York: Oxford University Press.

Rauktis, M. E., Huefner, J. & Cahalane, H. (2011). Perceptions of fidelity to family group decision-making principles: examining the impact of race, gender and relationship, *Child Welfare,* 90(4), 41–60.

Roby, J. L., Pennell, J., Rotabi, K., Bunkers, K. M. & de Uclés, S. (2014). Contextual adaptation of family group conferencing model: Early evidence from Guatemala, *British Journal of Social Work* [Advance Access], 1–17 doi:10.1093/bjsw/bcu053

Rauktis, M. E., Bishop-Fitzpatrick, L., Jung, N. & Pennell, J. (2013). Family group decision making: Measuring fidelity to practice principles in public child welfare, *Children and Youth Services Review,* 35, 287–295. doi: 10.1016/j.childyouth.2012.11.001

Roy, K. M. & Vesely, C. K. (2010). Caring for the family child: Kin networks of young low-income African American fathers, in R. L. Coles & C. Green (eds), *The myth of the missing Black father* (pp. 215–240). New York: Columbia University Press.

Sheets, J., Wittenstrom, K., Fong, R., James, J., Tecci, M., Baumann, D. J. & Rodriguez, C. (2009). Evidence-based practice in family group decision-making for Anglo, African American and Hispanic families, *Children and Youth Services Review,* 31, 1187–1191. doi:10.1016/j.childyouth.2009.08.003

Strang, H., Sherman, L. W., Mayo-Wilson, E., Woods, D. & Ariel, B. (2013). Restorative justice conferencing (RJC) using face-to-face meetings of offenders and victims: Effects on offender recidivism and victim satisfaction. A Systematic Review. *Campbell Systematic Reviews.* doi:10.4073/csr.2013.12

Smithgall, C., Jarpe-Ratner, E. & Walker, L. (2010). *Looking back, moving forward: Using integrated assessments to examine the educational experiences of children entering foster care.* Chicago, IL: Chapin Hall, University of Chicago.

Sullivan, D. & Tifft, L. (eds) (2006). *Handbook of restorative justice: A global perspective.* New York: Routledge.

U.S. Department of Health and Human Services, Administration for Children and Families, Administration on Children, Youth and Families, Children's Bureau [USDHHS]. (2013). *Child Maltreatment 2012.* Available from_www.acf.hhs.gov/programs/cb/research-data-technology/statistics-research/child-maltreatment

Van Pagée, R., van Lieshout J. & Wolthuis, A. (2012). Most things look better when arranged in a circle: Family group conferencing empowers societal developments in the Netherlands, in E. Zinsstag & I. Vanfraechem (eds) (2012). *Conferencing and restorative justice: International practices and perspectives* (pp. 217–230). Oxford: Oxford University Press.

van Wormer, K. S. & Walker, L. (eds) (2013). *Restorative justice today: Practical applications*. Los Angeles, CA: Sage.

Wang, E. W., Lambert, M. C., Johnson, L. E., Boudreau, B., Breidenbach, R. & Baumann, D. (2012). Expediting permanent placement from foster care systems: The role of family group decision-making, *Children and Youth Services Review*, 34(4), 845–850. doi:10.1016/j.childyouth.2012.01.015

Weatherburn, D. & Macadam, M. (2013). A review of restorative justice responses to reoffending. *Evidence Base*, 1, 1–18. Retrieved from http://journal.anzsog.edu.au/publications/4/EvidenceBase2013Issue1.pdf

Weigensberg, E. C., Barth, R. P. & Guo, S. (2009). Family group decision making: A propensity score analysis to evaluate child and family services at baseline and after 36-months, *Children and Youth Services Review*, 31, 383–390. doi:10.1016/j.childyouth.2008.09.001

Zinsstag, E. & Vanfraechem, I. (eds) (2012). *Conferencing and restorative justice: International practices and perspectives*. Oxford: Oxford University Press.

12

RESPONDING DIFFERENTLY TO NEGLECT: AN ECOLOGICAL APPROACH TO PREVENTION, ASSESSMENT AND TREATMENT

Justine Harris and Robyn Mildon[*]

Introduction

When we talk about child neglect, we usually link it inextricably to the physical abuse of children. We talk about child physical abuse and neglect as if they are synonymous and inseparable. While subtypes of abuse (for example, physical abuse, emotional abuse, neglect) clearly coexist and are rarely seen in isolation, subsuming physical abuse and neglect can create unhelpful assumptions that they have the same aetiology and responsiveness to change (Tsantefski & Connolly 2013). This is important because if we respond to neglect as if it is the same as physical abuse, we lose a potential opportunity to tailor our responses in ways that might result in better outcomes for children. In this chapter, we look at the particular nature of neglect and consider how we might respond in these more nuanced ways. We review the current knowledge on risk factors in child neglect, the contributing factors within the child's ecology and the implications for community-wide prevention and individualized approaches to assessment and treatment.

Child neglect is the most common type of child maltreatment and is also more likely to recur than other forms of maltreatment, even after involvement with child protective services (Connell et al., 2007; Jonson-Reid et al., 2013; U.S. Department of Health and Human Services

---

[*] Justine Harris is senior advisor for Evidence in Practice and Policy at the Centre for Evidence and Implementation, Victoria Australia. Robyn Mildon is the head of the Centre for Evidence and Implementation and is an associate professor at the University of Melbourne, Australia.

[USDHHS], 2012). In the United States, in the 2012 report on maltreatment, more than 78 per cent of substantiated cases were for children who had experienced child neglect compared to 18 per cent for physical abuse and 9 per cent for sexual abuse (USDHHS, 2012). Stoltonborgh and colleagues' (2013) meta-analysis on the international prevalence of neglect in the general population, which included almost 60,000 participants, found more than 15 per cent of children in the general population were estimated to experience neglect (Stoltonborgh et al., 2013). In a US study the authors estimated that at least 12 per cent of all American children will have a substantiated child protection finding, usually for neglect, before they reach their 18th birthday (Wildeman et al., 2014). Babies and toddlers are also more likely to experience neglect than any other form of maltreatment (Connell-Carrisk & Scannapieco, 2006).

Neglect has various definitions but is generally defined as an omission of a behaviour rather than as a commission of behaviour, as in the case of physical or sexual abuse (Sagatun & Edwards, 1995). A recent comprehensive definition explains neglect as 'a child who has suffered harm or the child's safety or development has been endangered as a result of a failure to provide for or protect the child. Acts of omission can include failure to adequately provide for the child's basic physical needs (physical neglect) and/or failure to supervise, obtain necessary health or mental health care, abandonment, and educational neglect' (Canadian Incidence Study of Reported Child Abuse and Neglect, Public Health Agency of Canada, 2010).

Despite high prevalence rates, limited quality research has been conducted in an attempt to understand the causes of child neglect and how to effectively intervene, compared to the body of work focusing on physical and sexual abuse of children (Dubowitz, 2007; McSherry, 2007; Stoltonborgh et al., 2013). Reasons for this lack of research includes its insidious and chronic nature compared to child physical abuse, which means it is often neglected or ignored by professionals despite its association with significant child mortality and long-lasting morbidity (Hobbs & Wynne, 2002). The resulting harm accumulates over time compared to discrete incidents in child physical abuse – for example a burn or broken limb, which naturally evokes a strong response, or child sexual abuse, where there are clear cultural prohibitions against sex with children (Dubowitz, 2007). As a result, neglect is not viewed to be as serious as physical abuse or sexual abuse (Dubowitz, 2007). Another impediment is that child physical abuse often occurs simultaneously, and it becomes the focus or priority of service involvement unless neglect is severe (Dubowitz, 2007).

More recently the 'risk paradigm' has increased the use of actuarial tools in identifying child maltreatment. Actuarial tools have proven to predict maltreatment better than clinical judgement alone as they are able to accurately forecast client behaviour, including neglect (Shlonsky & Wagner, 2005). For example, structured decision making includes a neglect index which is completed alongside an index for physical abuse. These tools reduce the discounting of neglect, because neglect is given equal priority and is not potentially overshadowed by specific incidents as the tools focus on whether there is likely to be a recurrence. While these actuarial assessments are useful for identifying cases where neglect is likely to recur, the risk factors used offer little guidance on how to intervene and how these individual risk factors interact to increase risk for children and families of ongoing neglect. In fact, that is not the intention of these instruments.

While neglect is increasingly identified, very few programmes have been shown to reduce neglect. Programmes for maltreatment which are delivered to families where neglect is identified have generally been evaluated on their ability to reduce physical neglect only. Perhaps these approaches are equally as effective for abuse and neglect. However, because the aetiology and responsiveness to change appear different or more complex in families with neglect than in families where abuse has been identified, we hypothesize that a different or additional approach is required. To respond appropriately to working with families where neglect is present, it is important to first understand the unique neglect risk factors for that child and family. Further still, understanding these risk factors can provide avenues at both a family and community level to prevent child neglect occurring rather than it being traditionally the domain of child protection alone.

A social-ecological view of risk, assessment and intervention

Child neglect has historically been viewed as a problem related solely to the parents' individual functioning; therefore, interventions were aimed within that system. As an examination of the risk factors reveals, however, child neglect is not solely an issue of an uncaring parent or lapse in parental ability (Krugman, 2014). There has been a growing paradigm shift in the field with increased recognition that child neglect is multicausal with contributing factors from a number of systems that are interrelated and need to be addressed if child neglect is to be reduced. Swenson and Chaffin's (2006) influential article on child maltreatment describes these system influences within the child's social ecology and their relationship to abuse. This focus on the child's natural ecology is a key to both assessment and effective intervention in child neglect. This conjecture is supported in the intervention literature as programmes that successfully reduce child neglect address a number of these determinants (Barlow et al., 2006).

Basic assumptions of a social-ecological model

The theory of social ecology (Bronfenbrenner, 1979) is well established in social work and the social sciences. It holds the view that human development involves an exchange between the environment and an individual. Within the context of environment or the social ecology, individuals coexist within multiple systems (Swenson & Chaffin, 2006). For example, systems in the life of an infant might consist of immediate family, extended family, neighbourhood and community. The relationship between the child and the systems in the social ecology is reciprocal and bi-directional (Swenson & Chaffin, 2006). A child's behaviour influences their parents and others in the system, and the actions of the other systems influence the child. To understand the impact of each of the systems in a child's social ecology, the proximity of each system to the child and family needs to be considered (Swenson & Chaffin, 2006). For example, the parental system is frequently most proximal to the child as it usually influences the child 24 hours per day, seven days per week. Wider family can represent the next closest system. Social-ecological theory has direct application to child neglect as there is evidence that dynamic, interactive relationships of children, parents, families and their environmental contexts shape the likelihood of infant neglect (Belsky, 1993; Bronfenbrenner & Morris, 2006).

Correlates of child neglect within each system

The following is a review of the correlates of child neglect in each system. We provide a summary and an update of evidence outlined in Swenson and Chaffin's (2006) article relating to child, parent, family and community factors which have been shown to correlate with child neglect. It is important to note that we are summarizing correlations, not causation. The following categorizations do not imply that each domain has an equal causal role or an order of importance, but rather, they assume that there are multiple spheres of influence on parental functioning (Belsky, 1993). Some of the risk factors listed for child neglect have been identified by research based on nonexperimental and correlational studies, so they are able to provide valuable information to practitioners working to identify neglected children and for researchers seeking to launch inquiries into new areas of investigation (Peterson et al., 2014). However, it limits the guidance that the research can provide for the development and implementation of effective policies and programmes. To design effective prevention and treatment policies and interventions, a continued understanding of the causal mechanisms of neglect is required (Peterson et al., 2014).

Risk Factors are broken down into dynamic risk factors (potentially changeable factors such as substance abuse by parents) and static risk factors (factors that collectively can predict neglect but are not amenable to intervention such) – for example, the age of parent.

Child factors

Static rick factors

Age of the child: Swenson and Chaffin (2006) concluded that age correlates highly with child neglect, with preschool children being especially vulnerable (Connell-Carrisk & Scannapieco, 2006). This makes sense given that parents are able to leave older children unsupervised, whereas younger children require more caretaking and are more dependent on their parents, as opposed to schools or the community (Swenson & Chaffin, 2006).

Disability: Children who have special caretaking needs, such as chronic medical conditions, developmental disabilities or physical disabilities are reported to be at higher risk for neglect (Connell et al., 2007). Having a child with a disability may contribute to levels of family stress, resulting in higher rates of involvement with child protection. However, Govindshenoy and Spencer (2007) concluded that 'the evidence base for an association of disability with abuse and neglect is weak. Psychological and emotional problems and learning difficulties appear to be associated with abuse but this association might arise because these conditions share a common aetiological pathway with abuse. There is limited evidence that physical disability predisposes to abuse' (p. 552). Therefore, more research is required to determine what, if any, association there is between neglect and disability.

Parental factors

Swenson and Chaffin (2006) concluded that parental factors are associated with neglect. Those who commit acts of child maltreatment are most often parents (80 per cent according to the U.S. Department of Health, Administration for Children & Families, Children's Bureau, 2013), and this is especially true in cases of neglect. An estimated 92 per cent of children are neglected due to the behaviour of a biological parent, compared to 64 per cent of children who get abused (Sedlak et al., 2010). Young mothers, in particular, are at a heightened risk for neglecting their children (Slack et al., 2004).

Dynamic risk factors

Substance use: Substance abuse in parents is associated with a significantly elevated risk of child neglect, with over half of parents who neglect their children meeting the criteria for a substance abuse disorder (Chaffin, Kelleher & Hollenberg, 1996). Children whose parents abuse drugs and alcohol are almost three times more likely to be neglected than children of parents who do not abuse substances (National Center on Addiction and Substance Abuse [NCASA], 1999). A recent report suggests that 63 per cent of all cases of child neglect had comorbid substance abuse in the parents (USDHHS, 2013). Parental substance abuse contributes to neglect in a number of ways, including the impaired care by the parent(s) when under the influence of drugs or alcohol, the resulting parenting difficulties for the other parent (Ammerman et al., 1999), the time using it, the time involved in looking for it and the money spent on it (Cash & Wilke, 2003). The caseworkers' perceptions of caregivers' substance abuse may also influence their perceptions of neglect and its severity (Berger et al., 2010). In summary, a number of studies have described an elevated rate of substance abuse in parents who neglect their children, controlling for at least some moderating factors (Petersen et al., 2014).

Parenting skills: Parents where neglect was substantiated were rated to have less knowledge of parenting overall on topics such as child development (Burke et al., 1998), children's needs and/or unrealistic expectations of children (Connell-Carrisk & Scannapieco, 2006). They also had fewer parental skills, such as impulse control, communication, problem solving and coping with stress (Connell-Carrisk & Scannapieco, 2006). They were rated as less warm and empathetic (Connell-Carrisk & Scannapieco, 2006). Poor parenting can be a result of a number of contributing factors, including the parent's mental health (Scannapieco & Connell-Carrick, 2005), low intellectual functioning (Connell-Carrick, 2003) and the parent's own experience of being parented (Éthier, Couture & Lacharité, 2004). These descriptive findings are not surprising, but they do not permit conclusions about causality, and Petersen and colleagues (2014) conclude that more research is needed to identify the specific constructs of parenting that are most relevant to child neglect for the purposes of identifying at-risk families and designing and implementing effective prevention and intervention efforts.

Parental mental health: Caregivers who were substantiated for neglect were also found to have a history of depression, of attempted suicides and of abuse and neglect in their own childhood (Chaffin et al., 1996; Connell-Carrisk & Scannapieco, 2006). The findings of the few existing prospective studies provide some evidence that maternal depression may play a causal role; however, it is unclear if the impact of neglecting one's children results in depression or whether the depression existed prior (Petersen et al., 2014).

Parental empathy: Several researchers have found that parental lack of empathy is associated with child neglect (Schatz & Lounds, 2007) and suggest that sensitive, empathetic mothering is not part of the caregiving environments of maltreated infants (Cicchetti, et al., 2011). Mothers who neglect are less able to 'read' and respond to their babies' emotional cues or to engage in emotional perspective taking (Dubowitz et al., 2005), and they are less expressive, offer little exchange of emotional information and acknowledge their infants less than do non-neglectful mothers (Gaudin, et al., 1996). This may reflect limited skills in interacting with their children (de Paúl & Guibert, 2008). Adolescent mothers, in particular, have shown less empathy in interactions with their babies (Schatz & Lounds, 2007).

Static risk factors

Age of mother: Young mothers are more likely to neglect their infants than are older mothers (Whitman et al., 2001). It is hypothesized that the aetiology of infant neglect by young mothers may in part be due to their lack of developmental readiness for parenthood but also by their disproportionate exposure to risk conditions compared to women who delay parenting until adulthood. Young mothers tend to experience difficult life circumstances linked to neglect, such as a maternal history of childhood maltreatment, poverty, social isolation and solo parent status, which, when compounded with their maturity, may compromise their ability to demonstrate empathy and provide adequate care (Borkowski, Whitman & Farris, 2007; Slack et al., 2004).

Relationship status: There is fairly consistent evidence that rates of child neglect are higher in families without two biological parents; however, it is not clear how these alternative family structures act as causal factors in neglect (Petersen et al., 2014). More research is required to make sense of what the contribution of relationship status is on neglect, as well as the impact that other risk factors have on this – for example, on parenting skills and social support.

Education levels of parents: Poorer rates of education in parents are found to correlate with neglect. In one study of over 900,000 children and their families, the risk of death and hospitalization was significantly higher among children with the lowest parental education level (Beiki et al., 2014). This finding could be related to the increased likelihood that parents who have low educational levels also have other risk factors, such as poverty, low parenting skills and financial and other stresses.

History of maltreatment: As noted above, adolescent mothers' childhood history of abuse and neglect is a risk factor for infant neglect. Bartlett and Easterbrooks (2015) found a correlation between maternal childhood histories of multiple maltreatment and the likelihood of infant neglect, which reduced with maternal age. However, the majority of adolescent mothers who were maltreated have not continued a pattern of maltreatment with their children (Bartlett & Easterbrooks, 2015). The increased risk of child neglect from parents who themselves experienced abuse may result from poor knowledge of appropriate parenting skills, higher rates of depression and less confidence in their ability to parent (Pears & Capaldi, 2001).

Family

One of the most significant risk factors for abuse is *family poverty* (Peterson et al., 2014; Swenson & Chaffin, 2006). Families living below the poverty line are 22 times more likely to be reported for maltreatment, mainly neglect, compared to families with higher incomes (Sedlak & Broadhurst, 1996).

Higher rates of neglect are reported in families who have poorer home environments with environmental stressors such as overcrowding, recent stressful experiences and hazardous or unsanitary home conditions (Connell-Carrisk & Scannapieco, 2006). Family poverty was also the strongest predictor of re-referral to child protective services (Connell et al., 2007). McSherry (2004) comments that poverty and neglect need to be understood as reciprocal, circular and interdependent. For example, it is the characteristics of the family – such as their ability to handle stress, access to social support and their parenting skills – that intersect with their financial hardship.

Static risk factors

Family composition: This is also an independent risk factor in the occurrence of child neglect. One study of child fatalities from neglect found that children living with adults not related to them were six times more likely to die of maltreatment from unintentional injury than those living with two biological parents (Schnitzer & Ewigman, 2008).

Social characteristics

Dynamic risk factors

Research on mothers who neglect their children found they have poorer social climates, including less social support, isolation and poor functioning within their social relationships, including less emotional support

(Connell-Carrisk & Scannapieco, 2006). The relation between social support and parenting quality was a key finding in Bartlett and Easterbrooks' (2015) study, offering further evidence of the impact of social support on neglect risk. Social support served as a buffer against infant neglect, promoting resilience – that is, reducing the intergenerational cycle of maltreatment (Armstrong et al., 2005).

Social violence was also found to be significant in neglect (Connell-Carrisk & Scannapieco, 2006). Social violence comprises the amount of violence within the home – including domestic violence and a history of violent behaviour, such as criminal behaviour (Connell-Carrisk & Scannapieco, 2006).

Community

Chronic neighbourhood poverty is a strong risk factor for neglect (Jonson-Reid, Drake & Zhou, 2013). Swenson and Chaffin (2006) listed three characteristics of communities that correlate with physical abuse and neglect. These include communities where there is economic disadvantage instability and poor organization (Molnar et al., 2015), as well as a lack of resources in the neighbourhood (i.e. poverty, lack of access to child-care) (Coulton, Korbin & Su, 1999). Child maltreatment rates, including neglect, are also higher in neighbourhoods with lower levels of positive social processes (Molnar et al., 2016). Molnar and colleagues found consistent associations between social processes and neglect after accounting for neighbourhood structural characteristics, provide empirical support for Coulton et al.'s (2007) theorization that social processes influenced the effects of such structural characteristics. They concluded that having a larger neighbourhood social network of family and friends nearby, and having neighbours who get to know the children and their parents, were associated with a lower likelihood of maltreatment.

Summary of risk and causal factors

There are a number of causal factors and risk factors across various systems that play a part in the occurrence of child neglect. Many of the risk factors are interrelated, and seldom are they present in isolation. Studies have shown that the presence of multiple risk factors can dramatically increase the likelihood of child abuse and neglect (Petersen et al., 2014). For each family there will be a range of individualized factors across more than one system that will have an impact. For example, a parent who abuses substances may also have limited social support, have financial problems and be living in an isolated area in an attempt to flee an ex-partner. Swenson and Chaffin (2006) conclude that based on a social-ecological model and a multi-determined aetiology for child maltreatment, effective interventions should consider a range of systems.

Static risk factors are of interest as they give information on who should be targeted, such as teenage mothers, but do not provide guidance on how to change the situation. Dynamic risk factors are helpful in providing targets for intervention.

Implications for prevention approaches

There are very few successful approaches that prevent child neglect at a community level. To be effective, a U.S. Advisory Board argued that child protection must become part of everyday life, so that it is embedded, seemingly naturally, in the social fabric – an ordinary function of the settings in which children and their families live, study, work and play (McDonnell et al., 2015). A neighbourhood-based child protection system is required to support families and make child protection a shared responsibility. An example of such an approach is Strong Communities, piloted in South Carolina, which aims to prevent child maltreatment and improve children's safety (McDonnell et al., 2015). This initiative promotes family and community well-being in order to prevent child abuse and neglect. The general approach is two-pronged. First, outreach workers organized communities to 'keep kids safe' by watching out for one another. Outreach staff recruited volunteers and engaged community organizations' and primary institutions in collaborative efforts to develop and implement localized action plans. The evaluation results group found small but significant effects on the comparison measures, providing evidence for the effectiveness of the Strong Communities intervention, including specific findings that suggest a reduction in incidences of neglect (McDonnell et al., 2015).

Other prevention approaches aiming at increasing access to parenting services have been found to be effective at reducing maltreatment (Molnar et al., 2016). For example, Triple P, randomized communities to condition, implemented an evidence-based parenting interventions as a prevention strategy and demonstrated positive impact of reducing child maltreatment indicators, including substantiated child maltreatment, child out-of-home placements and child maltreatment injuries (Prinz, et al., 2009).

Other prevention-based programmes target high-risk client groups, for example Nurse-Family Partnerships (NFP), which is a prenatal and early infancy project replicated across the United States, the United Kingdom and Australia. NFP is one of the most recognized evidence-based programmes addressing child neglect. Research on the NFP prenatal and early childhood home visitation approach by nurses showed that it reduces the number of subsequent pregnancies, the use of welfare, child abuse and neglect and criminal behaviour on the part of low-income, unmarried mothers for up to 15 years after the birth of the first child (Olds et al., 1997).

Implications for effective assessment and intervention

In order to be effective at preventing or reducing the recurrence of neglect assessment, interventions and service responses need to address the salient and proximal causes of child neglect across these various social systems (Swenson & Chaffin, 2006). Adopting an approach that addresses a number of systems can initially seem overwhelming as the number of casual factors is potentially large. However, successful programmes will target only the unique factors that impact each family; thus, assessment is focused on identifying the major malleable factors in each system that are amenable to treatment for that family (Swenson & Chaffin, 2006). This approach acknowledges the complex interplay of factors that can compromise parents' ability to offer appropriate care to their children (Turney & Taylor, 2014). Interventions offered are targeted at core, central, relevant and changeable factors by utilizing empirically validated techniques, such as parental substance abuse and low parenting skills (Swenson & Chaffin, 2006), as opposed to targeting variables that are not changeable (e.g. age, parental history of abuse) or peripheral or that have a week prognosis (Swenson & Chaffin, 2006).

Assessment

As stated above, assessment involves reviewing the impact of all key systems (Swenson & Chaffin, 2006). Strengths and weaknesses are determined within each system (e.g. individual child, parent, family, community). Thus, the assessment will include direct contact with people from each system. Based on the assessment, the practitioner selects critical treatment targets and determines the major reasons for the presenting problem. Individualized assessments tools may be useful in measuring specific treatment targets, such as parenting skills, or treatment progress, such as the use of the child neglect index, which specifies type and severity of neglect, which can then be used to set treatment targets for individual families and assess treatment progress (Trocme, 1996).

Intervention

While there are a number of evidence-based approaches aimed at reducing child maltreatment, which include treating families who have neglected children, few report outcomes related to the reduction or elimination of neglect, instead reporting on reductions in child physical abuse. As previously mentioned neglect is harder to substantiate and measure than physical abuse and therefore is more difficult to report on as a programme outcome. Few programmes or approaches are aimed at neglecting families. There are nevertheless some exceptions:

> *SafeCare*: SafeCare is a structured training curriculum for parents with children under the age of six who are at risk of or have been reported for child maltreatment and specifically neglect. There is a sizeable evidence base for SafeCare (Whitaker, et al., 2012). Randomized trials within the child welfare system and with families at risk for maltreatment show positive results (Whitaker, et al., 2012). By addressing health and safety, along with positive parenting, SafeCare addresses risk factors for both child neglect and physical abuse.

> *Multisystemic Therapy-Building Stronger Families (MST-BSF) and Multisystemic Therapy-Child Abuse and Neglect (MST-CAN) (Schaeffer et al., 2013; Swenson et al., 2010)*: MST-CAN is designed to help families with complex problems that have come under the guidance of child protective services specifically due to physical abuse or neglect. Meanwhile, MST-BSF focuses on cases with co-occurrence of physical abuse or neglect with parental substance abuse. Relative to families who received an alternative programme, mothers who received MST-BSF were three times less likely to have another substantiated incident of maltreatment over a follow-up period of 24 months after referral. The overall number of substantiated re-abuse incidents in this time frame also was significantly lower among MST-BSF families. These promising preliminary outcomes support the viability of a more rigorous (i.e. randomized) evaluation of the MST-BSF model. Swenson and colleagues (2010) conducted a randomized effectiveness trial of MST-CAN for physically abused youth. Five assessments over a period of 16 months showed MST-CAN was significantly more effective than an alternative service in reducing parental behaviours associated with maltreatment.

> *Families Activity Improving Relationships (FAIR)*: FAIR is an intensive community-based treatment model that combines evidence-based components of behavioural interventions shown individually to

produce positive outcomes for parenting and substance use. The results from a recent pilot are promising and suggest that FAIR is useful for families referred for substance use and child neglect (Saldana, 2015).

Adopting an evidence-based programme

Ideally, adopting an evidence-based programme and implementing the programme as intended is more likely to guarantee successful outcomes. There are few programmes, however, that have empirical support for reducing neglect specifically and few that address the interplay of causal factors that are indicated in neglect. In situations where a proven programme cannot be adopted, a components approach may be necessary. Descriptive data on common approaches used in child neglect helps to identify treatment processes and child/family/caseworker characteristics associated with outcomes. This 'practice-based evidence' can then be used to support quality improvement efforts and to facilitate the implementation of evidence-based practices in a range of service contexts (Garland et al., 2014). Research is nevertheless needed to test the impact of these practice elements with attention to the coordination of these elements (e.g. selection, sequencing, evaluating) and tailoring treatment for specific families (Chorpita et al., 2005).

Components from the field of neglect and maltreatment that appear promising in reducing neglect when working with individual families include the following: a never-ending focus on engagement of key players, especially family (for a full review, see Cunningham & Henggeler, 1999); safety planning, which includes interpersonal safety as well as safety from home hazards; an ecological assessment; goal setting; addressing concrete problems within the family (see DePnfillis, 2006); skills building, especially parenting skills; the provision of target health information; substance abuse treatment if required; and establishing appropriate social support. These components should be delivered by home visitors with cultural competence and who take a strengths-based approach.

Programmes delivered should also be embedded in a process of continuous quality improvement (CQI) to support caseworker fidelity to the treatment approach. This has been critical to favourable outcomes in existing evidence-based programmes (Henggeler, 2011; Lorch & Pollak, 2014; Rubenstein et al., 2014). A CQI approach ensures that services are clear about the outcomes they are intending to achieve, the problems that need to be solved and the intended client group, as well as simultaneously creating a system of indicators to monitor and measure outcomes and the quality of provision of the service components.

Conclusion

Child neglect occurs more frequently than any other form of child mal-treatment but is studied less. Poverty, access to housing, childcare, mental health services and transport can impact on the ability of parents to care for their children. Static factors help in identifying abuse but in them-selves do not provide enough guidance for assessment or treatment. The growing paradigm shift in the field with increased recognition that child neglect is multi-causal with contributing factors from a number of interre-lated systems which need to be addressed to reduce neglect has produced a more robust view of neglect. Swenson and Chaffin's (2006) article sum-marizes the need for an increased understanding of the impact of multiple factors on neglect, such as poverty, unemployment and housing, as well as individual and family characteristics in order to intervene success-fully. Programmes that target these casual drivers across various systems are proving to be more successful than programmes targeting only one system. Practitioners in the field can be guided by general principles of programmes that work with maltreatment and those that are specific for neglect. Important areas to cover include safety, skills building, parenting, teaching health and developmental information, and ensuring families have appropriate social support. However, as the use of these components has not been tested, it is essential that a CQI system is developed to deter-mine their impact on reducing neglect.

In summary, there is robust evidence that a systemic approach needs to be adopted to prevent or reduce the recurrence of neglect. It is time to move the emphasis from identifying neglect and its likely recurrence to a more purposeful focus on policies and programmes and to providing social-ecological responses to reducing child neglect that will ultimately better support families.

References

Ammerman, R. T., Kolko, D. J., Kirisci, L., Blackson, T. C. & Dawes, M. A. (1999). Child abuse potential in parents with histories of substance use disorder, *Child Abuse & Neglect*, 12, 1225–1238.

Armstrong, M. I., Birnie-Lefcovitch, S. & Ungar, M. T. (2005). Pathways between social support, family well-being, quality of parenting, and child resilience: What we know, *Journal of Child and Family Studies*, 14(2), 269–281.

Barlow, J., Johnston, I., Kendrick, D., Polnay, L. & Stewart-Brown, S. (2006). Individual and group-based parenting programmes for the treatment of physi-cal child abuse and neglect, *Cochrane Database of Systematic Reviews*, 3. Art. No.: CD005463. doi:10.1002/14651858.CD005463.pub2.

Bartlett, J. D. & Easterbrooks, M. A. (2015). The moderating effect of relationships on intergenerational risk for infant neglect by young mothers, *Child Abuse & Neglect*, 45, 21–34.

Beiki, O., Karimi, N. & Mohammadi, R. (2014). Parental education level and injury incidence and mortality among foreign-born children: A cohort study with 46 years follow-up, *Journal of Injury and Violence Research*, 6(1), 37–43.

Belsky, J. (1993). Etiology of child maltreatment: A developmental ecological analysis, *Psychological Bulletin*, 114(93), 413–434.

Berger, L. M., Slack, K. S., Waldfogel, J. & Bruch, S. K. (2010). Caseworker-perceived caregiver substance abuse and child protective services outcomes, *Child Maltreatment*, 15(3), 199–210.

Borkowski, J. G., Whitman, T. L. & Farris, J. R. (2007). Adolescent mothers and their children: Risks, resilience, and development, in J. G. Borkowski, J. R.Farris, T. L. Whitman, S. S. Carothers, K. Weed & D. A. Keogh (eds), *Risk and resilience: Adolescent mothers and their children grow up* (pp. 1–34). Mahwah, NJ: Lawrence Erlbaum.

Bronfenbrenner, U. & Morris, P. A. (2006). The bioecological model of human development, in W. Damon & R. M. Lerner (eds in chief) & R. M. Lerner (vol. ed.), *Handbook of child psychology: Vol. 1. Theoretical models of human development* (6th edn) (pp. 793–828). Hoboken, NJ: Wiley.

Burke, J., Chandy, J., Dannerbeck, A. & Watt, J. W. (1998). The parental environment cluster model of child neglect: An integrative conceptual model, *Child Welfare*, 77(4), 389–405.

Cash, S. J. & Wilke, D. J. (2003). An ecological model of maternal substance abuse and child neglect: Issues, analyses and recommendations, *American Journal of Orthopsychiatry*, 73(4), 392–404.

Chaffin, M., Kelleher, K. & Hollenberg, J. (1996). Onset of physical abuse and neglect: Psychiatric, substance abuse, and social risk factors from prospective community data, *Child Abuse & Neglect*, 20, 191– 203.

Chorpita, B. F., Daleiden, E. L. & Weisz, J. R. (2005). Identifying and selecting the common elements of evidence based interventions: A distillation and matching model, *Mental Health Services Research*, 7, 5–20.

Cicchetti, D., Rogosch, F. A., Toth, S. L. & Sturge-Apple, M. (2011). Normalizing the development of cortisol regulation in maltreated infants through preventive interventions, *Development and Psychopathology*, 23, 789–800.

Coulton, C. J., Korbin, J. E. & Su, M. (1999). Neighborhoods and child maltreatment: A multi-level study, *Child Abuse & Neglect*, 23, 1019–1040.

Coulton, C. J., Crampton, D. S., Irwin, M., Spilsbury, J. C. & Korbin, J. E. (2007). How neighborhoods influence child maltreatment: A review of the literature and alternative pathways, *Child Abuse & Neglect*, 31(11–12), 1117-1142.

Connell, C. M., Bergeron, N., Katz, K. H., Saunders, L. & Tebes, J. K. (2007). Re-referral to child protective services: The influence of child, family, and case characteristics on risk status, *Child Abuse and Neglect*, 31(5), 573–588. http://dx.doi.org/10.1016/j.chiabu.2006.12.004

Connell-Carrick, K. (2003). A critical review of the empirical literature: Identifying correlates of child neglect, *Child and Adolescent Social Work Journal*, 20(5), 389–425.

Connell-Carrick, K. & Scannapieco, M. (2006). Ecological correlates of neglect in infants and toddlers, *Journal of Interpersonal Violence*, 21(3), 299–316.

Coulton, C. J., Crampton, D. S., Irwin, M., Spilsbury, J. C. & Korbin, J. E. (2007). How neighborhoods influence child maltreatment: A review of the literature and alternative pathways, *Child Abuse & Neglect*, 31(11–12), 1117–1142.

Cunningham, P. B. & Henggeler, S. W. (1999). Engaging multiproblem families in treatment: Lessons learned throughout the development of multisystemic therapy, *Family Processes*, 38, 265–281.

de Paúl, J. & Guibert, M. (2008). Empathy and child neglect: A theoretical model. *Child Abuse & Neglect*, 32(11), 1063–1071.

Dubowitz, H. (2007). Understanding and addressing the 'neglect of neglect': Digging into the molehill, *Child Abuse & Neglect*, 31, 603–606.

Dubowitz, H., Newton, R. R., Litrownik, A. J., Lewis, T., Briggs, E. C., Thompson, R. et al. (2005). Examination of a conceptual model of child neglect, *Child Maltreatment*, 10, 173–189. doi:10.1177/1077559505275014

Easterbrooks, M. A., Jacobs, F. H., Bartlett, J. D., Goldberg, J., Contreras, M. M., Kotake, C. & Chaudhuri, J. H. (2012). *Initial findings from a randomized, controlled trial of Healthy Families Massachusetts: Early program impacts on young mothers' parenting*. Washington, DC: Pew Charitable Trusts.

Éthier, L. S., Couture, G. & Lacharité, C. (2004). Risk factors associated with the chronicity of high potential for child abuse and neglect, *Journal of Family Violence*, 19(1), 13–24.

Gardner, R., Hodson, D., Churchill, G. & Cotmore, R. (2014). Transporting and Implementing SafeCare a Home-Based Programme for Parents, Designed to Reduce and Mitigate the Effects of Child Neglect: An Initial Progress Report, *Child Abuse Review*, 23, 297–303. doi:10.1002/car.2338

Garland, A. F., Accurso, E. C., Haine-Schlagel, R., Brookman-Frazee, L., Roesch, S. & Zhang, J. J. (2014). Searching for elements of evidence based practices in children's usual care and examining their impact, *Journal of Clinical Child and Adolescent Psychology*, 43, 201–215.

Gaudin, J., Polansky, N., Kilpatrick, A. & Shilton, P. (1996). Family functioning in neglectful families, *Child Abuse and Neglect*, 20, 363–377.

Govindshenoy, M. & Spencer, N. (2007). Abuse of the disabled child: A systematic review of population-based studies, *Child: Care, Health and Development*, 33(5), 552–558.

Henggeler, S. W. (2011). Efficacy studies to large-scale transport: The development and validation of Multisystemic Therapy programs, *Annual Review of Clinical Psychology*, 7, 351–381. http://dx.doi.org/10.1146/annurev-clinpsy-032210-104615

Hobbs, C. J. & Wynne, J. M. (2002). Neglect of neglect, *Current Paediatrics*, 12, 144–150.

Jonson-Reid, M., Drake, B. & Zhou, P. (2013). Neglect Subtypes, Race, and Poverty Individual, Family, and Service Characteristics, *Child Maltreatment*, 18(1), 30–41. doi:10.1177/1077559512462452

Krugman, S. D. (2014). Advocacy and child neglect, *Pediatric Annals*, 43(11), 278–281. http://dx.doi.org/10.3928/00904481-20141022-12

Lorch, J. A. & Pollak, V. E. (2014). Continuous quality improvement in daily clinical practice: A proof of concept study, *Plos One*, 9(5), e97066–97011. doi:10.1371/journal.pone.0097066

McDonell, J. R., Asher, B. & Melton, G. B. (2015). Strong communities for children: Results of a multi-year community-based initiative to protect children from harm, *Child Abuse & Neglect*, 41, 79–96.

McSherry, D. (2007). Understanding and addressing the neglect of neglect: Why are we making a mole-hill out of a mountain? *Child Abuse & Neglect*, 31(6), 607–614.

McSherry, D. (2004). Which came first, the chicken or the egg? Examining the relationship between child neglect and poverty, *British Journal of Social Work*, 34(5), 727–733.

Molnar, B. E., Goerge, R. M., Gilsanz, P., Hill, A., Subramanian, S. V., Holton, J. K., Duncan, D. T., Beatriz, E. D. & Beardslee, W. R. (2016). Neighborhood-level social processes and substantiated cases of child maltreatment, *Child Abuse & Neglect*, 51, 41–53.

National Center on Addiction and Substance Abuse (NCASA) of Columbia University (1999). *No safe haven: Children of substance abusing parents*. New York. Funded by the Edna McConnell Clark Foundation PRIMERICA Financial Services, Inc. Samuel M. Soref and Helene K. Soref Foundation.

Olds, D. L., Eckenrode, J., Henderson, C. R., Jr, Hanks, C., Cole, R., Tatelbaum, R., McConnochie, K. M., Sidora, K., Luckey, D. W., Shaver, D., Engelhardt, K., James, D. & Barnard, K. (1997). Long-term effects of home visitation on maternal life course and child abuse and neglect: Fifteen-year follow-up of a randomized trial, *JAMA*, 278(8), 637–643. doi:10.1001/jama.1997.03550080047038

Pears, K. C. & Capaldi, D. M. (2001). Intergenerational transmission of abuse: A two-generation, prospective study of an at-risk sample, *Child Abuse & Neglect*, 25, 1439–1461.

Petersen, A. C., Joseph, J. & Feit, M. (eds) (2014). *New directions in child abuse and neglect research*. Washington, DC: Institute of Medicine and National Research Council.

Prinz, R. J., Sanders, M. R., Shapiro, C. J., Whitaker, D. J. & Lutzker, J. R. (2009). Population-based prevention of child maltreatment: The U.S. Triple P system population trial, *Prevention Science*, 10(1), 1–12.

Public Health Agency of Canada (2010). Canadian Incidence Study of Reported Child Abuse and Neglect – 2008: Major Findings. Ottawa.

Rubenstein, L., Khodyakov, D., Hempel, S., Danz, M., Salem-Schatz, S., Foy, R., ... & Shekelle, P. (2014). How can we recognize continuous quality improvement? *International Journal for Quality in Health Care*, 26(1), 6–15. doi:10.1093/intqhc/mzt085

Sagatun, I. & Edwards, L. (1995). *Child abuse and the legal system*. Chicago, IL: Nelson-Hall.

Schatz, J. N. & Lounds, J. J. (2007). Child maltreatment: Precursors of developmental delays, in J. G. Borkowski, J. R. Farris, T. L. Whitman, S. S. Carothers, K. Weed & D. A. Keogh (eds), *Risk and resilience: Adolescent mothers and their children grow up* (pp. 125–150). Mahwah, NJ: Lawrence Erlbaum.

Scannapieco, M. & Connell-Carrick, K. (2005). Focus on the first years: Correlates of substantiation of child maltreatment for families with children 0–4, *Children & Youth Services Review*, 27(12), 1307–1323.

Schnitzer P. G. & Ewigman, B. G. (2008). Household composition and fatal unintentional injuries related to child maltreatment, *Journal of Nursing Scholarship*, 40(1), 91–97.

Sedlak, A. & Broadhurst, D. (1996). The third national incidence study of child abuse and neglect (NIS-3). Washington, DC: U.S. Department of Health and Human Services.

Sedlak, A. J., Mettenburg, J., Basena, M., Petta, I., McPherson, K., Greene, A. & Li, S. (2010). *Fourth National Incidence Study of Child Abuse and Neglect* (NIS–4): Report to Congress. Washington, DC: U.S.D.H.H.S., Administration for Children and Families.

Slack, K. S., Holl, J. L., McDaniel, M., Yoo, J. & Bolger, K. (2004). Understanding the risks of child neglect: An exploration of poverty and parenting characteristics, *Child Maltreatment*, 9, 395–408.

Shlonsky, A. & Wagner, D. (2005). The next step: Integrating actuarial risk assessment and clinical judgement into an evidence-based practice framework in CPS case management, *Children and Youth Services Review*, 27, 409–427.

Stoltenborgh, M., Bakermans-Kranenburg, M. & van Ijzendoorn, M. (2013). The neglect of child neglect: a meta-analytic review of the prevalence of neglect, *Social Psychiatry and Psychiatric Epidemiology*, 48(3), 345–355. http://dx.doi.org/10.1007/s00127–012–0549-y

Swenson, C. C. & Chaffin, M. (2006). Beyond psychotherapy: Treating abused children by changing their social ecology, *Aggression and Violent Behavior*, 11(2), 120–137. http://dx.doi.org/10.1016/j.avb.2005.07.004

Swenson, C. C., Schaeffer, C. M., Henggeler, S. W., Faldowski, R. & Mayhew, A. M. (2010). Multisystemic therapy for child abuse and neglect: A randomized effectiveness trial, *Journal of Family Psychology*, 24, 497–507.

Trocmé, N. (1996). Development and preliminary evaluation of the Ontario child neglect index, *Child Maltreatment*, 1, 145–155. doi:10.1177/1077559596001002006

Tsantefski, M. & Connolly, M. (2013). Violence toward children, in A. Taylor & M. Connolly (eds), *Understanding violence: Context and practice in the human services* (pp. 131–141). Christchurch: Canterbury University Press.

Turney, D. & Taylor, J. (2014). Interventions in chronic and severe neglect: What works? *Child Abuse Review*, 23, 231–234.

U.S. Department of Health and Human Services, Administration for Children & Families, Children's Bureau. (2013). *Child maltreatment 2012*. Washington, DC: Author.

Whitaker, D. J., Ryan, K. A., Wild, R., Self-Brown, S., Lutzker, J. R., Shanley, J. ... & Hodges, A. E. (2012). Initial implementation indicators from a statewide rollout of SafeCare within a child welfare system, *Child Maltreatment*, 17, 96–101.

Whitman, T. L., Borkowski, J. G., Keogh, D. A. & Weed, K. (eds) (2001). *Interwoven lives: Adolescent mothers and their children*. Mahwah, NJ: Lawrence Erlbaum.

Wildeman, C., Emanuel, N., Leventhal, J.M, Putnam-Hornstein, E., Waldfogel, J & Lee. H. (2014). The prevalence of confirmed maltreatment among US children, 2004–2011, *JAMA Pediatrics*, 168, 706–713.

13

POSITIVE LEADERSHIP IN CHILD PROTECTION

Robyn Miller[*]

Introduction

Child protection work has long been challenged by the social control aspect of the role, the structural context of family disadvantage and the harmful effects of intervention that some children experience. In many English-speaking jurisdictions, a negative perception of child protection has developed, reinforced often by the media. Yet from within child protection systems, a contrary picture emerges of committed, highly motivated practitioners and leaders who seek to reform systems to enhance prevention and early intervention and to meaningfully improve practice for vulnerable children. Talented social workers doing extraordinary work are not often featured in newspapers. The front line, where creative leadership integrates social justice values and anti-oppressive practice in challenging and often traumatic circumstances, is nevertheless alive and well.

Using the example of practice reform efforts in Victoria, Australia, this chapter will explore the ongoing attempt to build capacity within a supportive culture that encourages good practice and greater access to expertise for frontline practitioners. Supporting frontline practice has never been more important, as services are challenged by growing demand and increased expectations that workers will provide safety for all vulnerable children. The authorization of the development of practice leadership within the Victorian system, as distinct from management, began in 2006 with the inaugural state-wide Principal Practitioner position. It was situated within the wider legislative and policy reforms over the last decade. The 'every child every chance' reforms both enabled the reinvigorated focus on practice and were underpinned by a vision of creating a public health approach to child protection. A public health approach to

---

[*] Dr Robyn Miller is the CEO of MacKillop Family Services, Victoria, Australia.

child protection requires a collective, structural analysis which considers the underlying social determinants – in particular, housing, maternal and child health, access to early children's services, employment services and the development of epidemiological intelligence to plan effective responses (Munro & Parton, 2007).

Changing the practice culture in Victoria to engage more with families and to be more informed by research on child development and trauma required concurrent planning and actions that were motivated by the rights of children to safety and well-being. Supporting families in their local communities and respecting the importance of culture required multiple changes in policy, inter-sectorial partnerships, legislation, programme design, operations and training – led both centrally, 'top down', and by local, regional experts, 'bottom up'. A clear finding that emerged from research on this phenomenon was that the energy to drive and sustain the reform process required coordination and senior leadership that modelled partnership, consultation, critical reflection and rigorous evaluation of the data. Leadership was a critical enabler of strengthening practice to be more evidence informed and emotionally intelligent, in order to more effectively make a difference to children and families (Miller, 2014).

The reforms required separate family service agencies in local areas to be coordinated and to partner with one another in a more integrated system to reach families in need earlier. This was a radical redesign of the service system, and ultimately with increased funding, 24 Child FIRST sites were introduced in sub-regional catchments throughout Victoria from 2007 to 2009. *Community-based child protection practitioners* were also co-located with these family services, non-statutory practitioners. This new statutory practice leadership role was created by the child protection programme to improve ease of liaison and information sharing, between child protection and family services, to enable shared assessments and joint work with children and families. As community-based child protection practitioners provide consultation on complex cases in Child FIRST and work collaboratively, there has been a marked improvement in local communication processes and, most importantly, in the experience of families (KPMG, 2011).

Managing child protection

Buckley (2009) explored the challenges involved in the management of child abuse work, particularly noting that relationships between professionals and involuntary clients tend to be adversarial rather than collaborative. Buckley distinguishes between surface issues and depth issues. Surface issues consist of the law, policies, procedures, performance indicators and auditing tools which combine to provide a visible frame-work for the delivery of services and which can be promoted by some to be addressed by 'technical rationality' (p. 29).

> The 'depth' issues ... are more subtle and include the ideological basis for the work, the dynamics that occur within and between professions and organiza-tions, the nature and quality of relationships between practitioners and service users, the struggle to balance helping relationships with statutory obligations, variable thresholds for intervening with families, 'buck passing' between profes-sionals and agencies, power differentials, gender, fear, panic, stress, burn-out, intimidation and lack of confidence that the system is doing more good than harm.

Buckley stresses that these

> depth issues will not be ameliorated by the introduction of mandatory report-ing or other regulatory measures; they need to be addressed by training, skill development, supervision and capacity building within a supportive frame-work. (p. 30)

The inherent tensions in the child protection role, given the well-publicized risks involved if the wrong decision is made, can make practitioners fearful that they are *damned if they do and damned if they don't*, which may contribute to a high turnover of frontline staff. The child and family welfare field is also generally beset by the problem of fragmented and procedural forms of supervision that limit the reflective and decision-making abilities of practitioners. From the UK perspective Reder and Duncan (1999; 2004), note this is a recurrent theme in child death and serious case reviews over the last 30 years. They also note that communication problems are recurrent in serious adverse events:

> In some networks, a 'closed professional system' seemed to have evolved, where groups of workers developed a fixed view about the case and became inaccessi-ble to contrary information or observations. (Reder & Duncan, 1999, pp. 16–17)

A significant aspect of this problem, in human services and also in other professions, is that people are reluctant to revise embedded beliefs, biases and assumptions which inform key decisions (Larrick, 2004). This directly impacts on families and children who are engaged with services. Munro (2002, p. 159) noted that '[t]here is no simple antidote to this weakness. Child protection workers can be aware only of how they are likely to err and consciously try to counteract it'. This underscores the need for quality supervision and other opportunities for learning and professional support.

The Report of the Protecting Victoria's Vulnerable Children Inquiry (Cummins et al., 2012) listed as one of seven key challenges for Victoria emerging from the available performance information: 'the need for improved and consistent practice quality' (p. 91). Cognizant of this, and in contrast to earlier patterns of appointing the most experienced practitioners into managerial, policy and central leadership positions to oversee and manage the 'business', in Victoria there has been a deliberate strategy to create a senior practitioner stream. This has been supported by the provision of post-graduate training on practice and supervisions skills and on social work leadership.

After earlier pilots were successfully evaluated (KPMG, 2011), the practice leadership stream was implemented state-wide from 2012. The newly created 'senior practitioner' position in every small team of five or six practitioners works in partnership with the team manager. The new positions of 'practice leaders' work across a cluster of teams – along with the 13 'principal practitioners', who actively engage with the most complex cases around the state in conjunction with the child protection managers in each region. Group 'reflective practice' sessions are provided monthly, in addition to individual supervision. This innovative way of operating, while challenging in its scale and implementation, has markedly increased the capacity for live supervision in the field, secondary consultation and for less experienced practitioners to co-work the most complex cases with a senior practitioners.

Reder and Duncan (1999) describe the phenomena of the exaggeration of hierarchy where decisions are made by supervisors and others with too little information; where there is role confusion; and where workers make selective interpretations of the history. In responding to these challenges, strengthening practice is clearly an important aspect of managing child protection, and writers have summarized fundamental knowledge areas that are important to safe practice that can be reinforced and negotiated in supervision. For example, Connolly and Morris (2012) identify four key knowledge areas that could create learning environments for supervisors and practitioners, including what is now a well-developed child protection knowledge base drawn from research; a practice skills repertoire that includes communication skills, ethical and relational skill sets, solution-finding and advocacy skills and cross-cultural competencies; analytical thinking and the nature of complex critical reasoning; and the professional context where child protection operates across interdisciplinary professional systems (Connolly and Morris, 2012).

Increasingly it is recognized that good outcomes with families with complex needs require skilled relationship-based practice (Miller, 2007a; 2008). Engagement with families needs to be informed by a dynamic synthesis of knowledge – what we can draw from research relating to abuse and neglect and the impact of violence on the development of children and what we can draw from a good reading of the history and the experiences of this particular child and family. Such engagement would include systemic understandings of the family history and contemporary trauma; strengths and protective factors; family values and culture; the parents' own experience as children; their history as a couple and importantly their history of parenting other children; previous history with child protection, police and other institutions; capacity to change and their motivation to change. As Connolly and Morris (2012, p. 142) note, 'this requires a depth of assessment and intervention that is beyond ... "conveyor belt" practice, requiring also a depth of knowledge about family and parental functioning, children's development, and the ways in which abuse and neglect intersect with these'. This rich integration of research and practitioner knowledge has the potential to motivate strategic thinking and planning about how the system could better help the most vulnerable children.

Systems across international jurisdictions have also begun to introduce practice leadership positions to strengthen practice at the frontline. An important role of practice leadership is to help child welfare systems shift from a compliance mentality to one of reflective practice decision making. This requires a learning culture that is authorized by the most senior leaders' supporting the facilitation of ongoing critical reflection. The need for this has been acknowledged for some years:

> the challenge ... is that of creating a climate wherein individual practitioners can be encouraged to engage in what Kemmis terms 'a collaborative exchange of learning'. When such a body of knowledge is developed around reflective practice then... child protection teams become a more effective force for the protection of children. (Clark 1988, p. 226)

It could be argued that the responsibility for embedding thoughtful, relationship-based practice essentially rests with management as messages from senior leaders provide the context within which practice strengthening occurs. The need to support and develop the expertise of inexperienced frontline practitioners is complex, and fostering organizational leadership that enables good supervision and management is crucial. Fiona McColl (2009, p. 128) strongly challenged the lack of critical reflection in child protection systems as contributing to the retention problems of experienced frontline practitioners and noted that other community services are becoming 'increasingly risk aversive and proscriptive'.

Reclaiming core social work practices and values and withstanding the dominance of managerialist discourses has been an important feature of child protection reform efforts in recent years (Lonne, Parton, Thomson & Harries, 2009; Connolly & Smith, 2010; Goodman & Trowler, 2012).

According to Lonne et al. (2009 p. 51), managerialism and the increased proceduralizing of child protection work has curtailed professional discretion, requiring practitioners to increasingly follow detailed procedural guidance. While acknowledging the negative impact of managerialism, and of adversarial practice cultures that have characterized English-speaking jurisdictions, Connolly and Smith (2010, pp. 14–15) also note the importance of generating partnerships between managerial and practice leadership. Although the development of performance measures in child welfare has been the subject of criticism, it was found that when used in conjunction with a professional reform package, such measures can play an essential part in preparing the ground for change. Increased discipline in both practice and financial management provided the organizational capacity to embrace reform and a sense of internal confidence that change was possible. It is notable that despite the increasing demand on the Victorian child protection system over the past decade, through the practice and operational reforms, retention improved significantly and the exit rate of frontline practitioners almost halved (Miller, 2014). Harnessing the strengths of both managerial and professional leadership embraces the notion that solutions to wicked problems may rest beyond single leadership models to models of adaptive leadership (Head & Alford, 2015), something we will return to later in the chapter.

In the reclaiming of social work in child welfare, frameworks for practice have been developed that return the focus of practice to the child and family (Connolly, 2007; Stanley, McGee & Lincoln, 2012; Goodman & Trowler, 2012). Practice change and development has also been critical to Australian reform efforts. The best interests case practice model (BICPM) (Figure 13.1) was first launched in 2008 in Victoria as a practice model across child protection, family services and out-of-home care after exhaustive consultation and authorization from both the statutory and non-government sectors and peak bodies (Miller, 2014). It focuses on how practice cultures need to shift towards a more consistent model of engagement with families, partnering with other services, intervening early in cases of abuse and neglect and preventing harm to achieve meaningful change for the child. This is in contrast to the episodic assessment of families and monitoring of the perceived risk, through a procedural, task-focused approach. The fragmentation that occurs when child protection is focused on episodic risk can lose sight of the child's experience. The required paradigm shift, is towards a *practice* orientation, rather than the historically dominant paradigm of episodic responses to ever increasing demand.

The promotion and endorsement of the BICPM state-wide, across the non-government family services sector and out-of-home care agencies as well as child protection, enabled a shared language and understanding about the importance of a 'strength-based and forensically astute'

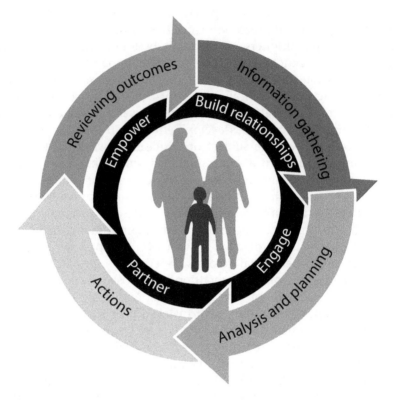

Figure 13.1 The best interests case practice model
Source: Department of Human Services, 2012.

approach to *engaging* with families where children are at risk (Miller, 2009). It was a conscious decision to reclaim core social work practices and values and to embrace a *case work* discourse rather than a discourse of managerialism. The change of position title from *child protection case manager* to *child protection practitioner* was deliberate and intended to reflect the ethos in the BICPM. This is not to minimize the need for good case management skills. Rather, it reflects a commitment to the value of case work and the practice skills of practitioners who have frequently only a brief window of opportunity to work with families in such a way that engages the parents in change rather than in a power struggle or angry avoidance.

The practice reforms in Victoria also aimed to increase evidence-informed practice. Thought leadership was an important part of articulating *how* practitioners could understand risk and engagement in safety. The dominant paradigm of risk assessment in the dynamic and uncertain life events of vulnerable families had previously led child protection to a siloed focus on the risk of *immediate* harm to children. The visual image of the child and family at the centre of the framework intends to give very clear messages about the need for a child focus, as well as responsiveness to family. The core purpose is to work towards positive outcomes for children and families regarding safety and well-being.

There has been very deliberate attention in the Victorian model paid to retaining a professional judgement focus that engages practitioners in the critical analysis of risk and requires a commitment to ongoing, embedded professional learning. The acknowledgement of *cumulative* harm and impact of neglect and family violence (Miller, 2007b) was also heightened during the reforms. Practice was found to have improved in multiple dimensions over the period of reform, and while acknowledging areas for improvement and ongoing demand and capacity challenges, the overall success of the reforms in Victoria is clear (Miller, 2014). The importance of a shared language and a coherent understanding of trauma, risk and child development across sectors has been a key finding in understanding the reforms, as has the importance of supporting practitioners to integrate research into practice, through modelling and live supervision by senior practitioners with the most complex cases. In short, leaders and practitioners at all levels 'walking the talk' have been critical to effecting change.

Leadership in in the context of wicked problems

The identification of child abuse and neglect as a 'wicked problem' is now well established (Devaney & Spratt, 2009; ARACY, 2008). 'Wicked problems' are those intractable problems that seem to defy solutions, no matter how hard services work to resolve them. Head and Alford (2015, p. 712) suggest that 'rational-technical approaches assume that efficient and effective achievement of objectives can follow from adequate information, carefully specified goals and targets, and choice of appropriate methods'. The managerial audit culture (Power, 1996) that has largely dominated child protection services with its rational-technical approach, its focus on administrative control and dominant risk paradigm, has certainly challenged the effective delivery of services for vulnerable children and their families. Indeed, there has never been a more important leadership opportunity in child protection to confront the challenges and to move beyond paradigms of risk. Although the challenges are considerable, writers have expressed a cautious optimism that wicked problems can nevertheless be responded to by thinking differently about problems – working collaboratively, thinking carefully about implementation and exploring models of leadership that support more nuanced and flexible organizational systems (Head & Alford, 2015).

Figure 13.2 The seven C's of reform leadership

Practice leadership and language can trap us in particular ways of seeing things, or it can liberate us to see things in new ways, creating different meanings and understandings. This in turn can shift belief systems and motivate different organizational behaviours. The practice reforms developed in Victoria have brought together important professional ideas and communicated them in ways that resonate with practitioners. The reforms also created a rich context for identifying key elements of organizational leadership, resulting in the development of the *seven C's of reform and leadership* (Miller 2014): commitment, collaborative leadership, critical reflection, congruence, coherence, champions and community (Figure 13.2). Elements of the seven C's are interconnected, making a contribution individually and collectively to organizational change.

The seven C's of reform leadership

Commitment

Reforming child protection requires an intentional and enduring commitment to change. As Connolly and Smith (2010, p. 27) note, 'decades of forensic practice will not change easily', and leaders need to appreciate that embedding change takes time – five to seven years according to some writers (Lonne et al., 2009). Building partnerships in the change process is important, where communication and trust develops over time. Reserves of energy are often required to work through issues when there is conflict and/or criticism and when leadership involves perseverance and commitment to remaining positive over the long haul. This includes balancing the day-to-day demands of a busy child protection system with the ongoing embedding and sustaining of reform efforts.

Commitment is also required for the integration of research into practice and the development of knowledge-based practice frameworks, including ethical approaches 'that can help workers navigate their way through the murky relational dimension of practice' (Connolly & Morris, 2012, p. 48). Knowledge frameworks also need to demonstrate a commitment to the rights of children and families and to models of continuous improvement, where the views of service users are both sought and considered in the development of services.

Collaborative leadership

According to Head and Alford (2015, p. 725), collaboration helps to address wicked problems when 'there are multiple parties with differential knowledge, interests, or values'. This is certainly the context within which child protection operates, and collaborative leadership has the potential to inspire and authorize reform. It supports the sharing of information and power and builds collaboration into governance processes, advocating for resources and collectively evaluating reform efforts. Collaborative leadership engages staff across the organization, creating a sense of 'one team' (Connolly & Smith, 2010), and fosters meaningful partnerships across the sector. Functional collaborations across sectors creates a 'collaborative advantage' that better understands the problems, promotes the possibility of finding 'provisional solutions' and creates a stronger context for good implementation through coordinated actions and shared contributions (Head and Alford, 2015, pp. 725–726). As Agranoff (2007) notes, it is rare for one organization to have a monopoly on solutions – collaboration provides a richer solution context when collaborative relationships are strong.

Critical reflection

The importance of critical reflection has been identified strongly in the child protection and social work literature now for some time (Morley, 2014; Munro, 2011; Jones, 2004), and supervision has been identified as a site for critical reflection (Egan, Maidment & Connolly, 2016). Critically reflective leaders bring a further dimension to the role, enabling a deeper understanding of the problems at both the practice and policy levels. Organizational policies and practices can have unexpected consequences that are not always helpful in providing good outcomes for children. Reflective leaders review the policies on and responses to systems to ensure that they are not creating or maintaining problems. Reviewing practice outcomes becomes part of a reflective learning process that is modelled throughout the system, providing a context of collaborative learning and knowledge sharing across sectors.

The 'reflective practice' sessions for frontline practitioners in Victoria inevitably explore the implicit assumptions, potential biases, blind spots and stuck points experienced by practitioners, but they do so in a way that does not shame the worker who is presenting the case. The aims are to build on the strengths of the practice and the practitioner, to notice these out loud and to explore stuck points and gaps in practice to develop a constructive way forward, with the child and family at the centre. Skilled facilitation is critical.

Generally, these sessions involve some sharing of knowledge, but the greatest value from the participants' feedback is that there is a safe environment to 'think' and 'feel' about what they are 'doing'. They generally leave feeling more confident and positive about the work, even if it has become clear during the session that decisions and direction need to change (Miller, 2010).

Congruence

The demands of a busy child protection system can create many stressors for frontline workers. Child protection work is unpredictable, and uncertainty often permeates practice. Reform efforts that land on the frontline can seem disconnected – yet another demand that threatens to compromise their day-to-day work. An integrated reform package may not look that integrated to busy practitioners who are faced with implementing new ideas. Connecting the dots between reform strategies, creating a shared language about the reforms and connecting the reforms to their underpinning evidence base creates a 'big picture' congruence that will make better sense to the workers on the ground. Seeing how the reform efforts fit together in ways that benefit children and families has the potential to engage and motivate the organization to embrace and embed change.

For example, the practice approach in the BICPM is deemed 'child focused and family centred', which challenged the dichotomy that child protection was focused on children and family services were focused on supporting parents. This congruent message across sectors, all publications, and both training and practice resources contributed to a shift in the practice culture.

Coherence

Connected to the notion of congruence, coherence is about being logical and consistent in the messaging relating to organizational vision, strategic direction and reform (Connolly & Smith, 2010). A transparent and shared vision needs to be clearly articulated, connecting workers to the organization's key priorities in ways that are logical and understandable. Communicating complex ideas in simple and accessible ways is not easy, but it is critical for organizations that are confronted with multifaceted demands. Consistency of vision and the messaging of priorities over time can be essential to the embedding of change. As Connolly notes in the preface to this volume, reform has to be given the time to work. Waves of reform efforts can create reform fatigue, and workers will not expend their precious energy reserves on change that is transient. Multiple reform efforts – particularly when they lack coherence – can also undermine external confidence in the organization. Promoting a coherent and consistent reform agenda will have benefits within and outside the organization.

Champions

John Maxwell (2013) suggests that if you really want to build an organization's potential, then you need to focus on growing leaders. Identifying people who share a commitment to the promotion of cultural reform and to have the capacity to lead is essential. Child protection systems are large and complex, and they often rely on frontline services that are well functioning and inherently self-regulating (Connolly & Smith, 2010). Trying to control everything from the top fails to harness the rich contributions of people at all levels of the organization. Champions who positively influence reform efforts and who resolve disputes and find creative local solutions are critically important to successful change at the local level. It is then the role of the transformational leader to inspire, enable and empower champions to influence local engagement in ways that create local dialogue and action (Head & Alford, 2015).

Practice leaders in Victoria provided supervision and case consultation that challenged narrow risk assessment and 'mother blame', and they equally challenged the rule of optimism and naive practice regarding offenders and dangerous parental behaviours. Leaders championed the need to be aware of the child development literature and to understand the impact of trauma on the child's development at different ages and stages. Practitioners were encouraged to review their decisions and focus on understanding risk assessment as an ongoing process that needed to be continually updated and reviewed. Thousands of practice resources were printed and are also available online so that every child protection, family services and out-of-home care practitioner had access to more detailed resources that were up to date with the research evidence but written with practical guidance about 'what to do'. At the systemic level in Victoria, without central and local champions, the changes to the way services were delivered to families through new partnerships and protocols would not have been possible.

Community

Developing communities of practice – like-minded people who are inter-dependent in achieving good outcomes – can really support collaborative reform agendas in child protection. Communities of practice have become a means through which organizations and groups can improve their per-formance. In essence, 'communities of practice are groups of people who share a concern or a passion for something they do and learn how to do it better as they interact regularly' (Wenger-Trayner, 2015, p. 1). Within the child protection context, and guided by the broader vision, they can become multidisciplinary and inclusive professional networks that sup-port and inspire the effort required for reform. They can close the policy, research and practice gaps through intentional dialogue, shared under-standing and mutual support that specifically target the achievement of change on the ground. Relationships across traditional research, policy and practice silos create strong networks of support and energy for the change effort, potentially generating sustained buy-in at all levels of the organization.

Although we have seven C's of reform leadership in this chapter, it could easily have been eight C's – with the inclusion of the idea of 'com-passion'. Managing change and developing responsive systems requires the kind of compassionate leadership that is attuned to the interests and needs across the system: the needs of vulnerable children and families; the needs of workers who strive to mobilize change in the face of significant pressures; and the needs of systems that are subjected to waves of criticism and challenge.

Conclusion

It is clear that moving beyond the risk paradigm requires leadership at mul-tiple levels of the child protection system. We need practitioners who will provide innovate responses to children and families, who will challenge oppressive systems and who develop reflective practice skills. We need practice leaders and supervisors who will create the kind of environment within which innovative practice thrives. We need senior managers who are cognizant of the negative influence of risk-averse paradigms and who will work towards the reinforcement of organizational messages that move beyond discourses of risk. Finally, we need political leaders who will think beyond political cycles with the kind of long-term vision that gives reform a chance to influence organizational cultures in deep and meaningful ways.

References

Agranoff, R. (2007). *Managing within networks: Adding value to public organizations.* Washington, DC: Georgetown University Press.

Australian Research Alliance for Children & Youth (ARACY) (2008). *Inverting the pyramid: Enhancing systems for protecting children.* Commissioned report by the Allen Consulting Group. Available at www.eccq.com.au/wp-content/uploads/2012/02/inverting-the-pyramid_2009.pdf

Buckley, H. (2009). Reforming the Child Protection System: Why we need to be careful what we wish for. *Irish Journal of Family Law*, 12(2), 27–31.

Clark, R. (1988). *Reflecting on child protection decision making.* Master's Thesis, University of Melbourne.

Connolly, M. (2007). Practice frameworks: Conceptual maps to guide intervention in child welfare, *British Journal of Social Work*, 37(5), 825–837.

Connolly, M. & Smith, R. (2010). Reforming child welfare: An integrated approach, *Child Welfare*, 89(3), 9–31.

Connolly, M. & Morris, K. (2012). *Understanding child and family welfare: Statutory responses to children at risk.* London: Palgrave Macmillan.

Cummins. P., Scott, D. & Scales, B. (2012). *Report of the protecting Victoria's vulnerable children inquiry.* Department of Premier and Cabinet- State of Victoria. www.childprotectioninquiry.vic.gov.au/report-pvvc-inquiry.html

Devaney, J. & Spratt, T. (2009). Child abuse as a complex and wicked problem: Reflecting on policy developments in the United Kingdom in working with children and families with multiple problems, *Children and Youth Services Review*, 31, 635–641.

Egan, R., Maidment, J. & Connolly, M. (in press). Supporting quality supervision: Insights for organizational practice. *International Social Work*.

Head, B. W. & Alford, J. (2015). Wicked problems: Implications for public policy and management, *Administration & Society*, 47(6), 711–739.

Humphreys, C., Holzer, P., Scott, D., Arney, F., Bromfield, L., Higgins, D. & Lewig, K. (2010). The planets aligned: Is child protection policy reform good luck or good management? *Australian Social Work*, 63(2), 145–163.

Jones, M. (2004). Supervision, learning and transformative practices, in N. Gould & M. Baldwin (eds), *Social work, critical reflection and the learning organization.* Aldershot: Ashgate Publishing.

KPMG (2011). *Evaluation of child and family services reform, evaluation summary report.* Department of Human Services, Victoria.

Larrick, R. P. (2004). Debiasing, in D. J. Koehler & N. Harvey (eds), *Blackwell handbook of judgment and decision making* (pp. 316–337). Malden, MA: Blackwell.

Lonne, B., Parton, N., Thomson, J. & Harries, M. (2009). *Reforming child protection.* London: Routledge.

Maxwell, J. C. (2013). *How successful people lead.* New York: Centre Street.

McColl, F. (2009). Where have all the social workers gone? Critical reflection and child protection, *Advances in Social Work and Welfare Education,* 11(1), 127–130.

Miller, R. (2007a). *The best interests principles: A conceptual overview.* State Government of Victoria, Melbourne. Online www.dhhs.vic.gov.au

Miller, R. (2007b). *Cumulative harm: A conceptual overview, Best interests series.* State Government of Victoria, Melbourne. Online www.dhhs.vic.gov.au

Miller, R. (2009). Engagement with families involved in the statutory system, in J. Maidment & R. Egan (eds), *Practice Skills in Social Work and Welfare, More than Just Common Sense.* Crows Nest, NSW: Allen & Unwin.

Miller, R. (2008, 2012). *Best interests case practice model: Summary guide.* State Government of Victoria, Melbourne. Online www.dhhs.vic.gov.au

Miller, R. (2010). Practice reflection: The knowledge and skills that child protection practitioners need today, *Advances in Social Work & Welfare Education,* 11(2), 116–119.

Miller, R. (2014). Promoting cultural reform in Victorian child protection and family services through the Best Interests Case Practice Model, PhD thesis, LaTrobe University, Melbourne.

Morley, C. (2014). *Practising critical reflection to develop emancipatory change.* Surrey, UK: Ashgate.

Munro, E. (2002). *Effective child protection.* London: Sage Publications.

Munro, E. & Parton, N. (2007). How far is England in the process of introducing a mandatory reporting system? *Child Abuse Review,* 16(1), 5–16. ISSN 1099–0852

Munro, E. (2011). *The Munro review of child protection: Final report, A child-centred system.* London. Available at www.gov.uk/government/uploads/system/uploads/attachment_data/file/175391/Munro-Review.pdf

Power, M. (1996). *The audit explosion.* Demos: London.

Reder, P. & Duncan, S. (1999). *Lost innocents: A follow-up study of fatal child abuse.* London: Routledge.

Reder, P. & Duncan, S. (2004). Making the most of the Victoria Climbie inquiry report, in N. Stanley & J. Manthorpe (eds), *The age of inquiry: Learning and blaming in health and social care.* London: Routledge.

Stanley, T., McGee, P. & Lincoln, H. (2012). A practice framework for assessments at Tower Hamlets Children's Social Care: Building on the Munro Review, *Practice: Social Work in Action.* doi:10.1080/09503153.2012.712677

Wenger-Trayner, E. & Wenger-Trayner, B. (2015). *Communities of practice: A brief introduction,* 24(4), 1–12 Available at http://wenger-trayner.com/wp-content/uploads/2015/04/07-Brief-introduction-to-communities-of-practice.pdf

14

CONCLUDING THOUGHTS: INFORMAL AND FORMAL SUPPORT FOR VULNERABLE CHILDREN AND FAMILIES

*Marie Connolly**

Introduction

What is clearly evident from the chapters in this book – and what practitioners intrinsically know – is that families are becoming more diverse and are looking after their children in challenging times. Parents from different cultural and social backgrounds have to draw upon increasingly complex support networks to meet the needs of children. It is also clear that the issues are challenging from a broader systems perspective as child welfare systems struggle to meet the needs of vulnerable children.

In this book, we have argued that moving beyond the risk paradigm requires a determined shift in focus from the needs of highly bureaucratized systems and the domination of 'issues management' (Tingle, 2015, p. 26), towards a renewed focus on the holistic needs of vulnerable children and their families. While this is not necessarily a new idea – indeed it rests at the heart of countless reform strategies – it nevertheless seems difficult to achieve. In this concluding chapter, we will explore whether part of the difficulty lies in the *nature* of the support that would be more responsive to the needs of vulnerable children. First though, we will say one or two words about issues management.

The domination of 'issues management'

In Chapter 2 Beddoe and Cree talked about the concept of moral panic and its centrality in driving child protection industries internationally. There is no question that within these tabloid times, organizations

* Marie Connolly is a professor and chair of social work at the University of Melbourne, Australia.

charged with the responsibility of protecting children have the added bur-
den of having to protect the system against media attack, whether valid
or exaggerated. Within this context, it is easy to see how child protection
systems can become consumed by their own issues as they spend valuable time dousing fires within a 24/7 news cycle. The importance of issues
management should not be underestimated. It is like managing a ship in a
major storm; the stakes are high, and poor management can have serious
consequences. It is, however, the way in which issues management influences and drives the bureaucratization of the child protection industry
that creates difficulties for the systems themselves and the families who
end up as receivers of risk-dominated practice (Buckley, in Chapter 6). Yet,
as we've seen in earlier chapters, professional child- and family-centred
practices do exist despite the tremendous challenges that workers and
families confront in risk-dominated systems. The next question, however,
is whether formal support services are actually what vulnerable children
and families need.

Formal and informal support for vulnerable families

Over the past decades child protection agencies under pressure have
increasingly relied on the professional provision of support services
through non-government agencies. These days, child protection services
often have well-developed referral mechanisms that help to connect
families to support services, and in general, formal support options are
privileged as the best way of responding – if indeed the family receives a
response at all. An assumption that the way forward is primarily through
the delivery of professional services does, however, underplay the important role that informal support networks have in finding solutions to
complex family issues. There are limitations in over-relying on formal,
bureaucratic solutions (Apple et al., 2001). Formal strategies and professional frameworks may lack relevance for families trying to cope with
broad-ranging issues that challenge their ability to parent. Indeed, Melton
(2013) argues from a US perspective that no matter how well formal programmes are packaged, they often have little logical relation to the needs
and hopes of the children and families for whom they are intended.
According to McLeigh (2013, p. 18), 'there remains a disconnect between
what we know parents need and what is available to them'. When
services lack relevance for children and parents, there is a greater likelihood that offers of support will be resisted (Cameron, 2013). The development of social support systems has been identified as an important
factor in a parent's ability to nurture their child's well-being (Burke
et al., 1998). Parents can feel isolated when they lack social networks.

Kinship caregivers, for example, often report feeling isolated in their carer role at the very time they need greater social support (Strozier, 2012). The provision of a professional caseworker in these situations is not a sustainable solution, nor is it likely to be what the family wants. Building sustainable and enduring support through family and community networks is one way of creating a richer balance of support for families (Connolly et al., 2016).

Facilitating and nurturing informal support

Child protection systems generally have a blind spot where the development of informal support networks is concerned. McLeigh, however, suggests that professional programmes 'should be viewed as *entry points* for engaging families in community activities so that they can become active participants, develop social connections, identify supports, and give back to their communities' (2013, p. 20, original emphasis). Support needs to be natural and local and based within community webs of reciprocity that will endure over time. Natural helpers can provide a new approach to helping, people who understand their communities, the cultural networks that sustain them and the personal commitment to improving their neighbourhoods:

> Natural helpers are more likely to provide support in the recipient's natural environment. They can support families who have been or would be unable or unwilling to receive services in more traditional settings. This can allow for more effective and comprehensive monitoring of child safety. The monitoring is more likely to include all family members and, possibly, members of their support networks. (Apple et al., 2001, p. 255)

Families access support in diverse ways: from many different sources, from the local community, from relatives and friends and from the Internet and social media. Social support plays an important but not yet well-understood role in the protection of children, and currently, few child protection resources target informal support development. Professional services clearly have an important role in working with complex family issues, and we need to continue to build universal and targeted services in ways that meet the diverse needs of families. This will require a review of the kind of formal and informal supports that are provided to vulnerable children and families. In this book, we have promoted an approach to the work that is located in a child welfare tradition – one that positions professional work with children and families in the context of their communities, including their cultural communities. This involves being responsive to families and cultures (Connolly et al., 2016). In recent years, professional services have been strongly focused on child-centred practice. While attention to the child's needs, interests and rights is clearly important, it is vital that we do not diminish the role of parents and extended family as solution-finders for children at risk. Child-centred practice alone can unintentionally create authoritarian approaches to practise. When integrated with a family-responsive approach, however, we have the potential to better protect the child through the harnessing of family and community support systems. This also suggests the need for us to think again about how we foster new preventative ideas that will support vulnerable children and their families in an increasingly complex world. Mobilizing and resourcing informal support networks might be a critical next step in the development of sustainable child welfare systems.

References

Apple, K., Bernstein, S., Fogg, K., Fogg, L., Haapala, D., Johnson, E., Johnson, R., Kinney, J., Nittoli, J., Price, D., Roberts, K., Smith, R., Steele, T., Strand, K., Trent, E., Trent, M., Trent, V. & Vignec, R. (2001). Walking our talk in the neighborhoods, in E. Walton, P. Sandau-Beckler & M. Mannes (eds), *Balancing family-centred services and child well-being: Exploring issues in policy, practice, theory and research* (pp. 252–285). New York: Columbia University Press.

Burke, J., Chandy, J., Dannerbeck, A. & Watt, J. W. (1998). The parental environment cluster model of child neglect: An integrative conceptual model, *Child Welfare*, LXXVII(4), 389–401.

Cameron, G. (2013). Creating positive systems of child and family welfare: Questions and suggestions, in G. Cameron, M. Fine, S. Maiter, K. Frensch & N. Freymond (eds), *Creating positive systems of child and family welfare: Congruence with the everyday lives of children and parents* (pp. 283–301). Toronto, ON: University of Toronto Press.

Connolly, M., Kiraly, M., McCrae, L. & Mitchell, G. (2016). A kinship care practice framework: Using a life course approach, *British Journal of Social Work*, Advance Access, published 9 May 2016, 1–19. doi:10.1093/bjsw/bcw041

McLeigh, J. D. (2013). How to form alliances with families and communities, *Child Abuse & Neglect*, 37, 17–28.

Melton, G. B. (2013) 'Programs' aren't enough: Child protection must become part of everyday life, *Child Abuse and Neglect*, 37, 1–7.

Strozier, A. L. (2012). The effectiveness of support groups in increasing social support for kinship caregivers, *Children and Youth Services Review*, 34, 876–881.

Tingle, L. (2015). Political amnesia – How we forgot how to govern, *Quarterly Essay*, 60. Black Inc. Books: Collingwood VIC.

INDEX